NORTHMET

A History of the North Metropolitan Electric Power Supply Company
the North Metropolitan Electric Power Distribution Company and
the North Metropolitan Power Station Company

by

N C Friswell

© N C Friswell 2000

First published in 2000
by N C Friswell
19 Clarence Road
Horsham
RH13 5SJ

All rights reserved

ISBN 0-9538592-0-7

Printed by
A A Sotheran Ltd, Redcar, Cleveland.

PREFACE

I have been asked why I have written this history of Northmet. As the work went on I began to ask myself the same question, but without getting a clear answer. Having joined the Northmet sub-area of Eastern Electricity a few years after nationalisation, I became increasingly impressed with the legacy left by the pre-nationalisation Company. It was only when I transferred to another Area Board that I realised just how good Northmet must have been.

An article by the late Cecil Melling, who had been Eastern Electricity's first Chairman brought it all back to me. Privatisation was creating fresh turmoil in the Electricity Supply Industry, the wheel was being reinvented and it seemed that the history might be lost. Sure enough the Electricity Association, careless of the history in its archives, disposed of much material, most irretrievably.

This history is an attempt to redress the balance. No doubt there were other electricity companies in Britain as good as Northmet, but this is the one we knew. Although I am the author of the book, it would not have been possible without all the help and reminiscences of former employees of the Company and the Sub-Area. I am sincerely grateful to all of them.

Electricity generation and distribution is a technical business and it is technology that has changed and is continuing to change. I have, therefore, included much technical description in order that it can be properly recorded. If the story is a bit light in other areas it is because of a lack of information.

Whatever your interests I hope that you enjoy this account of an interesting enterprise.

ABBREVIATIONS

Abbreviations of various types are used in this account. For convenience they are:-

AC	Alternating current
AEC	Associated Equipment Co
Ah	Ampere-hour (measure of battery capacity)
BEF	British Electrical Federation
BET	British Electric Traction Company
BT-H	British Thomson-Houston Co
CATE	Control Alarm and Telemetry Equipment
CEB	Central Electricity Board (1920-1947)
CEGB	Central Electricity Generating Board (1947 on)
cp	candle power
d	pence (pre-decimalisation)
DC	Direct current
ELO	Electric Lighting Order
F	temperature in degrees Farenheit
ft	foot
GEC	General Electric Co (of Britain)
hp	horse power
HP	High pressure or Horse Power (depending on context)
Hz	Hertz (frequency, cycles per second)
IEE	Institution of Electrical Engineers
in	inch
kV	kilovolt
kVA	kilovolt-ampere
kW	kilowatt
L&ST	London and Suburban Traction Co
lb	pound (avoirdupois)
lb/h	pounds per hour
LGB	Local Government Board
LGOC	London General Omnibus Co
LNER	London and North Eastern Railway
LP	Low pressure
LPTB	London Passenger Transport Board (1933-47)
LRTA	Light Rail Transit Association
LT	London Transport
MET	Metropolitan Electric Tramways
MCC	Middlesex County Council

MVA	megavolt-ampere
MW	megawatt
NMPSCo	North Metropolitan Electricity Power Supply Co
Northmet	Used variously for the three North Metropolitan electricity companies
PAX	Private Automatic telephone Exchange
PC	Privately contributed contributions (in footnotes)
PLA	Public lighting attendant
psi	pounds per square inch
rpm	revolutions per minute
SF6	Sulphur hexafluoride (gas insulation for switchgear)
sq in	square inch (used for pre-metrication cable sizes)
STC	Standard Telephones & Cables Ltd
swg	standard wire gauge
TRLS	Tramway and Light Railway Society
UDC	Urban District Council
UERL	Underground Electric Railways of London Ltd
unit	kilowatt-hour (kWh)

No attempt has been made to convert imperial units of measurement to metric units nor have monetary values (in pounds shillings and pence) been converted to decimal or present-day values.

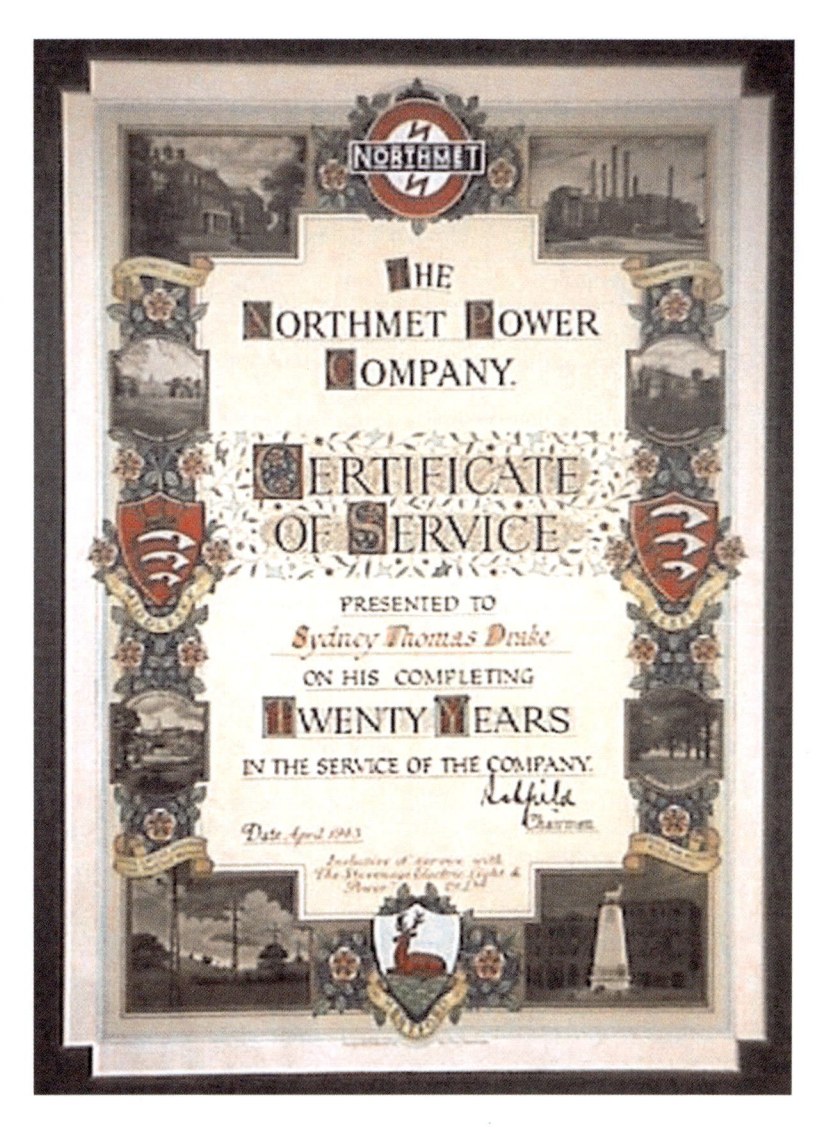

Frontispiece: **Long Service Certificate awarded to S T Drake**
[*C J Thody*]

CONTENTS

	INTRODUCTION	1
1	ORIGINS	5
2	CONSTITUTION	29
3	GENERATING STATIONS	36
4	THE SOUTHERN UNDERTAKINGS	79
5	THE WESTERN AREA	103
6	THE NORTHERN UNDERTAKINGS	118
7	HEAD OFFICES	144
8	SHOWROOMS	157
9	COMMERCIAL MATTERS	176
10	ORGANISATION, OFFICES & PROCEDURES	180
11	THE POWER SYSTEM AND ITS OPERATION	195
12	PUBLIC LIGHTING	215
13	TRACTION SUPPLIES	220
14	BIOGRAPHICAL NOTES	227
15	NORTHMET AT WAR	240
16	NATIONALISATION	252
	INDEX	265

INTRODUCTION

The Northmet Company was formed in 1899. It started with small local power stations but in 1900 it was the first electricity company in the London area to obtain authorisation to supply power in bulk to other authorities. When Brimsdown power station was opened in 1904 its main generating plant comprised turbo alternators at a time when reciprocating engines were still being installed elsewhere.

In 1913, when the first Ljungstrom turbo-alternator was demonstrated at Stockholm, engineers from Northmet and Brush visited that city. Northmet bought the demonstration machine and installed it at Willesden, while Brush acquired the right to manufacture the machine in England. Subsequently Northmet bought five larger Brush-built Ljungstrom sets and installed them at Brimsdown and Willesden.

Brimsdown and Willesden were operated in parallel which was a novel arrangement at the time. As the system was extended northwards into Hertfordshire the towns of Hertford, St. Albans and Stevenage were interconnected with a link to Luton and, in 1922, synchronising of the frequency with the time was introduced and controlled from a master clock at Willesden, later transferred to Brimsdown. During the 1920s Acton Lane (another station at Willesden) and Barking were connected to the Northmet system although neither were owned by Northmet.

A suction coal handling plant was installed at Brimsdown in 1923 and a year later a boiler was equipped for pulverised coal firing. In 1924 Northmet supplied power to the British Empire Exhibition at Wembley, which continued to 1925. An Outside Department was set up in 1921 at New Southgate to control stores, mains and meter departments. In 1926 a new meter repair and test facility was installed with an annual throughput of 10,000 meters, rising to 75,000 post-war.

In 1926 Northmet designed a new power station, Brimsdown B, alongside the existing station which became Brimsdown A and new 33 kV outdoor switchgear was installed to handle the increased output. The new station was designed for an ultimate output of 150 MW to be achieved in three stages using boilers fired with pulverised coal. The first stage was commissioned in 1928 with two 25 MW turboalternators, the one generating at 33 kV being the largest set in the country to generate at this voltage. Electrostatic precipitation was installed at Willesden in 1929.

The second stage of Brimsdown B was commenced in 1930. Again two 25 MW turboalternators were installed but several innovative features were built into the pulverised-fuel boilers to improve their efficiency in both steam raising and superheating. Steam receivers were of welded construction and the welds examined by X-rays. Flue gas washing plant was provided for three boilers and an electrostatic precipitator for the fourth. A new type of 33 kV metalclad outdoor switchgear was installed before the power station extension was commissioned in 1932.

Shortly afterwards it was decided to rebuild Brimsdown A with new generating plant and two forced-circulation boilers in a new boiler house. In 1938 the Company purchased two Loeffler steam generators from Czechoslovakia and had two more made in this country. These Loeffler boilers were of all-welded construction and were the first of this type to be installed in the country, being designed to operate at 2000 psi and 940F. The boilers supplied a single cross-compound generating set, the low-pressure side first being supplied from the old boilers in 1937 and the complete set supplied from the high-pressure boilers in 1938. Both alternators generated at 33 kV. A further new type of 33 kV outdoor switchgear with three phases in a single tank was commissioned.

Work on the final stage of Brimsdown B began in 1939, but was delayed by the war, the complete plant being first put on load in 1943. In contrast to the earlier stages of Brimsdown B, this final stage was designed on similar lines to Brimsdown A with two larger Loeffler boilers supplying a 60 MW cross-compound generating set.

The generating plant at Willesden was increased and pulverised fuel firing was introduced in 1926. To make best use of the existing space, compact Brush Ljungstrom generating sets were installed, the last in 1932.

In 1938 a plan was prepared to shut down the station and build a new one of larger rating. This work was also delayed by the war, but the new plant was commissioned before the end of the war. Two 32 MW generating sets were supplied by five boilers, three of which were of the La Mont forced-circulation type operating at 1300 psi and 950F.

By the outbreak of the Second World war Northmet's last generating station, Rye House, was being designed. It was completed by the British Electricity Authority.

The Company was one of the first users of 33 kV switchgear and cables. Some of these items, especially cables, were a little before their time and frequent failures resulted in some of them being downgraded to 11 kV (the general adoption in the mid-1920s by British manufacturers of the Hochstaedter 'H' type of cable construction, with metallic screens to even out the electrical stresses, solved this problem).

The Northmet Power company took underground cable laying and jointing very seriously. All joints were plumber-jointed including those at low voltage and consumers were provided with an earth bond to the lead sheath. Very good records were kept of cable laying and jointing and statistical analysis of cable and jointing failures was made to find out what was the likely cause.

Engineers at the Company were also responsible for the development of under-floor electric heating. Their first attempts in this field were with air raid shelters during the Second World War. They also developed the use of thermal storage heaters and improved the designs to those we know today. Some of the earliest design were installed at Wherstead, the Headquarters of Eastern Electricity, just after nationalisation.

On the Commercial side the Northmet company was well known for the large number of showrooms it had in each of its Districts and its very large contracting departments. By promoting the sale of appliances and installing wiring it built up electricity sales. It sold high quality appliances and had a reputation for only doing high class work.

The Northmet company, which had over 300,000 consumers by the late 1930s, had management problems few others in the electricity supply industry had to cope with. Under the 1882 Electricity Act it had to keep records of all capital works and expenditures under either supplies to Electricity Act or Electricity

Order consumers. In theory Local Authorities had the right to take over all Electricity Order consumers (mainly domestic) after 21 years at a price related to the investment in the supply system. This meant that the Company had to keep very good records and accounts.

The sheer size of the Northmet transmission and distribution system meant that day to day operation was very complex. As it developed, the Company operated the high voltage system through a Control Centre at Northmet House. In the urban areas especially, communication with the Control Room was by telephone through a private telephone system using the pilot and telephone cables normally laid alongside high voltage and extra high voltage cables. In addition there was an elaborate system of control of prearranged switching of circuit breakers using application forms to allow control engineers to check load flows and ensure safety of operation. Under fault conditions control engineers were able to advise engineers in the field and speed up restoration of supplies. Very few other electricity companies were so well organized.

CHAPTER 1: ORIGINS

Parliament thought that they were ahead of the game. There had been early electric lighting installations in public places and large country houses. It could be foreseen that a legislative framework would be needed and this was based on experience with railways, tramways and gas distributors. The 1870 Tramways Act introduced the concept of the Provisional Order granted by the Board of Trade and confirmed by Parliament. The consent of the local authority was required. The tenure was 21 years after which the undertaking could be purchased by the local authority at cost. There was, at this time, a marked advance in municipal socialism[1]. It was a period of concern about the dangers of monopoly that could make a killing at the expense of the general public. Monopolies should be regulated. Better still, they should be municipal enterprises because profit made by private companies was regarded in some circles as a loss to the community. In the event, the desire for municipal ownership caused the dismembering of some systems of tramways without any advantage to the ratepayers or the travelling public.

In 1875 local authorities had been given powers and responsibilities regarding roads. Although owners of properties adjacent to the highway theoretically owned the ground beneath the road surface, only the local authority had powers to lay pipes and other structures in the surface substrata. Even the local authority's rights were limited to public lighting and did not allow the sale of gas or electricity to consumers[2]. Anyone else who wanted to put anything under the highway needed an Act of Parliament. In 1878 there were 34 Private Parliamentary Bills seeking powers to supply electricity in various towns.

The early legislation for electricity suppliers reflected the thoughts of the day. A Parliamentary Committee was appointed and the result was The Electric Lighting Act of 1882, the title reflecting the main use envisaged for electricity at that time. The 1882 Act continued with the principles of the Tramways Act. A system was devised where local authorities could apply for Provisional Orders allowing them

---

[1] *The Progress of Electrical Enterprise* by E Garcke, Electrical Press Ltd, 1907
[2] Hinton (Lord) of Bankside: *Heavy Current Electricity in the United kingdom*, Pergamon Press, 1979. ISBN 008 023246 9, p13.

to supply electricity within their own area (but not outside it). The capital to install a power station and the distribution cables had to be found and, in most cases, this was a matter for the Local Government Board (LGB) to sanction a municipal loan. Such permission was not a foregone conclusion; many local authorities found that the LGB would not allow them to borrow money for proposed schemes.

Companies could also apply for provisional electric lighting orders. In this case the local authority had the power to take over the undertaking after 21 years at cost price. In 1888 this was changed to 42 years and the price had to include an allowance for goodwill, &c, reflecting the value of the undertaking as a going concern. Whether this threat of takeover affected the enthusiasm of promoters is a moot point. It is probable that 21 years was considered by most investors to be a lifetime away.

Although Parliament's first Electric Lighting Act was in 1882, very few schemes were put forward until the late 90s. In many cases they were coupled with tramway electrification. Tramway companies had had similar buy-out clauses imposed on them and, just as electrification of the horse-drawn tramways was becoming technically practicable, their time was running out. They were disinclined to invest heavily in electrification only to have their assets bought out, at cost, in the near future by the local authority.

Electric lighting had also not been a complete success technically. Arc lamps were very bright. They were attractive for prestige street lighting and other public places but unsuitable for private homes. Houses, workshops and side streets had to wait for the development and general acceptance of the incandescent lamp.

Electric lighting and electric tramways together gave a worthwhile load for an undertaking. It was often, therefore, local authorities with tramways that made the first steps toward electricity supply. Although electric motors for other purposes were available, the use of motors in factories was generally rather belated and they were not considered in the early days as justification for an Electric Lighting Order (ELO).

The 1890s were also notable for the battle of the systems. Should an electricity supply company use direct current (DC) or alternating current (AC)? If the locality had a tramway and distances were not great, DC was often chosen. It had

ORIGINS

the additional advantage that when the load was light, at night, batteries could be used, being recharged when the generators were started up again. Alternating current was favoured by a few and became almost essential for those companies set up to supply a larger area.

London, as always, was in the forefront but most of the towns of Middlesex and Hertfordshire were well behind. The inter-relationship between early electricity supply and tramway electrification was complicated in this area because the London County Council operated most of the inner-London trams and the North London routes which were ripe for electrification were company owned, extending across local authority boundaries.

One of these companies facing the electrification of their horse tram system was the North Metropolitan Tramways Company, soon to become the Metropolitan Electric Tramways[3] (MET). They would need a source of electricity if their schemes were to be realised.

The British Electric Traction Company Ltd (Reg no. 49,855) had been formed in 1896 and was involved in the acquisition or leasing of existing tramway undertakings and initial promotion of new schemes with a view to working them by electric traction. This was done through subsidiary companies.[4] The Metropolitan Tramways and Omnibus Company (also shortly to become the Metropolitan Electric Tramways Co) was associated with BET. At a BET meeting in 1898 mention was made of the benefits of having a Light Railway Order and an ELO for the same place (Merthyr)[5] so it was obviously in the corporate mind that BET would have to be involved in electricity supply as well as electric traction.

On 19[6]th April 1899 the North Metropolitan Electrical Power Distribution Company, Limited[7] (Reg no. 61,692) was registered with a capital of £50,000 in £10 shares (2,500 preference), to "carry on the business of electrical engineers and contractors, electricians, suppliers of electricity, electrical apparatus manufacturers, mechanical and chemical engineers, tramway and light railway proprietors, carriers, &c". The first subscribers (each with one share) were : G J

---
[3] For a complete history of MET see C S Smeeton *Metropolitan Electric Tramways*.
[4] *Electrical Review* vol 42, p721 3/6/1898
[5] *Electrical Review* vol 43, p875 9/12/1898
[6] Garcke's Manual 1902-3 gives the date as 12th April
[7] Referred to henceforth as 'the Distribution Company'.

Somerville, electrical engineer; C Walmsley, accountant; E Garcke, director; C H Dade, assistant secretary; W E Singleton, solicitor; M E Sheerboom, clerk; J Renwick, clerk. "The first directors (to number not less than three nor more than five) are to be nominated by the subscribers; qualification £100; remuneration as fixed by the company. Registered office, Surrey House, Victoria Embankment, WC".[8] The North Metropolitan Electric Power Distribution Company was formed as a subsidiary of MET. Emile Garcke was Managing Director of BET, and continued to have a wide influence in electricity supply and electric tramways for decades to come.

The Middlesex County Council initially had had different ideas about both tramways and electricity distribution. It resolved to oppose the provisional ELOs then being applied for by Twickenham, Finchley and Hendon Councils[9]. A similar resolution with regard to light railways had been arrived at, the intention being a standstill, presumably while a policy was being developed.

Parliament had still not quite got it right. There had been an amending Act in 1888 and in 1889 the Electric Lighting (Clauses) Act laid down the principles under which electricity suppliers would be granted provisional ELOs (except in London). Undertakings were not allowed to associate or amalgamate nor to supply or lay down lines outside their own concession[10].

By 1899, things were starting to stir in the area north of London. A number of local authorities were considering electric lighting, mostly, at this stage, with the intention of applying for their own Provisional Orders. Part of this exercise included, of course, opposing any applications that the fledgling Northmet, or any other company might make. Behind all this was the County Council's standstill.

On 14th July 1899, the *Electrical Review* reported that the Secretary of the North Middlesex Electrical Supply Association had asked the Friern Barnet Council to grant them an interview but the Council replied that it still intended to lodge an objection to the proposed order[11]. It is not clear who or what the North Middlesex Electrical Supply Association was.

---
[8]   *Electrical Review* vol 44, p781 12/5/1899
[9]   *Electrical Review* vol 43, p934 23/12/1898
[10] Hinton (Lord) of Bankside: *Heavy Current Electricity in the United kingdom*, Pergamon Press, 1979. ISBN 008 023246 9, p40.
[11] *Electrical Review* vol 45, p55 14/7/1889

A week later it was reported that at a meeting of the East Barnet Valley District Council, a letter was read from the North Metropolitan Electric Power Distribution Company Limited, stating the intention to apply (before 21st December next) for a provisional order to supply electrical energy for public or private purposes within the urban district of East Barnet Valley. It was decided to write to the Board of Trade, intimating that the Council objected to the proposed scheme[12].

Northmet was not the only supplier interested in the area. At a meeting of the Enfield District Council on 13th July 1899 notices of intended application for provisional electric lighting orders to supply Enfield with the electric light were received from Edmundson's Electricity Corporation Ltd, as well as the North Metropolitan Electrical Company. The matter was referred to a committee[13].

Meanwhile, out in Hertfordshire, Hertford Corporation resolved to dispose of its provisional order of 1891 to the Municipal Electric Supply Company[14]. In Barnet, the District Council had obtained a provisional order in 1893 but the area of that order was restricted to the Barnet Local Board District as then constituted. It was decided in 1900 to obtain a new provisional order covering the whole of the Council's district[15] and both orders were transferred to the new Northmet Electric Power Distribution Company. Supply commenced in September 1900. Barnet generating station was erected by the North Metropolitan Electrical Power Distribution Co Ltd in 1900. In May 1905 bulk supply from the Northmet Supply Company commenced, that company officially taking over the power station in 1906. Subsequently the station was converted into a substation.[16] The area of supply was later extended to the whole of Barnet District.

Hornsey District Council also appointed an expert to advise them as to the question of an electric installation. The Council already had a provisional order granted in 1898[17] and many offers had been made by private companies to take it over. Just to make quite sure, the Council also decided to ask those companies for definite offers[18].

[12] *Electrical Review* vol 45, p100 21/7/1899
[13] *Electrical Review* vol 45, p145 28/7/1899
[14] *Electrical Review* vol 45, p272 18/8/1899
[15] *Electrical Review* vol 45, p800 17/11/1899
[16] *An Outline History of the Northmet Power Company* by E T Kingsbury and Evelyn Boys, 1946.
[17] The Borough of Hornsey Electricity Undertaking *A Brief History 1903-1939.*
[18] *Electrical Review* vol 45, p844 24/11/1899

The Middlesex County Council were still opposing applications for an electric lighting order by the Enfield District Council (as the main roads and bridges were affected) and applications by Harrow, Heston, Teddington, and Twickenham. The application for a provisional order by the North Metropolitan Electric Power Company for powers to generate and supply electricity in the areas of the Edmonton and Hendon Unions was also opposed[19].

During 1899 the Middlesex County Council joined with the Urban District Councils in the County (with the exception of Finchley) to obtain light railway orders[20]. This had the effect that the local UDCs could not now rely on tramway load. Finchley's application to run its own tramways was rejected on 14th March 1900 and, as a result, the UDC opposed whatever the County put forward for many years after. Middlesex became the tramway authority for the County in 1901 and was able to set up a network of lines in collaboration with the Metropolitan Electric Tramways Company.

When these Middlesex Light Railways were planned, it was proposed to build a separate generating station for each group of routes. The Hendon and Stonebridge Park depot sites were chosen for their suitability for generating stations, and other sites considered were at Finchley, Wood Green, Edmonton, Alexandra Park, Winchmore Hill and Friern Barnet. Most were in residential districts, and the district councils usually objected.[21]

Another company, the North Metropolitan Electric Power Supply Company[22], was set up under a private Act of Parliament in 1900 specifically to supply in bulk to authorised undertakers over an area of 326 square miles (later extended to 345 square miles). The separate statutory company was necessary because a company supplying under an ELO, such as the Northmet distribution company, could only supply within the area of the ELO, not outside it. Each of the ELO areas which the distribution company supplied had to be kept separate. This continued until nationalisation[23], leading to some complex administrative and accounting procedures.

---

[19] *Electrical Review* vol 45, p1055 29/12/1899
[20] *Metropolitan Electric Tramways* by C S Smeeton, Light Rail Transit Association, 1984. ISBN 090 043394 9, p29.
[21] *Metropolitan Electric Tramways* by C S Smeeton, Light Rail Transit Association, 1984. ISBN 090 043394 9, p195.
[22] Referred to henceforth as 'the Supply Company'.
[23] Personal communication, E Wright.

ORIGINS

When the original area of the Supply Company was authorised, powers to distribute electricity were held by local authorities or other companies in respect of Barnet, Finchley, Harrow, Hendon, Hertford, Hornsey, St.Albans and Walthamstow which presented the prospect of affording all or some of these authorised undertakers with supplies in bulk. Moreover, it was known that the North Metropolitan Tramways Company contemplated electrifying their extensive system of horse tramways. A certain number of factories had been established along the banks of the River Lee which runs from Hertford through Ware, Hoddesdon, Cheshunt, Waltham Cross, Enfield, Edmonton and Tottenham and then on to join the Thames at Limehouse and Blackwall. Apart from Hertford there were no authorised undertakers for these districts[24].

In St Albans, the City Council had been granted an ELO on 12th August 1898 which, together with an additional order for four Rural District Council parishes, was transferred by the corporation to a local company (St Albans & District Electric Supply Company Ltd) in 1905. The Northmet Supply Company took over that local company in the same year but, because the supply company was constituted under an Act, the St Albans City ELO system was kept separate from the rural system. The main substation was the common source of supply where the two systems were metered. Meter accounts, wages and all works had separate allocation numbers until nationalisation[25].

The Supply Company acquired two further sites for generating stations. The smaller one, which was developed first, was on the bank of the River Lee in Hertford near the Great Northern Railway, and was opened on 20 November 1901. For the first few months it was operated by the Distribution Company. The larger 12.25-acre site, the freehold of which was owned by Trinity College, Cambridge, was alongside the River Lee Navigation at Brimsdown in the parish of Enfield. This was destined to become the large central station which supplied the power requirements of the Metropolitan Electric Tramways and a large area of West Essex, South Hertfordshire and North Middlesex. In 1902, the MET had estimated that Brimsdown would cost £103,000.[26]

---

[24] *Outline of the History of the Northmet Power Company* by E T Kingsbury and E Boys, 1946 1899
[25] Personal communication, E Wright.
[26] *Metropolitan Electric Tramways* by C S Smeeton, Light Rail Transit Association, 1984. ISBN 090 043394 9, p35.

The first large power consumer (other than the tramways) to be connected to the Company's system was the Edison Swan Electric Company who started to take supply at Ponders End in December 1906[27]. Simultaneously with the construction of the power station, rotary converter substations were built at Edmonton, Wood Green and Finchley, to be supplied from Brimsdown, and at Hendon, to be supplied from Willesden, all feeders being at 10 kV.

At the end of June 1901, representatives of Wood Green, Tottenham, Edmonton, Southgate and Enfield District Councils met in conference to consider a joint scheme for electric power for the districts. A joint committee of the several districts had been appointed the previous year, and preliminary arrangements were made for promoting a Bill in Parliament for the necessary powers. However, owing to an adverse vote of the ratepayers of Enfield and Edmonton, the "combine" had been abandoned at the cost of £240 to each of the five authorities. The meeting this time resolved that "in view of the expressed opinion of this conference that the supply of electricity could be generated much cheaper by larger than by smaller undertakings, it is desirable that the Joint Committee of the District Councils of Edmonton, Southgate, Tottenham and Wood Green be reconstituted to take into consideration the proposed use of electricity in their respective areas."[28]

2: **Electricity for tramways was one of the reasons for the formation of Northmet: MET trams bound for Palmers Green** [*Author's collection*]

---

[27] *An Outline History of the Northmet Power Company* by E T Kingsbury and Evelyn Boys, 1946. 1906
[28] *Electrical Review* vol 49, p16 5/7/1901.

It was felt at that time that the public interest demanded that the generation and supply of electricity should be in the hands of local authorities rather than of private companies. When Tottenham District Council discussed the matter the following week they decided that the Council should not join with any committee until their application for a provisional ELO had been decided. The Edmonton District Council, at their meeting also decided to apply for a provisional order for electric lighting[29].

By October, Enfield Council were asking Mr R Hammond to advise upon the agreement submitted by the North Metropolitan Electrical Power Distribution Company Limited and the proposals of the Provincial Electric Light and Traction Company Limited[30].

Meanwhile East Barnet UDC instructed a Mr P W Adams to report upon the electric lighting of the district. The Council already had a provisional order and had been approached by the North Metropolitan Power Distribution Company who wished to give a supply 'in bulk' and by companies who desire to establish a complete undertaking[31].

Wood Green, who seem to have been a bit behind by comparison with their neighbours, also passed a resolution to apply for a provisional order for electric lighting[32].

By the end of 1901, Northmet's Hertford power station had just opened and the site for Brimsdown had been acquired. The intention was to lay a trunk main from Hertford to Cheshunt[33].

Although Enfield were at least prepared to consider dealing with Northmet, Edmonton[34] and Tottenham[35] District Councils decided to oppose to the utmost the Bill of the North Metropolitan Electric Power Supply Company which

---

[29] *Electrical Review* vol 49, p58 12/7/1901
[30] *Electrical Review* vol 49, p714 1/11/1901
[31] *Electrical Review* vol 49, p751 8/11/1901
[32] *Electrical Review* vol 49, p751 8/11/1901
[33] Bourne R: *Hendon Electric Supply Company* (1985), p9
[34] *Electrical Review* vol 49, p1086 27/12/1901
[35] *Electrical Review* vol 50, p179 31/1/1902

sought powers to generate and supply electricity in Tottenham, Edmonton, Enfield, Wood Green and Southgate.

Hornsey had not been involved with the other Councils and had decided to go it alone. By 1902 contracts were being let for pipework and mechanical coal-handling plant for the UDC's electricity works[36] and generation started in March 1903. Hornsey Borough Council continued to supply electricity locally independent of Northmet until nationalisation, bulk supplies being taken from the London & Home Counties Joint Electricity Authority and the Central Electricity Board from 1929[37].

At Wood Green in 1902 a deputation of well-known tradesmen attended a meeting of the District Council for the purpose of submitting to the local authority their views regarding electricity supply. The deputation contended that, though it was in favour of electric light for the district, the best and cheapest means to obtain it would be through the agency of a company. It urged the Council to call a public meeting of ratepayers before committing itself to an extensive municipal scheme. According to the deputation, in 1901 fifty two British towns lost £84,632 and their ratepayers were saddled with loans amounting to over five million pounds. This sum was unproductive, and was not represented by assets of an equal amount. Allowing depreciation at 3%pa on £5,458,272, which would amount to £163,747, the total loss to the ratepayers in those 52 towns on last year's trading alone was £248,379. The deputation contended that the Borough Funds Act of 1872 required that a meeting should be held, but the Council were advised there was no need to comply with that Act[38]. Towards the end of the year Wood Green Council decided to apply for an ELO[39] which was granted in 1903.

Southgate District Council also received a petition from 34 influential gentlemen in the parish, stating that they observed with alarm the action the Council had taken in the electric power matter by opposing the North Metropolitan Electric Power Distribution Company's Bill before Parliament, and demanding that a public meeting of ratepayers be held to state their wishes. It was agreed that the

---

[36] *Electrical Review* vol 50, p25 3/1/1902
[37] The Borough of Hornsey Electricity Undertaking *A Brief History 1903-1939.*
[38] *Electrical Review* vol 50, p385 7/3/1902
[39] *Electrical Review* vol 51, p892 28/11/1902

chairman should confer privately with the signatories as to the intentions of the Council with regard to electric power[40].

All this had come about because in January 1902, Northmet had promoted their private Bill. As well as extending the limits of supply authorised by Parliament, the Bill was to extend the area of supply to Willesden and allow the erection of a generating station as well as to raise £250,000 additional capital. The Bill came before the examiners of the House of Commons on 24th January 1902 for proof of compliance with standing orders and was ordered to go forward for first reading[41]. The Middlesex County Council petitioned against the Bill but this was disallowed by the Court of Referees except as against those provisions of the Bill which authorised interference with main roads and county bridges vested in the MCC[42]. The Parliamentary committee decided not to allow the proposed extension of the company's area of supply into the urban district of Willesden[43].

Petitions against the Northmet Bill were deposited in the Private Bill Office of the House of Lords by the Wood Green, Edmonton and Tottenham Urban District Councils[44]. The North Metropolitan Electric Power Supply Company Ltd countered by petitioning in opposition to the Electric Lighting Orders Confirmation Bill No1, the orders granted under the Bill being to the local authorities of Edmonton, Tottenham and Wood Green[45].

Finchley's application to run its own tramways had been rejected but they decided in 1902 to go ahead with their own electricity supply scheme for which they applied to the Local Government Board for leave to borrow £35,000 for the first portion of the scheme. There were objections on behalf of the ratepayers, the local Finchley Electric Lighting Company Limited and Northmet, the last offering to to supply electricity at 3¾d per unit, and to give the Council power to purchase in 14 years or less[46]. This was followed by a dispute between the Council who had a ELO but were not yet using it and the local company who, it seems, had no authority but was pushing on with its work and booking up orders rapidly. Notwithstanding recent decisions of the High Courts, overhead

---

[40] *Electrical Review* vol 50, p423 14/3/1902
[41] *Electrical Review* vol 50, p167 31/1/1902
[42] *Electrical Review* vol 50, p678 25/4/1902
[43] *Electrical Review* vol50, p851 23/5/1902
[44] *Electrical Review* vol 50, p1010 20/6/1902
[45] *Electrical Review* vol 50, p972 13/6/1902
[46] *Electrical Review* vol 51, p18 4/7/1902

conductors were carried across two public highways[47]. Finchley UDC threatened to cut the Finchley Electric Lighting Company's wires, and at an appeal, their Lordships decided that what was vested in the local authority was so much of the area above, and so much below, as was necessary for ordinary use as a street, and that the wires in question, which were carried across the roadway at a height of 30 ft, were clearly outside the Council's area of use. They accordingly allowed the appeal, and granted a perpetual injunction with costs against the Council[48].

By November 1902 Finchley Council were looking for contractors to supply boilers, balancer sets, crane, batteries, mains, street lighting, &c. Finchley, like Hornsey, continued their own municipal electricity undertaking independent of Northmet until nationalisation.

In July 1902, Southgate UDC decided to operate the electric lighting order which it had obtained[49] while Cheshunt UDC was negotiating with the British Insulated Wire Company as to the lighting of the town by electricity[50]. Edmonton resolved to invite three electrical engineers to submit reports and estimates of the costs of schemes for carrying out the electric lighting order of the Council, and an estimate of the annual expenses and revenue. The Northmet Supply Company and other firms were to be invited to submit their terms for supplying electrical energy in bulk and, alternatively, for supply and distribution complete for all purposes[51]. In the event the UDC offered Messrs Hammond and Hawtayne a fee of 50 guineas each to submit reports on and estimates of the cost of schemes for carrying out the recently obtained provisional order.

In Tottenham the District Council considered a recommendation from the Electric Lighting Committee to appoint Mr W C C Hawtayne as expert electrical engineer, to work with the Council's engineer in preparing and carrying out a scheme under the provisional order which had been obtained by the Council. It was proposed that the subject should be referred to a committee of the whole Council. The Chairman said that it would be disgraceful to adopt the Committee's recommendation when, by accepting the terms of another firm, Kincaid, Waller & Manville, the ratepayers would be saved £1875. In the course

---

[47] *Electrical Review* vol 51, p662 17/10/1902
[48] *Electrical Review* vol 52, p282 13/2/1903
[49] *Electrical Review* vol 51, p105 18/7/1902
[50] *Electrical Review* vol 51, p143 25/7/1902
[51] *Electrical Review* vol 51, p507 19/9/1902

of the discussion, the Chairman admitted that he had been carrying out work under Messrs Kincaid. It was alleged that the Chairman had said that if Kincaid's did not get the job it would be thousands out of his pocket. The chairman said the statement was false. The Committee's recommendation was adopted[52].

In still relatively-rural Hertfordshire a conference was held at Hitchin on 19th November 1902 with representatives of the Stevenage UDC, to decide if the ELOs of both towns should be transferred to Crompton & Co Ltd. The Stevenage representatives recommended that an agreement should be entered into with Crompton's for carrying out the undertaking. The Councils would have the option of purchase at the end of 14 years. It was pointed out that it would be hopeless for the Stevenage Council to carry out the order itself. The terms were considered reasonable, and in the end the report of the delegates was adopted[53].

Meanwhile negotiations were going on in St Albans for Northmet to take over the City's ELO[54] and provide electric lighting[55] and at Ware negotiations were proceeding with the electric supply company for the leasing of the UDC's provisional order for electric lighting[56].

At Cheshunt the UDC decided on 15th January to negotiate with the Northmet to take over and work the Council's ELO, on terms similar to those secured by Ware UDC[57].

In East Barnet the Council adopted an electric lighting scheme, having had a provisional order granted in 1899. It was proposed to generate electricity with the aid of a dust destructor. The estimated cost would be £14,000[58]. A LGB inquiry was held at New Barnet to consider an application from the UDC for the loan of £14,000. The mains of the company supplying the adjacent district of High Barnet were on the boundary of East Barnet Valley, and offers had been made to the UDC to supply energy to the area at 3.25d per unit, against 7d proposed to be charged under the local authority scheme. The supply was immediately available and the residents not only in the compulsory area, but also in the important

---

[52] *Electrical Review* vol 51, p822 14/11/1902
[53] *Electrical Review* vol 51, p900 28/11/1902
[54] *Electrical Review* vol 51, p621 10/10/1902
[55] *Electrical Review* vol 52, p18 2/1/1903
[56] *Electrical Review* vol 51, p1030 19/12/1902
[57] *Electrical Review* vol 52, p141 23/1/1903
[58] *Electrical Review* vol 52, p63 9/1/1903

residential district of Hadley Green, on the threshold of which the company's mains were also laid, could be supplied. There was strenuous opposition both within the Council chamber and among the ratepayers, to the Council's scheme.

It appeared from the evidence that the members of the Council were about equally divided in opinion but, because one member was absent at the critical division, a decision was arrived at in favour of the speculation, by a majority of one. Col Bentley, a resident at Hadley Green, whose house was already wired and waiting for current, gave evidence at the enquiry against the scheme. Councillor Wood said that property owners were dead against it.

The only evidence in favour of the loan, was from a Mr Ambler, who believed that there was a possibility of the electricity being supplied at a profit. The opposition was mainly from an important section of the ratepayers. A memorial signed by 752 occupiers (representing more than half the rateable value) was presented to the LGB. The Barnet District Gas and Water Co opposed as large ratepayers, and pointed out that supplying electricity at a loss would mean that the gas company, as ratepayers, would be taxed to subsidise their own competitors. For the North Metropolitan Co, Mr Offor stated that the same terms would be charged as at High Barnet, and his company guaranteed that consumers in East Barnet Valley should not pay more than 3.75d per unit as a general average. He appealed to the Board to adopt the recent precedent of Faversham and recommend the Council to make terms with his company.

The evidence of Mr Adams, the Council's expert, showed that even at 7d per unit the undertaking would not yield a profit till the third year. He had no faith in the maximum demand system of charging, because there were no very large consumers in the district, and nobody would ever reach the lower rate (apparently oblivious of the fact that very small consumers, if they ran their lamps beyond an average of one hour per day, would reach the lower rate). Mr Adams made no allowance in his estimates for depreciation or antiquation of the plant, and contended that it was not necessary and was not good finance[59].

Mr Adams later alleged that the opposition was fomented by interested parties, and the signatures to the memorial obtained by gross misrepresentations. There was, he said, a strong feeling on the part of the Council against allowing their electric lighting powers to be absorbed by the vast group of companies with

---

[59] *Electrical Review* vol 52, p261 13.2.1903

which the North Metropolitan Power Distribution Co was associated. He thought that the group would be better employed in developing the undertakings they had already secured, rather than in continually launching out in fresh directions[60]. The ratepayers countered that they were not opposed to electric lighting, but simply to an impracticable scheme carried by reason of the fact that one of the six opposing councillors was ill when the vote was taken[61].

The *Electrical Review* commented that it would be interesting to see how the LGB would deal with the case, which presented many and obvious reasons against the proposed speculation by the UDC. There was no necessity for it because better terms and a prompter supply could be obtained from the company carrying on business in the adjoining district. The Council was divided in opinion and a very important section of the ratepayers was opposed to the scheme. On what principle, then, could the LGB sanction the undertaking? If its province was to protect the interests of the ratepayers by only sanctioning an outlay when satisfied of its prudence, necessity, and its being in accordance with the desires of the inhabitants of the district, it would be impossible to approve of the transaction as presented at the inquiry[62].

In the best traditions of arbiters, the LGB informed the UDC that, in view of the strong opposition of the ratepayers at the recent inquiry, and the division of opinion of the UDC itself, it would defer its decision until after the election of District Councillors in April next, so that ratepayers may be able to express their opinion on the question with the full knowledge of the facts revealed by the inquiry[63].

By June it was reported that East Barnet District Council was in negotiation with the Supply Company as to obtaining a supply of electricity in bulk. The company said that the price would be 1.25d per unit after 100 hours use per quarter of the ascertained maximum demand, which would be charged at 3.5d per unit. If the Council used their maximum demand for the equivalent of three hours per day, the average price would work out at 2d per unit. The agreement would be terminable by two years notice at the end of 12 years, or at the end of subsequent periods of seven years. If the Council agreed to a proposal for distribution to consumers, the general average price of the retail supply need not exceed 3.75d

---

[60] *Electrical Review* vol 52, p340 27/2/1903
[61] *Electrical Review* vol 52. p390 6/3/1903
[62] *Electrical Review* vol 52, p261 13/2/1903
[63] *Electrical Review* vol 52, p437 13/3/1903

per unit. This low price to the consumer was due to the relative economy of a uniform and comprehensive system[64].

Northmet did not, however, get it all their own way. In April 1903, Hornsey, who were developing their own supply system, decided to support a proposal contained in the Wood Green District Council's Bill which would enable Hornsey to supply electricity in bulk to Wood Green[65]. According to the *Electrical Review*, Wood Green went ahead and let contracts for underground mains and roadwork[66] but there was no electricity distribution in the district until the Council transferred its ELO to the Tottenham & District Gas Co ten years later.

At St Albans the UDC were in negotiation with the Distribution Company with a view to the transfer of its powers, but agreement could not be reached and the Council recommended withdrawal from all further negotiations with that company[67].

At Edmonton, the District Council received reports from Mr B Hammond and from Mr W C C Hawtayne with respect to the Provisional Order which had been obtained by the Council in 1902. Mr Hammond said that the undertaking would not be dependent upon electric lighting only, as the neighbourhood had ideal scope for a first-class motive power business. He referred to the large factories already established in the district, the bulk of which might be relied upon as users of electrical energy. The extent of the area for which the supply was to be given permitted the use of the low tension direct current system. Mr Hammond recommended that, at the outset, cables should be laid in certain streets, which would give a total of 6,200 yds of distribution mains. This would probably ensure consumers whose total demand would be equivalent to 15,000 8cp lamps. He estimated the maximum load at 300kW, including 15kW for public lighting and 55kW as motor load.

Mr Hawtayne, in his report, referred to the working-class character of the district, and said that if arrangements could be made with one of the several companies who undertook the wiring of premises on the easy payment system and if slot meters were adopted he had very little doubt that, within a few years, 17,000 to

---
[64] *Electrical Review* vol 52, p1044 19/6/1903
[65] *Electrical Review* vol 52, p573 3/4/1903
[66] *Electrical Review* vol 52, p929 29/5/1903
[67] *Electrical Review* vol 52, p573 3/4/1903

20,000 lamps of 8cp equivalent would be connected. He recommended the adoption of the three-phase alternating current system, and estimated the capital expenditure, if the Council were to provide their own power station, at £33,000, provision being made for generating plant of an aggregate of 375kW. A large profit, the report added, could not be expected.

Nothing was included in either scheme for public street lighting[68].

The District Council felt that the experts had considerably over-estimated the number of probable customers[69]. Sure enough, a fortnight later it was reported that six large firms which, it was hoped would be heavy power consumers said they would not take supply[70]. Eventually, Edmonton UDC transferred its Order to Northmet for £2800[71].

Over at Willesden in June 1903, it was expected that the District Council would be able to supply electricity "in a couple of weeks time"[72], but the Council had already decided to apply to Parliament for an Act allowing Willesden UDC to sell the electricity works and undertaking to the North Metropolitan Electric Power Supply Co[73]. Northmet would supply the Council with energy in bulk. Mr Ruthven Murray, the Council's electrical engineer, advised that the prices offered by Northmet for supplying energy were much below what the Council could reach for some years. He estimated that there would be a deficiency on the first three years' working of the Council's plant of £9672, as against £4893 if the company's offer were accepted. In accepting the arrangement, the Council still retained all the advantages of its provisional order and could at any future time generate on its own account[74].

On 22nd May 1903, the Select Committee of the House of Lords considered the Bill of the Willesden Urban District Council. The Bill sought power to take lands in Taylor's Lane, Harlesden, for a generating station and also powers to supply electrical energy in adjacent districts and for traction purposes. There were several opponents to the Bill, including the Gas Light and Coke Co whose

---

[68] *Electrical Review* vol 52, p870 22/5/1903
[69] *Electrical Review* vol 52, p963 5/6/1903
[70] *Electrical Review* vol 52, p1044 19/6/1903
[71] *Electrical Review* vol 59, p134 27/7/1906
[72] *Electrical Review* vol 52, p970 5/6/1903
[73] *Electrical Review* vol 52, p1007 12/6/1903
[74] *Electrical Review* vol 52, p657 17/4/1903

representative addressed the Committee in opposition to the electricity portion of the scheme, and said that on behalf of the Gas Light and Coke Co he had to ask that the same provisions should be inserted in the Bill for the protection of that company as had been done in the case of the Bermondsey and Woolwich municipal electric undertakings.

The Willesden District Council were seeking powers to erect a large generating station from which to supply adjoining local authorities, who were empowered to supply energy, and they further wished to supply any local authority, company or person owning or working any tramway, railway or light railway partly within and partly without their district. There was a considerable difference of opinion as to how far local authorities should be allowed to indulge in municipal trading, and he believed that the feeling of Parliament was that this sort of trading had already been allowed to go too far. If the Committee granted the request of the Willesden District Council, he asked that the Gas Light and Coke Co should be given protection against any probable loss which might ensue to them from the electric undertaking of Willesden. He would remind their Lordships that the Gas Co paid over £2000 a year in rates, and it would be monstrous, if there should be a loss on the undertaking, that it should be borne by the general body of ratepayers, among whom was the Gas Co

If municipalities were to go in for trading, they should do it on fair terms, and he would ask the Committee to agree to four propositions to secure that result. He would ask the Committee to say,
first, that the Willesden Urban District Council should not be allowed to supply energy to local authorities outside its own area;
second, that it should also be prevented from supplying electrical energy to tramways outside its own district;
third, that if it were allowed to supply electrical fittings at all, it should be put under an obligation not to supply them free; and
fourth, that a clause should be put in the Bill similar to that of the South Metropolitan Gas Co's clause, providing that the Council should, once a year, after the first year's working, cause to be laid before it a statement and balance sheet giving the accounts of the electrical undertaking, and that it should thereupon fix annually the charges to be made for the supply of energy in the ensuing year at such a rate that the revenue for the year should balance the expenditure. He explained that the last provision was necessary in order to

ORIGINS

guarantee that the expenditure should he met out of the revenue each year, and thus avoid any loss coming on the rates.

The Chairman said the Committee had decided that the Council should be restricted to the supplying of energy within its own area. They were of opinion that the last clause, asked for by Mr Browne with reference to an annual balance-sheet and the fixing of prices, should be inserted in the Bill. With regard to the question of the supply of electrical fittings, they were of opinion that the clause should remain in the Bill as drafted by the Council[75].

When the Northmet Bill came before the Examiner for Proof of Compliance with Standing Orders, it was found that the Orders had not been complied with. Accordingly it was referred to the Standing Orders Committee, who would decide whether the Bill could be allowed to proceed. The Bill empowered the UDC of Willesden to sell their generating station to the company, and the company would be empowered to enter into agreements to supply electricity in bulk from the station to the District Council, to the Harrow Road and Paddington Tramways Co, and to any new tramways or light railways within the area owned or worked by the Metropolitan Electric Tramways Co Ltd[76].

The Company eventually obtained its Act authorising them to acquire Taylors Lane power station and to afford a bulk supply to Willesden Council whose district remained outside the Company's limits of supply[77]. A substantial part of the output was supplied to tramways. A rotary converter substation at Hendon supplied the MET's route from Cricklewood to Edgware, which opened on the 3 December 1904[78].

The contract for the erection of Brimsdown power station had been placed in 1903 by the Metropolitan Electric Tramways and was taken over by Northmet in 1904 simultaneously with the starting of the electric tramways. On 22nd July 1904, the MET and BT-H inspected the new power station[79].

---

[75] *Electrical Review* vol 52, p912 29/5/1903
[76] *Electrical Review* vol 52, p1076 26/6/1903
[77] *An Outline History of the Northmet Power Company* by E T Kingsbury and Evelyn Boys, 1946.
[78] PC Bourne R
[79] *Metropolitan Electric Tramways* by C S Smeeton, LRTA, p44

It is reported that on 14th June 1906, British Insulated Wire Co won an emergency contract to supply and lay 9.25 miles of 11kV cable and 4.625 miles of 8-core telephone cable, both to be installed by the end of July. The job needed 230 men. History does not record the reason for this sudden unplanned requirement[80].

Cheshunt UDC agreed to Northmet supply in the district[81] in 1906 and Kingsbury transferred its order to Northmet about the same time[82]. The St Albans & District Electricity Supply Co informed the St Albans RDC that it intended to transfer its order to Northmet[83] (although no supply had started there at that time) and supply started in Enfield on 29th September[84]. In November 1906 Northmet applied for Provisional Orders for Hendon, Barnet, Edmonton, Ware, Hertford, Hatfield, Welwyn and St Albans[85] but they were not getting it all their own way because the Electricity Supply Co (of Scotland) won the rights to supply in Hitchin, Stevenage and Hendon[86].

Supplies for lighting, heating and general purposes commenced in Edmonton in July 1907 followed by Tottenham (December 1907), Kingsbury (October 1910) and Southgate (April 1911). All these supplies were afforded under Electric Lighting Orders which had been transferred to the Company.

By now Northmet was really a going concern, with a substantial traction load and various supply undertakings with power supplied from four generating stations.

The following statement of the units supplied at ten-yearly intervals from the commencement of supply shows the development which took place:-

Year Units supplied
1902 35,000
1912 29 millions
1922 65
1932 299

---
[80] D B Welbourn *Portrait of Burkwood Welbourne, an Engineer*, Pentland Press, 1996. ISBN 185821 3894, p34
[81] *Electrical Review* vol 59, p19 6/7/1906
[82] *Electrical Review* vol 59, p20 6/7/1906
[83] *Electrical Review* vol 59, p58 13/7/1906
[84] *Electrical Review* vol 50, p651 19/4/1907
[85] *Electrical Review* vol 59, p829 23/11/1906
[86] Bourne R: *Hendon Electric Supply Company* (1985) p15

1942 1,065
1945 1,142

The units sold in bulk to other Authorised Undertakers steadily increased from less than 1 million in 1904 to about 204 millions in 1938. In the two following years there was a decline in the bulk supplies due to the transfer to the Company of the undertakings of the Harrow and Hendon Companies but since then the increase continued and by 1945 the output for bulk supplies amounted to 212 million units[87].

Bulk supplies were afforded by the Company to other authorised undertakers as follows:–
Metropolitan Borough of Stoke Newington – April 1906 to March 1928;
Hendon Electric Supply Co Ltd. – January 1903 to September 1939;
Colne Valley Electric Supply Company – from October 1914;
Harrow Electric Light and power Co Ltd. – December 1920 to October 1937;
Welwyn Garden City Ltd. – from October 1921;
Tottenham & District Gas Company (Wood Green)–November 1922 to January 1933;
Stevenage Electric Light and Power Co Ltd. – November 1925 to November 1927;
Bedfordshire, Cambridgeshire & Huntingdonshire Electricity Company - from June 1927;
Hitchin Urban District Council – from October 1927;
Bishop's Stortford Epping and District Gas company - January 1929 to September 1933;
and the County of London Electric Supply Co Ltd. (for distribution in a small outlying part of their Essex area) – from January 1936.

In Northmet's early years the demand for industrial power developed slowly; in 1914 the units sold were less than 4 million. During the 1914–18 war the majority of the power consumers were engaged in the manufacture of munitions and their electricity requirements increased considerably and in 1917, the peak year, over 22 million power units were sold. From 1918 the power output dropped and it was not until 1925 that the figure of 1917 was overtaken. Subsequently there was a steady increase year by year and in 1943 the units sold

---

[87] *An outline history of the Northmet Power Company* by BT Kingsbury and Evelyn Boys

for power purposes amounted to 261 million. There was a slight drop in 1944 and a further substantial decrease in 1945 when the output for power purposes was 214 million units. The Company also supplied a large number of small factories whose consumption rose from 20 to 129 million units between 1932 and 1944. In 1945 these Supplies dropped to 117 million units. The Company was fortunate in having an area of supply which accommodated a large variety of industries with the result that the diversity of the power users was such that the aggregate output was not materially affected by fluctuations in the activities of any particular industry.

In the Parliamentary Session 1924–25 the Northmet Company promoted a Bill to authorise, amongst other things, the acquisition of 36 acres of additional land at Brimsdown, Enfield; the erection of a generating station thereon, and the raising of £650,000 on debenture or mortgage specifically for those purposes, in excess of the authorised borrowing powers which, at that time, were limited to one half of the issued share capital. The additional borrowing powers were asked for in order to secure the benefit of the Government guarantee under the Trade Facilities Acts.

The provisions for the additional borrowing were struck out of the Bill but the provisions in regard to the acquisition of the site and the erection of the station remained and were incorporated in the Act which received Royal Assent on 30th June 1925. At that time the unissued share capital and the unexercised borrowing powers were not more than sufficient to meet the liabilities in connection with the normal development of the Company's business.

The position was explained to the Trade Facilities Act Advisory Committee and application was made for the Government guarantee of loans amounting to £1,000,000 to a new company, the North Metropolitan Power Station Co Ltd, proposed to be formed with a small nominal capital and unlimited borrowing powers. The proposals were that Northmet should subscribe for the whole of the share capital in the new company which would then issue debentures or debenture stock to meet the cost of the station. The new company would lease the station to Northmet which would pay a rental sufficient to meet the interest and service charges in connection with the proposed issue of debentures or debenture stock.

The Trade Facilities Act Advisory Committee said that they were well disposed towards the scheme and would be prepared to recommend a guarantee, subject to the necessary legal formalities being proved to be practicable and subject to the general views of the Electricity Commissioners.

Counsels' opinion was obtained and they advised that there was no legal objection to the proposed scheme and the Commissioners informed the Advisory Committee that they were satisfied that the needs of Northmet required the erection of the proposed station and they did not object to the formation and registration of the proposed new Company if the application met with the Advisory Committee's favour.

The North Metropolitan Power Station Company Limited was registered on 5th May 1926 to construct and equip, or to enter into agreements for the construction and equipment of generating stations in any part of Great Britain and to lease generating stations to the Northmet Company. The authorised and issued capital of the Station Company was £100 (all held by the Northmet Company), the dividend being limited to 6% pa. The Company had unlimited borrowing powers. The outstanding loan capital of the Station Company at December 31, 1945 was £5,221,330. It was through the Power Station company that the extensions to Brimsdown were carried out and, eventually, Rye House was built.

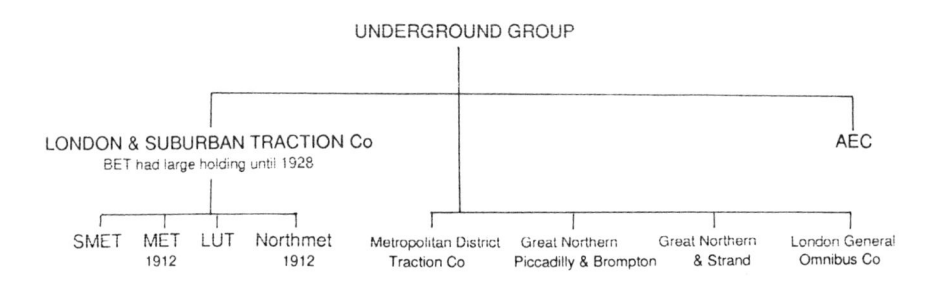

```
                          UNDERGROUND GROUP
                                 |
       ┌─────────────────────────┼──────────────────────────────────────┐
LONDON & SUBURBAN TRACTION Co                                          AEC
BET had large holding until 1928
       |
  ┌────┬────┬──────┐      ┌──────────────┬──────────────┬──────────────┐
SMET  MET  LUT  Northmet  Metropolitan District  Great Northern  Great Northern  London General
      1912       1912     Traction Co    Piccadilly & Brompton   & Strand       Omnibus Co
```

3: **Northmet ownership**

CHAPTER 2: CONSTITUTION

There were in all three Northmet companies. For simplification in this history they are referred to as the Distribution Company, the Supply Company and the Power Station Company.

"Who owns whom?" is a question often asked of modern companies. The situation was no less complicated 100 years ago. The North Metropolitan Electric Power Distribution Company was formed in 1899 by the Metropolitan Electric Tramways Co (MET) which was, in turn, a subsidiary of the British Electric Traction Co (BET).

The other Northmet was the North Metropolitan Electric Power Supply Company which was formed by Act of Parliament in 1900. That Act authorised the Company to supply electricity in bulk to authorised undertakers in an area of approximately 326 square miles. The Company was empowered by subsequent Acts and Orders to supply electricity for all purposes to domestic and other consumers in the specified areas which eventually extended to 345 square miles. In July 1903 MET acquired the Supply Company from BET.

When the Supply Company's original area was authorised, powers to distribute electricity were held by local authorities or other companies in respect of Barnet, Finchley, Harrow, Hendon, Hertford, Hornsey, St Albans and Walthamstow. This did, however, present the prospect of affording all or some of these authorised undertakers with supplies in bulk.

In addition, of course, the Distribution Company's owners, MET, were planning to electrify their extensive system of horse tram-ways.

At the same time, factories were being established along the banks of the River Lee from Hertford through Ware, Hoddesdon, Cheshunt, Waltham Cross, Enfield, Edmonton and Tottenham and then on to join the Thames at Limehouse and Blackwall. Apart from Hertford there were no authorised electricity undertakers for these districts and in 1902 the Supply Company promoted a Bill to authorise it to distribute electricity for all purposes in the more developed districts of Edmonton, Enfield and Tottenham and the adjoining districts of

Southgate and Wood Green, The Distribution Co had previously made an application for a Provisional Order for Enfield and similar applications were made by the local authorities for Edmonton, Tottenham and Wood Green about the time the Company's Bill was deposited.

These competing promotions were considered by a Select Committee of the House of Commons over a period of six days with the result that Parliament decided to grant the Provisional Order powers applied for by the local authorities and the Distribution Company and authorised the Supply Company to supply for power purposes subject to the consent of the respective local authorities which was not to be unreasonably withheld.

Stoke Newington, which was in the County of London, was added to the Supply Company's limits by the Company's Act of 1905 and that same Act authorised the Company to supply Alexandra Palace in Wood Green. It also extended the traction powers so that the Company could supply within their area for use outside. The Act also enabled the Company to take transfers of Electric Lighting Order undertakings and under this authority Electric Lighting Orders which had not been implemented were subsequently acquired for the districts of Edmonton, Kingsbury, Southgate and Tottenham.

The powers were extended by the Act of 1907 which authorised the Supply Company to supply for all purposes subject to the consent of the authorised undertakers, if any, in the whole of the area except the five districts in which the Company were authorised by the 1902 Act to supply for "power" purposes and certain other districts. By subsequent Acts the number of other districts excepted was reduced to four; Finchley, Hornsey, Stoke Newington and Walthamstow.

Prior to the passing of the 1907 Act further Electric Lighting Orders had been granted in respect of Ware (1905) Cheshunt, East Barnet, Hendon Rural, Wealdstone and Wembley (1906) but all these were subsequently revoked and supply afforded by the Company under its Act powers.

In November 1912 BET brought its interests in the London tramways companies and allied motor omnibus undertakings together by the formation of the London & Suburban Traction Co Ltd (L&STCo). This new company now held the majority of shares in MET, London United Tramways, Tramways (MET) Omnibus Co, South Metropolitan Electric Tramways and Lighting Co

(SouthMet), MET and, through the shares held by MET, all the ordinary shares of the Northmet Companies. The issued capital of L&STCo was £4,150,000 of which BET held 859,313, 'a large interest being held by Underground Electric Railway Co of London'[1]. It was at this point that control of Northmet effectively passed to the Underground group. [see family tree]

The group of companies included in the L&STCo transferred their offices to Electric Railway House, Broadway on 31st December 1915 in order to coordinate more fully their business with the management of the UERL and LGOC[2]. The constituent companies (MET, London General Omnibus Co, the two Northmet companies, SouthMet and the Tramways (MET) Omnibus Co) resigned from the British Electricity Federation although BET had a residual interest until 1928.

In 1922 the 'Order' undertakings for Barnet, Enfield, Hertford and St Albans, then held by the Distribution Co were vested in the Supply Company and the Distribution Company was dissolved.

By arrangement with the Hertfordshire County Council, Northmet applied for, and obtained, a further Act in 1925 which extended the limits of supply to the northern boundary of the County and the Company were authorised to supply for all purposes in this added area.

This still left a complicated situation because there were legal differences between the 'Order' undertakings and those districts supplied under the various Acts of Parliament. The differences of constitution meant that the 'Order' undertakings could, in theory at least, be taken over after different periods of time by the local authorities. If this happened compensation would have to be paid, so each undertaking had to keep separate accounts. There were also different technical requirements for much of Northmet's existence because the Electricity Supply Regulations (which governed the safety aspects of the business) applied to the Order undertakings. The Northmet Acts of Parliament had had similar, but not identical, requirements included in those Acts. This gave rise to particular complications at St Albans where the original City area was supplied under an Electric Lighting Order but the surrounding rural area was authorised under an Act.

---

[1] British Electricity Federation annual report, 31/12/1913
[2] British Electricity Federation agenda 34, 17/4/1916

Northmet was, therefore, able to supply for all purposes throughout the whole of the area, except, in the end, in Finchley, Hornsey, Stoke Newington, Walthamstow, Hitchin, Letchworth and Welwyn Garden City where the Company could only supply in bulk to those undertakings.

Wood Green was, for many years, supplied by the Tottenham & District Gas Co, but sold out to Northmet, the final transfer being completed in 1932. The Hendon company was taken over by Northmet in September 1936 and Stevenage in November 1927.

The Colne Valley Electric Supply Co Ltd distributed in the Parish of Pinner which was within Northmet limits and in other districts outside the Northmet area. Bulk supply was afforded by Northmet for distribution by the Colne Valley Company and their associated company, the Northwood Electric Light and Power Co Ltd.

The Welwyn Garden City Electricity Supply Co Ltd distributed in Welwyn Garden City, a bulk supply being taken from Northmet.

The Urban District of Baldock and part of the Rural District of Hitchin within Northmet's limits formed part of the area of the First Garden City Ltd, Letchworth, which generated its own requirements.

During 1928 BET disposed of its interest in London & Suburban and hence in Northmet to the Underground Electric Railways of London group. At the following BET Annual General Meeting it was reported that the L&ST shares had been paying no dividend at all. Lord Ashfield took over from Emile Garcke as Chairman and Managing Director of Northmet in 1929[3].

Soon after this, moves were started to create London Transport, mainly from the Underground group of companies[4], but initially the proposals were not acceptable[5]. Letters were exchanged with the Minister of Transport and terms agreed eventually. UERL's interests in AEC (the Associated Equipment Company, who made lorries and bus chassis) and Northmet were not included in the scheme[6], nor was the electricity supply undertaking of the South

---
[3] London Metropolitan Archive Acc/1297/UER1/6 Minute 3883, 3/10/1929
[4] London Metropolitan Archive Acc/1297/UER1/6 Minute 4026, 4/12/1930
[5] London Metropolitan Archive Acc/1297/UER1/6 Minute 4067, 20/3/31
[6] London Metropolitan Archive Acc/1297/UER1/6 Minute 4080, 1/5/1931

Metropolitan Electric Tramways which was sold to the London & Home Counties Joint Electricity Authority[7].

Under a scheme dated 5th July 1933, shares in Northmet and the vehicle manufacturers AEC were transferred to 12 named trustees in accordance with s88 of the London Passenger Transport Act, 1933[8] and they were floated as independent companies. The Underground group was formally wound up[9] after the formation of the London Passenger Transport Board in 1933, although Lord Ashfield remained chairman of Northmet as well as becoming chairman of LPTB. By this time Captain Donaldson was Northmet's General Manager and he visited the LPTB headquarters at 55 Broadway frequently to report on progress to Lord Ashfield.

Donaldson would be dressed in a country tweed suit in contrast to the conventional black or grey suits worn by LT Officers and staff. When he was asked how things were going with Northmet, he used to reply "Plenty of load". His cheerfulness was a welcome change from the usual mood at 55 Broadway, where the finances of the LPTB were not satisfactory (and the finances of the United Railways of Havana were much worse than those of the LPTB!). Supplying electricity during the continuous housing and industrial development of the north London suburbs was a rewarding business[10].

By nationalisation the five local authority undertakers in the Northmet area were Finchley, Hitchin, Hornsey, Stoke Newington and Walthamstow. Hitchin took a bulk supply from the Company but the remaining authorities either generated themselves or obtained their power elsewhere.

As electricity supply developed it was realised that sharing the bulk supplies from the most efficient power stations was far more economical than each undertaking having its own power station. The principle had been recognised from the earliest days by Northmet but, nationally, it led to the formation of the Central Electricity Board (CEB) and a move to amalgamation of electricity undertakings into Joint Electricity Authorities. The Electricity (Supply) Act was passed 23/12/1919 but without controversial "and dangerous" provisions for the

---

[7] London Metropolitan Archive Acc/1297/UER1/6 Minutes 4115 (1/10/1931) and Minute 4183.
[8] London Metropolitan Archive Acc/1297/UER1/6 Minute 4312, 28/7/1933
[9] London Metropolitan Archive Acc/1297/UER1/6 27/6/1935
[10] PC Bull A.

formation of District Electricity Boards with compulsory purchase powers for generating stations and main transmission lines. The Act provided for the appointment of Electricity Commissioners and the formation of Joint Electricity Authorities but with no compulsory powers[11]. However, new power stations had to be authorised by CEB. The concept of Joint Electricity Authorities continued to hang over Northmet and from 1930 to 1937 became mixed up with the local authorities' purchase rights under the Electricity Acts.

It was recognised that more power would be needed in the Lea Valley and for this purpose the North Metropolitan Power Station Company was formed. It was incorporated on 5/5/1926 initially to fund extensions to Brimsdown. In this way Northmet were able to take advantage of loans and government grants under the Trade Facilities Acts, 1921-26, designed to help alleviate the effects of recession and unemployment.

In 1930 the extension of Brimsdown was authorised and the following years saw expenditure of nearly £1m. In 1934 Brimsdown A was purchased by the Power Station Company at cost less depreciation. The following year it was decided to reconstruct Brimsdown 'A' (another £1m) and in 1938 the Power Station Company further extended Brimsdown 'B'.

Taylors Lane (Willesden) power station was purchased from the Supply Company in 1939 and leased back. The proposed reconstruction was costed at £1.25m.

Before the Second World War, the CEB and Northmet had considered the possibility of another new power station in the Lea Valley. In 1942 a site of approximately 90 acres was acquired by the Station Company in the Urban District of Hoddesdon for a proposed new generating station and on 2nd July 1945 the Central Electricity Board formally notified Northmet of the proposal under Section 6 of the 1926 Act for the construction of a new station on the site to be known as the Rye House Generating Station.

On 30th November 1945 application was made to the Electricity Commissioners for their consent under Section 11 of the 1919 Act and a copy of the application was sent on the same day to the Hoddesdon UDC in accordance with the Town & Country Planning Acts.

---

[11] British Electricity Federation agenda 41 (26/4/1920):

CONSTITUTION

At about the same time Northmet deposited a Bill in Parliament to authorise them to take on lease and operate the Rye House Station. However, on account of the objections lodged by the Hertfordshire County Council and the Local Authority against the erection of the Station, the Electricity Commissioners and the Minister of Town and Country Planning decided to hold a joint Local Inquiry on 26/27th March 1946. The result was that the consent of both parties was given on 22nd June subject to certain conditions and the Northmet Bill received Royal Assent on 6th November 1946.

Eventually, after these delays, the construction of Rye House power station (with buildings designed by Sir Giles Gilbert Scott) was begun although electricity generation did not start until well after nationalisation. Generation commenced in December 1951 with further units being commissioned in the following two years.

In the meantime nationalisation had taken place and the Northmet Companies ceased to exist from 1st April 1948. However, the ghost of the organisation continued for many more years in the form of a Sub-Area of the Eastern Electricity Board.

CHAPTER 3: GENERATING STATIONS[1]

When Northmet was formed in 1899 it was a electricity company without any generation but, then, it did not have any consumers either!

Barnet

Barnet power station was erected by the North Metropolitan Electrical Power Distribution Co Ltd. Supply commenced on 31st August 1900. The original plant consisted of two 160 psi dry back boilers, two 50kW Holmes DC generators each coupled direct to Reavill steam engines, and a Hart Battery. In 1901 the plant was increased by one 100kW Brush Universal set and one Babcock & Wilcox water tube boiler. In 1904 a second 100kW Brush Universal set was erected temporarily outside the station. In May 1905 the power station was transferred to the Northmet Power Supply Company and bulk supply commenced[2].

The batteries were removed in 1906-7 and a 10kV AC to 560/480 volt converter was installed, said to be the first made for this voltage. A second one was added in 1908. In 1909 the Babcock & Wilcox boiler was sent to Hertford and the old boiler house demolished. Subsequently the station was converted into a substation but the rotary converters stayed for the remaining DC consumers and tramway (and subsequently trolleybus) supplies.

Hertford

The Hertford power station was commissioned in 1901, for the Distribution Company to supply power to their authorised area. The station was transferred from the Power Distribution Co Ltd to the Supply Co in 1902 for £14,560/18/8d[3]. The original capacity of the station was 200kW. The first plant comprised two hand–fired Babcock and Wilcox water-tube boilers providing superheated steam at 400F to two Raworth "Universal" engines running at 300 rpm. Direct–coupled to each engine was a 100kW four-pole Brush compound

---
[1] Originally based on a paper by Bourne R, presented at the IEE's 1988 *History of Technology* meeting, the information has been supplemented from other sources, as indicated by the notes.
[2] Northmet Monthly Bulletin 7/26 Item 68
[3] Minutes of Northmet Supply Co Board Min 6 8/4/1902

generator of Mordey design. The output at 460 Volts was connected to a four-machine Brush Mordey set running at 1100 rpm comprising two balancers and two boosters. A 250 Ah Hart accumulator was provided.

By 1905 it seems that the plant was not in very good order. An inspection by A W A Chivers on 5th January 1905 for the British Electric Traction Co Ltd, resulted in the following report:

"GENERATORS. These consist of a two 100kW universal Brush sets. I saw No 2 set running which was very noisy when first started up, the noise no doubt being due to water in the cylinders. I understand these engines were supplied with new cylinders in June 1903, and that the drain holes in the new cylinders are only a quarter of an inch against one inch in the old cylinders. The smaller holes no doubt prevent the escape of water as readily as the larger holes

"I found the usual trouble which is common to this type of engine, viz air leakage at LP valve spindle, and explained to the engineer in charge, Mr Butler, the method proposed to overcome this difficulty.

4: **Hertford Power Station before extension** [*Hertford Museum*]

"Both engines were indicated in December of last year and the cards were good, with the exception of the poor vacuum line. The cards were decidedly better than those taken in December 1901, when the engines were new.

"The foundation for an additional 200kW set has been put in, but I notice that no provision has been made for the cable pipe. This will necessitate cutting through the engine room concrete floor.

"BOILERS. There are two boilers of the Babcock and Wilcox type capable of evaporating 3800 gallons per hour. They appear to be in good condition. Mr Butler told me that the inside condition is also good. They were inspected by the Vulcan Insurance Co's inspector in July and August of last year and the certificates show that they were in a satisfactory condition at that time.

"CONDENSING PLANT. This is a of the jet type by Blake and Knowles. It appeared to be in a rather bad state of repair. The link brasses were slack and noisy. The pumps have not been overhauled lately and their action seemed to indicate they were badly in need of such. The vacuum gauge at the engine indicated 22", at the condenser 23½". Mr Butler said he could get more by increasing the speed of the pumps, this was tried and the gauge stood at 23½" at engine and 25½" at condenser. No doubt the air leakage at L P valve spindle has much to do with such poor results, and it is quite conceivable that this plant uses a very large proportion of the total steam to obtain a fair vacuum. Under these conditions it is doubtful as to whether any economy is obtained by the use of condensing plant. I think there is little doubt but that it would pay better to run non-condensing at the light load periods, although I was informed the light load periods are of short duration, but even so, advantage should be taken of every opportunity to lower the generating costs. A coal consumption test would soon clear the matter up, and cost practically nil to carry out.

"FEED PUMPS. The exhaust pipe is a very poor job, and it should be altered. It would cost very little to make a permanent job of it.

"BATTERY. This is of of the Hart type, consisting of 250 cells and is rated at 320 Ah. It is not looking particularly healthy. Some of the plates show signs of sulphation and some in are buckled. The following are the charge and discharge rates recommended by the makers:-

GENERATION

Maximum emergency discharge 160 amps.
Maximum normal discharge 64 amps.
Maximum charge rate 48 amps.
Normal discharge 44 amps.
Normal charge 40 amps.

"This battery is used to take the day and night loads, the average maximum demands of which is about 50 amperes, but which varies considerably owing to the power load which it has to take.

"I have to point out that there is no regular attendant at the power house during the time that the battery is taking the load, consequently the voltage is constantly varying[4], and under these conditions the battery is not getting a fair treatment. It would be most useful if recording instruments were supplied. I think they would soon show the advisability of getting an attendant on the job.

"STAFF. As follows:-
1 fitter driver; 34/- per week of 56 hours, sixpence per hour overtime
1 pupil.
1 stoker, 30/- per week, sixpence per hour overtime when on morning shift.
1 jointer, sixpence per hour, no extra for overtime.
1 clerk at 25/- per week
1 lamp lighter 8/- per week

"Under the conditions which the station is worked I do not consider the generating staff adequate, and I would suggest getting either another pupil or an improver. In my opinion it is false economy to work with too small a staff.

"Mr Butler is not satisfied with his fitter driver, as he lacks interest in his work and as he is obliged to rely greatly on him for the running of the station a change might prove beneficial.

"WEIGHING MACHINES. There are no means of weighing coal on the works. Some means ought to be provided. A check on the coal delivered is sometimes made by the railway company, and has been found satisfactory.

---

[4] There is a handwritten annotation on the report: 'This is certainly to the detriment of the battery and will every day become more so as the plates become old' Initialled *R J H.*

"Comparative tests of coal consumption, condensing v. non-condensing, etc cannot be carried out satisfactorily without some means of weighing.

"It is impossible to ascertain the correct cost of fuel per unit generated. Mr Butler informed me that he has to make up 9 tonnes since June last, consequently he has had to charge over the amount actually used to make up the deficiency. This is unsatisfactory all round.

"REVENUE. Receipts. The receipts of the distribution company, for the quarter ended 30th September 1904 amount to £311/10/5 against £288 for the corresponding period in 1903. The increase is due entirely to lighting receipts. During the last three months, 28th September 1904 to 28th December 1904, the equivalent 8 cp connections have increased from 5479 to 6297, so that the receipts for the year 1904 will probably show good increase over the year 1903.

"Expenses. I find it impossible to make more than an approximate estimate of the expenses of the Distribution Company, for reasons stated below under "general" remarks. So far as the Supply Company is concerned I feel sure that economies are possible by close attention to the various points already referred to.

"GENERAL. The power house has been sold to the Supply Company who generate and sell in bulk to the Distribution Company at the following rates: 3 pence per Unit for the equivalent first 100 hours of supply of maximum demand, and one penny per unit for any further quantity.

"Mr Butler informed me he did not know for what quantity of current the Supply Company was entitled to charge the Distribution Company, whether it was the units generated or sold. As far as I have been able to ascertain, the Distribution Company have been paying for units generated. I have since read the agreement between the companies dated 25th March 1902 and the only construction I can put on it is that it is neither of these, but the units sent out.

"The following is an extract from the agreement, clause five: "All electrical energy required by the vendors for the purposes of the said Hertford Electric Lighting Order shall be delivered to them by the purchasers at the general switchboard of the vendors in the said generating station".

"By clause 1, all machinery and plant was agreed to be sold, other than and except for the switchboards, mains and other apparatus, as at the date of agreement was used by the distribution company, for the purpose off or in connection with the distribution of electrical energy from the generating station. That, I take it, means strictly all plant with the exception of the feeder panels and balancer. If this be a correct interpretation of the agreement then the distribution company must pay for units delivered at the feeder panels. Unfortunately there are no meters on the feeders, consequently the amount sent out and can only be estimated. It would be much more satisfactory if meters were supplied.

"Taking the quarter ended 30th September 1904 there were no less than 5577 units, or 25 per cent of the total units generated, used on works and lost in cables, boosters, battery and mains.

"It will therefore be seen it is impossible to ascertain exactly how each company stands until some agreement is made as to the number of units to be paid for by the distribution company. It seems very probable that the distribution company could make some claim on the supply company for current paid for and not really supplied, but then the difficulty arises how to ascertain the amount in the absence of meters."

The report was signed by A W A Chivers, 7th January 1905.

100kW of plant was added in 1906 and a further 500kW in 1913. A refuse destructor was erected and put into service in 1910 with a boiler and 100kW Brush set second hand from Barnet[5].

In 1913, the Great Northern Railway cut their loop line from Cuffley to Stevenage via Hertford North using electrically powered excavators. Two new boilers, a 625kVA turbine-driven alternator, a rotary converter and transformers were installed at Hertford to meet this extra load. The GNR work was finished by 1915 but the equipment was retained to provide the extra loads demanded by wartime work.

The final development of the station came in 1921 when a 1 MW Ljungstrom turbine was transferred from Willesden and some of the old plant was scrapped. A 240kW mercury arc rectifier was also installed. Generation ceased from the beginning of May 1926 but a 700kVA 750RPM BT-H rotary condenser had been

---

[5] Northmet Monthly Bulletin 5/26 Item 59

commissioned earlier the same year. The full load operation of that machine (connected to the 11kV system by a transformer) produced a voltage rise of about 4% between Brimsdown and Hertford along the 11kV transmission line.

When generation ceased it seems that the dust destructor became something of a bone of contention between Northmet and the Council[6]. There were plans for its purchase by the Council followed by arguments about its value.

St Albans

In 1908 two 150kW/200hp Brush Falcon sets and a refuse destructor were installed at the Campfields, St Albans and commenced operation on 26th September. Each of the engines drove two 75kW 265 volt DC generators arranged in tandem[7]. For some years, the whole supply of the town was given from this station. This installation was one of the earliest (if not the earliest in the country) to use refuse to produce steam in reasonable and regular quantities to supply electricity. The exhaust steam was used to heat the works and offices of the Salvation Army's Campfield Press, just across the road. Coal, if required to supplement the refuse, arrived by road, probably from the railway sidings at Sutton Road, at the far end of Campfield Road.

As the supply to the town outgrew the capacity of the destructor, two 95kW/120hp Sulzer diesel engines were installed in 1909 and again this was one of the first power stations in this country where diesel power was used. At this stage oil was very cheap so, when further extensions were needed in 1912, two additional 300HP diesel sets were ordered from Carels in Ghent. The second one left Belgium only a day or two before the Germans over-ran the district[8]. The new high–speed diesel engines were not a success and, were replaced in 1913 by a 275kW set of a considerably lower speed. A sister set was added in 1914, bringing the plant capacity up to 1040kW. Oil was delivered to a siding behind the Salvation Army factory on the other side of Campfield Road and piped under

---

[6] Northmet Management Committee Min 637 26/5/1927
[7] Northmet Monthly Bulletin 4/26 item 54
[8] *St Albans Electricity* Northmet commemorative booklet, 1934. There is some confusion whether there were one or two high speed sets. The St Albans commemorative booklet refers to two, as quoted, the Northmet monthly Bulletin 4/26 item 54, mentions only one.

the road to the power station[9]. The tanker siding would have been high enough to allow the oil tanks to be filled by gravity.

In 1918 a 500kW DC turbine-powered generator was installed with a surface condenser and separate cooling tower. At the same time an underfeed stoker was fitted to one of the original boilers to take the place of one of the refuse destructors. The turbine, built in Switzerland, had been intended for a German colony and was reputedly captured on the high seas before being diverted to Northmet!

Costs rose during the Great War and Northmet attempted to renegotiate the payment from the City Council for burning the refuse. No agreement could be reached and on 1st January 1923 the contract was terminated[10].

At the end of 1922 the Company started to take supply from Luton and during 1923 and 1924 major alterations took place, including high power links with Brimsdown and, later, with Taylors Lane. The original steam plant in the engine room was removed and two Mather & Platt 500kW Rotary Converters with two 560kVA transformers were installed in its place. The destructor boilers were also removed and transferred to Brimsdown and the old boiler house was converted into a modern transformer and switch room. In 1924/5 the two 95kW diesel sets were removed, one being transferred to Stevenage and the 500kW turbo generator and auxiliaries were transferred to Willesden. The remaining generating plant consisting of two 275kW Diesel sets and two 150kW Brush Falcon sets was subsequently sold. Voltage control at St. Albans Power Station had been carried out by the charge engineer. With the arrival of the rotary converters control was again by the charge engineer. 3kV AC supply was regulated by hand operation of the ratio regulators[11]. The Station ceased to generate as from 1st January 1930.

Willesden (Taylors Lane)

The first power station in Willesden was built at Acton Lane by the Metropolitan Electric Power Supply Company which had no connection with Northmet. The power station at Taylors Lane was built by Willesden District Council in 1903

---

[9] PC E Wright
[10] PC W Killick
[11] PC E Wright

with plant comprising two 300kW and one 600kW double-current generators[12]. The concept of the double–current generator was that DC was the most suitable supply for the majority of consumers but AC was almost a necessity for long-distance distribution because transformers could be connected to compensate for voltage drop. The double–current generator was similar in construction to a rotary converter with the addition of a prime mover. The original 300kW machines could give full output, either DC or AC, or any combination of DC and AC totalling 300kW. Excitation could be either shunt or compound giving a range of direct voltages from 480 to 560V with the former or 500 to 550V with the latter excitation. Three-phase alternating voltage was 61% of the DC value. The nominal voltages were 500 volts DC or 400 volts AC. Speed was 250rpm, giving 25 Hz with 12 poles.

In 1903, the Electricity Committee of the Willesden UDC decided to accept an offer made by the North Metropolitan Electric Power Distribution Co to purchase the Council's generating station and outstanding liability, and to supply it with energy in bulk[13].

Mr Ruthven-Murray, the Council's electrical engineer, advised that the prices offered for supplying energy were much below what the Council could reach for some years. He estimated that there would be a deficiency on the first three years' working of the Council's plant of £9672, as against £4893 if the company's offer were accepted.

The Company's proposals were:

1.To pay in cash:–

(a) the expenditure out of current account in respect of site, £128 14s 6d;

(b) the instalments and interest in respect of site already paid by the Council, £284 12s 2d;

(c) the instalments and interest in respect of buildings, machinery, &c, already paid by the Council, £1,325 6s 5d;

(d) a sum equal to 5%. on the £2,710 expended on site, £135 10s;

(e) a sum equal to 5% on the capital expenditure in connection with the electricity works, estimate £2,990: Total £4,864 3s. 4d.

2.To take over the outstanding liabilities of the Council in connection with the before-mentioned loans of £2,581 and £59,800 for buildings, &c.

---

[12] 48 PC R Bourne after *Electrical Times* vol 22 10/7/1902
[13] Electrical Review vol 52, p657 17/4/1903

GENERATION

3. To guarantee the Council against the deficiency for the first three years, estimated as £4,893 12s 1d, upon the understanding that should the agreement for bulk supply be terminated at the end of the first seven years, two-thirds of the amount of any such deficiency shall be repaid to the company, or if it is terminated at the end of 14 years, that one-third of such deficiency shall be so repaid, but if it is determined later, then there shall be no repayment. It is further understood that the full amount of the deficiency in either the first, second or third years shall be paid by the company, provided the limit of the total sum of £4,894 is not exceeded.

In the discussion on the terms, it was pointed out that the price to be charged by the company (which would be on a sliding scale), would work out at 2d per unit on the amount calculated to be sold in the first year. Taking into consideration financial charges, the Council could not generate under 4d per unit.

In accepting the offer, the Council still retained all the advantages of its provisional order, and could at any future time generate on its own account. Ethelbert Ruthven-Murray transferred to Northmet with the power station.

In 1905 AC generation was converted to 50Hz[14] and an additional 750kW double current generator was installed. Two 1000kW turbo generators were put into service in 1906 and further extensions were made from time to time until 1912 when the capacity of the plant installed in the original building was 4.5 MW. The 1912 plant included the first Ljungstrom turbine ever built. This was rated 1MW at 3000 rpm. A further extension was then put in hand, being completed in 1914. The plant installed was one 3000kW turbo-generator with 3 Babcock boilers. Between 1914 and 1926 three additional turbines and five boilers were added bringing the total capacity of the generating plant up to 25MW but, owing to the limited capacity of the boiler plant, it was not possible to carry a sustained load of more than 19MW so a large pulverised fuel boiler was constructed to enable the station to carry loads up to the capacity of the generating plant installed. The pulverised fuel firing was a novelty at that time but Northmet were known for embracing advanced techniques.

The original Ljungstrom turbine remained in use until 1921 when it was transferred to Hertford.

---

[14] Northmet Monthly Bulletin 2/26 Item 35

In 1929 a 12.5MW Brush–Ljungstrom turbo–alternator was installed in place of the old 3MW set and a 1000kW Met–Vick motor-generator was also put in. In 1932 a 10MW turbo alternator set was installed in place of the 6MW set which had been in service since 1919.

Taylors Lane and Brimsdown became "selected stations" under the South East England Electricity Scheme 1927, as adopted by the Central Electricity Board. In December 1938 the Company were directed by the Central Electricity Board to extend Taylors Lane at an estimated cost of £1,250,000 by the installation, ready for commercial operation in September 1941, of two 32MW turbo alternator sets, five 150,000 lb/h boiler units and two cooling towers.

Taylors Lane occupied a restricted site in a built-up area with very limited railway siding and coal-stocking facilities. Early in 1937, however, there had been an opportunity of acquiring some 5 acres of land separated from the main power station site by a roadway. The new site was adequate for the establishment of a coal store and for the erection of three reinforced-concrete cooling towers for a total station capacity of 96 MW provided that a steam cycle economical in circulating-water requirements was adopted.

In 1939 an official direction was received authorising the installation of two 32MW sets and ancillary plant. It was decided to provide two standard natural circulation boilers for the first turbo-alternator, and three forced circulation type for the second, one of these being standby for either set. The plant arrangement approximated to the unit principle in that there was no interconnection either on the steam or condensate pipework between the two machines, apart from the intermediate standby boiler connections.

Contracts were placed with the International Combustion Company for two Cantini natural-circulation boilers, and with John Thompson Water Tube Boilers Ltd, for three boilers of the La Mont type. All five boiler units were specified for a normal economic rating of 120,000 lb of steam per hour with a continuous maximum rating of 150,000 lb/h, the boiler stop-valve conditions being 1,400 psi and 960 F. As at Brimsdown (and for the same reasons) chain grate stoker firing was adopted, together with unified boiler control for the auxiliary system. The associated DC generators were driven through gearing from the main alternator shaft. The high degree of superheat necessitated close attention to the temperature control and, on all five boilers, surface type desuperheaters were installed between the primary and secondary superheater banks.

The contract for the first machine was placed with the Metropolitan-Vickers Electrical Company, and for the second with the English Electric Company. The 32 MW continuous maximum rated output of each main turbine comprised a 30 MW main alternator output, plus 2 megawatt auxiliary works power including one 700kW house alternator and the two DC generators each rated at 635kW and associated with the two boilers supplying the set. The voltage of generation of both main alternators was 33 kV.

The proposals involved the displacement of two 5 MW, one 6MW and one 10MW generating sets and nine boiler units having a total capacity of 227,000 lb/h. The dismantling of the old plant was commenced in April 1939 and completed about September when the demolition of the buildings was started preparatory to the reconstruction. Work on the reconstruction was delayed on account of shortage of labour due to the war and it was not until August 1943 that the first turbo set was run on load. Work on the second set was completed about the middle of 1944.

No 2 (English Electric) machine was the first high-pressure unit to be commissioned at this station, being placed on load in July 1943, in conjunction with one boiler of the forced-circulation type. The set operated initially at half capacity pending the commissioning of the second boiler in May 1944. Meanwhile No 1 (Metropolitan-Vickers) machine had been placed in service in January 1944, in conjunction with the first natural-circulation boiler, and was commissioned up to full load in August, when the second boiler became available[15].

During 1945, the station generated 195,150,810 units at an average thermal efficiency of 26.53% on the basis of units generated, corresponding to 24.57 on the "sent-out" basis. On this performance the station ranked highest in thermal efficiency in the group of stations generating between 100 and 200 million units per annum in the Electricity Commissioners' annual tabulation. The high-

---

[15] *Some Operating Experiences with High-pressure Steam Power Plant* by W. N. C. Clinch, MIEE, Divisional Controller, Eastern Division, British Electricity Authority. IMechE Proc 1949, vol 161 (WEP No.50)

pressure plant alone generated 185,940,330 units at an average thermal efficiency of 27.42%. The load factor averaged 33.17%.

The corresponding figures for 1946 were 228,539,170 units generated at an overall thermal efficiency of 27.12%, the load factor being 40.76%.
Week-to-week operating results, for the year July 1945 to June 1946 showed that higher plant-load factors were maintained. In one period of three weeks' operation during December 1945, the figure of 29% was reached or surpassed. Over the year, the overall thermal efficiency averaged 27.5% at an average running plant load factor of 65%.

Output from the station during 1947 was restricted by reason of the outage, for a period, of one of the main sets for rewinding the alternator rotor. Nevertheless the overall thermal efficiency recorded for the year represented the best annual performance to date, 195,565,800 units being generated at an efficiency of 27.67%, corresponding to 25.79% on the 182,307,309 units sent out.

For the months of March and April 1947, the station ranked first in order of merit of overall thermal efficiency in south-east England, with figures of 28.22% and 28.58% respectively. The corresponding "sent-out" figures were respectively 26.40% and 26.88%.

The turbogenerators had serious problems running up, with different expansions of the HP spindle and the casing. Attempts were made to alleviate the problems by the use of steam flange warming on one machine and end tightening gear on the other.

Serious tube failures occurred in each boiler after almost precisely the same number of steaming hours (approximately 1,500). These failures could not be attributed to high-pressure working as such, and subsequent modifications to the internal baffling corrected the faulty circulation through the tube banks concerned. The consequences of the failures which, in view of the working conditions, might have been serious, were fortunately unattended by any injury to personnel although the immediate effect of the tube burst was in each case the ejection of steam and water through the rupture, quenching the fire and scattering coal from the grate.

The three La Mont boilers at Taylors Lane exhibited the flexibility in operation and the quick steaming properties expected from the forced-circulation design. However, they also presented certain difficulties in operation, particularly in the early stages, which imposed limitations on boiler availability and, in consequence, upon overall station efficiency.

Early operating problems centred around the circulating-pump units. Each boiler was served by an electrically driven pump for normal operation, with a steam-turbine-driven standby unit, the operation of which was automatically controlled by the discharge pressure. The pumps were of the single-end design and the standing pump was therefore subjected to the full end thrust resulting from the difference between 1,400psi and atmospheric conditions, amounting to a load of some seven tons on the thrust bearing. The driving turbines were found to be incapable of providing adequate starting torque to overcome this end thrust and, to ensure safe operation pending suitable modifications, it was necessary to maintain the turbine-driven units in operation to the detriment of the cycle efficiency. The difficulty was overcome by the provision of a hydraulic thrust-relieving device which operated on the admission of steam to the standby driving turbine. This device added an additional complication but operated satisfactorily. Experience questioned, however, the desirability of double-ended pumps for forced-circulation boilers operating at that pressure[5].

The chain grates were capable of being put into a very high speed mode to clear the fire if a forced circulation pump failed (when the tubes would burst like machine gun fire). The boiler feed pumps were of the positive displacement type. Perhaps without thinking, the designers had also installed conventional feed regulating valves. The first time one shut with the feed pump running, the pump split open[6].

The low pressure boilers were of a very primitive pulverised fuel type. Initial ignition was by burning oil-soaked rags on the end of a pole inserted through a hole in the casing. One man was killed by blow-back as the casing was very near a wall and there was no escape.

On one occasion vacuum was lost on both 30MW machines due to loss of cooling water and the machines tripped. A passer-by called at the gatehouse reporting that there had been a loud crash in the cooling tower next to the footpath from Taylors Lane to the North Circular Road. It was a freezing cold night and the whole pack inside the tower had gradually become one mass of ice, eventually causing the complete internals of the tower to fall into the pond. Following this incident all cooling towers in UK were fitted with a de-icing ring of jets around the base of the tower to give a curtain of warm water.

Operational problems at Taylors Lane led to the station having something of a reputation. It was said that one shift charge engineer had ended up in a mental home. The two 32MW turbines were arranged with the main and auxiliary generators driven through a gearbox which split the drive. A problem with the gear ratios meant that when the main set ran at 50Hz, the auxiliary generator ran at 50.5Hz. This led to synchronising difficulties which could only be overcome by a strict sequence of operations, synchronising first the auxiliary generator with the station transformer before speeding up the machine to synchronise the main alternator with the grid. To shut down the machine in an emergency it was very easy to lose everything[16].

The Brush Ljungstrom machine was very little used in later years. Its cooling towers were of square all-wooden design.

5: **Fireless locomotive *Sir James* at Brimsdown [*CEGB*]**

---

[16] PC A D Winyard

Coal was delivered to Taylors Lane by rail and, as at Brimsdown, there was a fireless shunting locomotive. The locomotive boiler was just a well-lagged steam receiver charged with steam from the power station HP system through a reducing valve. Once charged up it could then go shunting for several hours before it needed to be recharged again.

One Saturday afternoon the locomotive at nearby Acton Lane broke down, meaning that the coal bunkers could not be replenished. Although the two power stations were nothing to do with each other officially, the charge engineer at Acton Lane rang his opposite number at Taylors Lane to see if he could help. The Taylors Lane loco was charged with steam and available. However, the only way of getting it to Acton Lane was over British Rail lines. A chat with the signalman and it was all arranged; off went the loco to Acton Lane. It did a lot of work there, more than had been expected and, on the way back it ran out of steam, stranded on the BR main line. There was a real rumpus with express trains bound for the north stuck in the London terminus while BR sent a locomotive out to the rescue. This, on a busy Saturday afternoon.

The Department of Trade and Industry gave consent for the construction of a 150MW gas turbine station at Taylors Lane and two 70MW sets were fully operating by 1981 but this was on a site across the road from the old Northmet station.

Brimsdown A

The contract for the erection of Brimsdown station was placed in 1903 by the Metropolitan Electric Tramways and was taken over by the Northmet Supply Co in 1904 simultaneously with the starting of the Metropolitan Electric Tramways. The Company had purchased 5 acres of land from Trinity College, Cambridge at £300 per acre[17].

When built, the station embodied some of the most advanced ideas of the day. It was one of the first all–turbine stations in England and the generators installed were the first turbo–alternators to be wound for 10,000 volts. The original plant consisted of three Brown Boveri/Parsons 50Hz 1MW turbo–alternators and two 100kW and two 50kW engines driving direct current generators, and supplying 115 volts for excitation and works power purposes. The boiler house was

---

[17] Northmet EPSCo Board Minutes Min 5 8/4/1902

equipped with six Babcock & Wilcox 15,000 lb/h water-tube boilers operating at 160 psi with superheat to 520 F. Circulating water was abstracted from the River Lee Navigation. The switchboard by BT-H/GE had motor controlled oil switches[18].

To supply the tramways there were eventually four 11kV feeders from Brimsdown to Tramway Avenue substation, situated behind the tram depot at Edmonton.

Extensions came thick and fast. A 1750kW BT-H/Curtis vertical turbo–alternator was installed in 1906. Two 20,000 lb boilers were added in 1910 and in 1912 there was installed a 3000kW Brush turbo–alternator. In 1914 two further 20,000 lb boilers were added and in 1918, in order to cope with the munition load, a Willans & Robinson turbo–alternator driving a 6.6kV Siemens alternator and two further 20,000 lb boilers were installed. The 6kV alternator was connected to an autotransformer to step the voltage up to 11kV.

In 1920 a scheme for modernising the station was put in hand and the general arrangements in the Engine Room were completely re–designed. This involved the scrapping of the four original turbines which had a total capacity of 4,750kW. In place of these four sets, two modern 5MW Brush Ljungstrom turbine generators were installed and an English Electric set similar to the 1918 Siemens equipment. Typical of Northmet, in the vanguard of development, the Brush Ljungstrom sets were among the largest at that time. At the same time four additional 20,000 lb. boilers were added. The generating capacity of the station was thus increased to 23MW which was supplied from 18 boilers with an aggregate evaporative capacity of 320,000 lbs.

The original coal handling was by means of a gravity bucket conveyor, grabbed from barges by means of a rail-mounted crane, weighed and passed into working bunkers. The ground stocks were distributed over a large area, making reclaiming expensive. With the 1920 extensions, a new coal handling plant was installed replacing the old rail-mounted electric crane which had lifted coal from barges on the River Lea navigation. The new Henry Simon pneumatic suction plant could handle 50 tons of coal per hour. A boom transferred coal from either the rail wagon tippler or canal barge to or from the dump. A conveyor took the coal to the bunkers above the boiler house. Once again Northmet had installed a

---

[18] Northmet Monthly Bulletin 3/26, item 44

first model of its type in the country. In later years at least three different types of coal were being used; B station boiler house no 1 needed fairly low-volatile coal, boiler house no 2 needed high volatile coal and the high pressure plant in both A and B stations needed coking coal to suit the chain grate stokers. Misdirection could lead to severe consequences as was demonstrated during the 1949 strike[19].

In 1925 a rail connection was put in off the Royal Small Arms siding of the LNER, so providing an alternative supply route. Shunting was done by means of a fireless locomotive[20]. This locomotive had no fire box. The steam tank was filled three-quarters full of water and superheated by a steam pipe from the station boilers. As the pressure reduced during use of the locomotive further steam flashed from the superheated water. The engine could handle loads up to 350 tons and normally had to be charged twice a day. Eventually there were two such locomotives, both built by Andrew Barclay. No 1 was much the older having been built for the Ministry of Munitions in 1917 and bought by Northmet in 1924. No 2 was bought new in 1930. The two Brimsdown locomotives were named Sir James (after Sir James Devonshire) and Lord Ashfield, maintaining a Northmet link long after the CEGB took over. They were in use until about 1968[21].

Coal by rail was handled by a rotary wagon tippler. The suction plant took the coal from the hopper under the tippler.

In 1926 the station staff consisted of 7 engineers and 120 waged employees.

Mr W W Lackie, Electricity Commissioner, visited Brimsdown on 14th August 1931, being met by Evelyn Boys and the resident engineer, E Zoller. As well as the power station, he was shown the new 132kV CEB line, then being erected to link Brimsdown to the Grid.

In 1933 the 3 MW machine in A station was replaced by a 7.5 MW BT-H unit which was entirely used for supplying works' power to the adjacent 'B' Station. In 1934 the 'A' Station plant was put on a care–and–maintenance basis at the request of the Central Electricity Board, and the 7.5 MW machine was moved to the 'B' Station as the 'house set'.

---

[19] PC R G Whillock
[20] Northmet Monthly Bulletin 3/26, item 44.
[21] Smeeton C S, *Metropolitan Electric Tramways* ISBN 0900433949.

6: Turbine hall at Brimsdown 'A' before reconstruction in 1935, showing the four 5MW sets [*IMechE*]

In July 1935 it was decided to build a new 'A' station. The Central Electricity Board directed that the station be extended at an estimated cost of £575,000 to be ready for commercial operation in September 1938. This gave the Company the opportunity to experiment on a commercial scale with high pressure plant. Space was available at the north end of 'A' Station for a limited extension to the boiler house, and for the addition of one bay to the turbine room and, with the concurrence of the Central Electricity Board, it was decided to proceed with investigations into the practicability of high-pressure plant on the basis of a 50-megawatt unit.

Two main considerations applying to the Northmet power station sites were the necessity to economise in the greatest possible measure in coal consumption per unit sent out (since both at Brimsdown and Taylors Lane coal supplies were largely rail-borne) and to reduce to the lowest practicable limit the circulating-water requirements. Development at both station sites necessitated additional cooling towers, and in both cases local requirements regarding circulating water make-up involved costly expedients.

At Brimsdown coal arrived by rail and river, by a spur from Brimsdown LNER station and by 100ton barges, horse drawn or by tug pulling four barges. There was an extensive system of conveyors taking coal to the various bunkers.

Studies of various high-pressure plants in operation on the Continent led to the decision to adopt for the pioneer plant at Brimsdown 'A' the 1,900 psi, 930 F reheat cycle. Designs by the Metropolitan-Vickers Electrical Company for a primary turbine for these conditions were in existence, a Met-Vick plant being in operation on the Continent in association with Loeffler boilers. The original design by Dr Loeffler was developed by the Vitkovice Mines Steel and Ironworks Corporation of Czechoslovakia and a licence to manufacture in Britain was held by the Mitchell Conveyor and Transporter Company.

Theoretical considerations indicated that, by comparison with the 315 psi 750 F cycle then operated at Brimsdown 'B', the fuel economy per unit generated was of the order of 17%. The reduction in circulating water quantity was likely to amount to 24%.

In collaboration with the two manufacturers, designs were developed on the basis of this steam cycle and type of boiler. It was foreseen that in a pioneer plant initial difficulties were likely to be encountered. However, even on a pessimistic view, the indications were that efficiencies should compare with the best achievements of the standard 600 psi, 850 F cycle[5].

The Loeffler boiler was essentially a superheater. The source of low-pressure steam for starting-up purposes, required for this type of boiler, could be provided by the retention of a number of the existing boilers in the station.

An inspection of the Loeffler boilers in operation at the Caroline Pit and Trebovice Power Stations of the Vitkovice Company was made before contracts were placed, and satisfactory reports were given by the operating staff upon the steaming characteristics and general control of the boiler in commercial operation. Two units were ordered from the Mitchell Company, each having a normal output of 175,000 lb of steam per hour, with a continuous maximum rating of 210,000 lb per hour, conditions at the boiler stop valve being specified at 2,000 psi and 940 F.

The generating plant was designed for a total output of 53MW at continuous maximum rating, the primary (high pressure) turbine being rated at 19MW, and the condensing (low pressure)unit at 34MW. These outputs included the 1,650kW house alternator coupled to the primary alternator, and the two 1,050kW 500V DC generators driven through gearing from the low-pressure alternator shaft. These latter were associated with the unified Ward-Leonard boiler control system. The generation voltage was 33kV in both main alternators.

The intermediate pressure of 160 psi was selected for the initial plant with the object of utilizing the eight 20,000/25,0000 lb low-pressure boilers retained from the original station for starting-up purposes. These sufficed to produce an output of 22MW from the condensing turbine, providing useful output on occasions when one or both of the high-pressure boilers were out of commission. In adopting this intermediate pressure, however, it was realized that the efficiency available from the initial steam conditions was not fully utilized, as theoretical considerations showed that the optimum values would be reached when the reheat pressure was in the range 325–350 psi.

The new plant displaced four 5MW sets. The 33MW LP set was put on commercial load for the first time in December 1937 and the 20MW HP set was put on load some months later.

The Brimsdown 'A' plant first went into full commission with both Loeffler boilers steaming on the 13th December 1938. The results obtained during the first few days' operation gave promise of achieving the anticipated performance. On four consecutive days, Tuesday 20th to Friday 23rd December which, incidentally, coincided with a period of unusually cold weather, the plant operated slightly below its normal economic rating at efficiencies in excess of 29% on the basis of generated units.

Although efficiencies in excess of 30% were logged occasionally and the plant proved itself to be capable of its designed performance at economic rating, this level of performance depended upon full boiler availability as no spare boiler unit was provided. Severe low-temperature deposits of a corrosive nature were experienced in the boiler plant at an early stage. Midland washed slack coals were employed on starting up the plant, and almost immediately intensive deposition (known as 'birds nesting') occurred on the convection superheater tube surfaces. Early in 1939, north-country coals were tried. Conditions in the superheater passes at once showed an improvement but within a few months severe corrosion of air-preheater elements became evident resulting in frequent boiler outages for cleaning or replacement. In the 1950s the air flow was reversed and coal changed to Hordern coal from Durham.

This phenomenon was not inherently associated with high steam pressure operation. As in many other boiler plants in the country, the formation of both high- and low-temperature deposits on the heating surfaces was experienced at an early stage, the effect being frequent boiler outages for cleaning, with consequent reduction of turbine-room rating.

The incidence of war militated against the achievement of performance at both 'A' and 'B' Station plants. Contact with the Czechoslovakian designers of the Loeffler plant was lost during the "teething trouble" stage, and war conditions prevented the use of suitable coals during the experimental stages. There were demands for increased output at the expense of efficiency as the national plant shortage became increasingly felt.

7: **Turbine hall at Brimsdown 'A' in 1948 showing 34MW machine with direct driven DC auxiliary generator** [*IMechE*]

All four turbine plants did, however, demonstrate that the economic advantages theoretically available from the use of high steam pressures and temperatures were obtainable in practice and marked a notable advance in British steam power-plant design and construction in this respect.

It had been expected that the steam conditions, and in particular the temperatures employed, would introduce problems in operation not all of which could be foreseen and provided for in the design stages. Both plants used steels containing 0.5% chrome and 0.5% molybdenum and were designed for base load[22]. In practice, the starting-up and shutting-down of the high-pressure turbines, and still more so a restart after a comparatively brief shut-down, proved to be somewhat delicate operations.

Running the machines in 'A' station was always tricky, the HP shaft being bent at least twice, possible more often. After the last of these incidents, Metropolitan Vickers advised that it would be the last time the shaft could be straightened[23].

It was the opinion of Captain Donaldson, Northmet's Chief Engineer, that the problem of corrosion of the air preheater might not have arisen had a pulverized-fuel plant been installed. At the time the installations at Brimsdown and Taylors Lane were started, dust had lost its terrors, but there was not sufficient room for the extracting equipment. Nevertheless, although it might have seemed difficult to install such equipment, he thought that if he could have his time over again, he would have done so[5].

The Loeffler boilers were very good at producing acid in the flue gases. During the early years of operation the life of a set of air heater cold-end plates was about six weeks. The station chemist had the task of researching into acid formation in flue gas as well as his normal duties of checking on coal and water qualities[24].

The pioneer plant at Brimsdown "A" was not equipped with barring gear in the first instance. Experience proved this to be essential to plant of this description and the gear was specified for the three subsequent machines. Similarly, for the pilot plant eccentricity gauges for observing rotor deflection during starting-up

---

[22] PC S Polliket
[23] PC S Polliket
[24] PC R G Whillock

were not originally provided; nor was there any ready means of observing differential axial expansion.

As outlined above, attempts were made to use the boilers for peak loads by bringing them up to power and shutting them down again quickly. Unfortunately the special steels used for the very high pressures could not deal with the rapid temperature changes and started to crack up. In the late 1950s, the main steam chest on the HP set, having suffered extensive cracking, was removed to London Transport's Lots Road power station where it was entombed in a loosely made refractory brick enclosure and induction heated. The Anglo Swedish Welding Company cut out the cracks and re-welded to steam chest. The heating, welding and cooling was done under the supervision of a metallurgist. The whole job took some two weeks, heating slowly so that welding could be done, further heating to relieve the stresses and a long slow cooling[25].

Around 1950 one of the original boilers which had been retained to supply steam for starting up purposes blew up, throwing lumps of iron and concrete far and wide.

In the 1960s the Loeffler boilers were converted from chain grate to oil firing, the oil tanks being built on the site of the old Babcock boilers.

In the winter of 1959/60, two severe busbar faults occurred resulting in catastrophic loss of supply to Eastern Electricity consumers and to London Transport. The switchgear was originally by Ferguson Pallin, being one of the first installations using reinforced concrete structures. The replacement, in line with the other switchgear at Brimsdown, was BT-H JB427 type.

The station continued in use with one 1938 40MW MetVick set supplied by just two oil fired boilers until around 1975 when it was decommissioned and the site, together with 'B' station was cleared for redevelopment.

---

[25] PC S Polliket

Brimsdown B

Although extensions to the two main generating stations at Taylors Lane and Brimsdown had been carried out from time to time, they became inadequate to cope with the increasing demand on the Company's system. At the end of 1925 it was decided to build a new station, to be known as Brimsdown 'B', and to use the existing 'A' station only as standby. The necessary sanction of the Electricity Commissioners was obtained to proceed with the first section of the new station. It consisted of two 25MW turbo alternators (the first single-line turbines of this rating in the UK to operate at 3000rpm[26]) together with a boiler house to contain five units each of 100,000 lbs per hour arranged in such a manner that two boilers would normally deal with one turbine, the fifth remaining as a spare for either of the two sets. The completed scheme was planned to consist of three such sections, ie, six 25MW turbines and three separate boiler houses. The boilers used pulverised coal firing, believed to be the second example of this technique which had been tried at Metesco's Willesden Acton Lane power station 25 years earlier[27].

8: **Brimsdown 'A' and 'B' stations with Loeffler boilers at 'A' station on the left** [*IMechE*]

---

[26] PC R G Whillock
[27] *Electricity Supply in Great Britain; A Chronology* The Electricity Council 1977 ISBN 0 85188 053 3

Oil cooled transformers had been widely used for many years but one oddity, perhaps another Northmet experiment, was the installation of a bank of three 15MVA single-phase water-cooled 11/33kV interbus transformers. These were for generator B1 which, unlike the others, generated at 11kV instead of 33kV[28]. In spite of most electrical engineers' dislike of mixing water and high voltage electricity, they never gave any problem so far as is known.

The other generator was the first direct wound 33kV alternator by Parsons.

When the station was put in hand the position in regard to the cooling water was a difficult one. Negotiations which had been carried on for 3 or 4 years with the Metropolitan Water Board with the idea of securing the use of the water in the King George Reservoir for cooling purposes had not reached a settlement. The station was, therefore, designed in such a manner that the pumping plant could take care of the requisite cooling water from any one of the three available sources; the River Lee Navigation, the King George Reservoir or cooling towers. The work on the foundations was started in February 1926 but, owing to the coal dispute which started in the following April, the construction work was slowed down. A full year was lost on account of the coal strike and its results so it was not until August 1928 that the first section of the plant was in operation.

In the grounds of the power station there was a concrete scale model of the King George Reservoir about 12' long. This was full of fish which enthusiastic lunch time anglers had caught in the river Lee and deposited in the model[29].

Work on the second section commenced in December 1930. In most respects the two sections were the same, the main difference being in the boiler house where there were four boilers each having a normal capacity of 175,000 lbs of steam per hour. One turbine was first put on load in April 1932 and the other in May 1932.

Directions from the Central Board in regard to the third station were received in June 1938 end the consent of the Commissioners about a month later. The estimated cost of the third section was £912,000 and the directions stated that it was to be ready for commercial operation in September 1941.

---

[28] PC R G Whillock
[29] PC S Polliket

Conditions at Brimsdown 'B' were favourable to the installation of a second high pressure plant like the one newly installed in 'A' station. Calculations showed that coal consumption per unit generated could be nearly 2% below the 'A' Station figure. A further reduction of about 3% in circulating water requirements could be expected.

Operating data from the pilot plant was not yet available in the design stages of this second installation, and in essential features the plant was similar to that installed at 'A' Station. The live steam reheater was, however, dispensed with. Subsequent experience showed this to be redundant at 'A' Station and a modified drive was adopted for the steam circulating pump unit. At 'A' Station this had been driven by an independent turbine deriving steam from the high pressure set and it exhausted into the de-aerator forming part of the low-pressure turbine condensate circuit. At 'B' Station the DC generator associated with each boiler unit was coupled through gearing to the shaft driving the steam circulating pump, the turbine being a self-contained condensing unit taking steam from the exhaust of the high-pressure set. There was, in theory, a small loss in overall thermal efficiency from this modification but it was adopted mainly from practical considerations, so that the high-pressure boilers and turbine could be operated apart from the condensing set[5].

Each of the two Loeffler boilers was specified to have a normal economic rating of 200,000 lb of steam per hour and a continuous maximum rating of 250,000 lb/h. Boiler stop-valve conditions, as at 'A' Station, were 2,000 psi, 940 F. Chain grate stoker firing was also adopted for this second installation.

The primary HP turbine in this installation was rated at 17 MW. The condensing (LP) set drove an alternator of 39 MW (both main alternators generating at 33kV) and the direct-coupled house alternator of 1,650kW. The two DC generators were each rated at 1,035kW. At continuous maximum rating the reheat pressure was 315 psi, which was the operating pressure of the existing plant in the station. Consequently, in the event of the high-pressure boilers being out of commission, the condensing turbine could be operated in conjunction with the existing boiler plant. On the other hand, with the condensing turbine out of commission, the high-pressure plant could exhaust into the existing low-pressure turbines.

Work on the excavations for the boiler house raft and the turbine room foundations was started in June 1939. Owing to war conditions there was unavoidably considerable delay in the progress of this work and it was not until February 1942 that the LP Turbine was put in permanent commission in conjunction with the existing LP boilers. The HP turbine was run up to speed in May 1943 but certain adjustments were necessary. The work on the HP boilers was delayed on account of the shortage of skilled welders and it was not until August 1943 that steam was raised on one of these boilers.

By reason of war delays, the first Loeffler boiler was commissioned in 1943, some months before the second unit was complete. Early operation led to modification of the second Loeffler boiler but load requirements were such that the first boiler could not be modified until September 1945, the second having been commissioned one month earlier. In January 1946, both boilers became available in the modified condition, and from that date only did the combined plant operate under variable intermediate-pressure conditions up to the design capacity.

During the short period of tandem operation isolated from the low-pressure system in the calendar year 1945, the plant generated 60,365,700 units at an overall thermal efficiency of 28%, although the running plant load factor averaged as low a figure as 38%.

Air heater corrosion troubles were not been experienced to the same degree at this station. Boiler availability was again the principal factor militating against maintained good performance. In this installation there was no spare boiler capacity provided, so boiler outage for cleaning or air-preheater element washing involved reversion to mixed-pressure operation or reduction of load to less than half capacity.

During 1946, 199,337,100 units were generated at a load factor of 37.9% with an overall thermal efficiency of 27.29%. The corresponding figures in 1947 were 180,789,200 units generated, load factor 34.4%, and overall thermal efficiency 28.97%. These figures were disappointing and comprehensive tests on boiler and turbine plant were being undertaken. In neither year had the average running plant load factor been higher than 48%, which figure is an indication of the restriction placed on the plant by boiler availability. Coal consumption in the middle to late forties topped 2000 tons per day[30].

In the calendar year 1947 the high-pressure plants at Brimsdown and Taylors Lane generated 54% of the Company's total output at an overall thermal efficiency of 27.13%. In comparison with the level of performance of the pre-war low-pressure plant, there was a saving of 74,000 tons of coal in the year. The annual saving in overall costs of production was £260,000, inclusive of capital charges, so that general financial considerations also justified employment of the high-pressure cycles.

The outbreak of war so soon after the commissioning of the pilot plant, and when the subsequent plants were in their early stages of manufacture, was unfortunate because it reduced the number of Northmet and manufacturers' personnel available to investigate the numerous initial problems as closely as their nature warranted. Lack of free choice in the purchase of coal also impeded research into the combustion problem, which was the principal difficulty in operating the original Loeffler boilers.

9: **Control room at Brimsdown 'B' station** [Alick Barnett]

[30] PC S Polliket

Generator G6 was a 900psi/900 C Richardson Westgarth 60MW turbine hydrogen cooled to a Brown Boveri design. It was installed at the north end of B station engine room and started up in 1955. This was a very successful installation[31].
By February 1969, G6 was the only unit in 'B' station that was regularly on load. The two boilers and the turbine at Brimsdown 'B' continued in use until 1974. The first two generators, out of use, were removed although the newest, G6, was still running. Eventually it was removed to CEGB's store at Elstow in Bedfordshire as spares for similar machines in the region.

In the control room in the 1960s there was a fault level "Simulator" which was used by Control Engineers to check that plant fault ratings were not exceeded.

In 1975 engineers in the then Enfield District of Northmet Sub-Area were trained at Brimsdown in the operation of the four 33kV Switchgear Groups which had quite complex interlocking arrangements. By the time generation ceased, Eastern Electricity assumed control of the 132kV system.

Work started in 1976 to establish Brimsdown North 132/33kV Grid Substation with two 90 MVA Grid Transformers (ex Borehamwood Grid) and 2000 Amp GEC Switchgear. This was to allow the de-commissioning of Groups 1,3 & 4, and the consolidation of Group 2 (the youngest Group having been commissioned in 1955 with G6). There was a hotch potch of five existing Grid Transformers at Brimsdown, one 60MVA, two 45 MVA, and two 20 MVA, all dating from the 1940's and before. The original Brimsdown North scheme only allowed for the de-commissioning of the two 20 MVA units. Northmet Planners were seemingly reluctant to replace obsolete plant.

Demolition of the Power Station equipment commenced in earnest in 1979. It could only be part demolished as the Control Room needed to be maintained because of the control/relay panels for Group 2 and for Brimsdown "A" 132/11kV substation. Operationally this presented many major challenges to keep the lights on for many thousands of customers while major demolition work was carried out. The cooling towers and the two main Brimsdown Station boiler chimneys were demolished, the towers by explosive changes and the chimneys by cutting round the base and pulling down by steel hawsers attached around the chimney tops. It was reported as frightening to watch, as the hawsers broke twice

---

[31] PC S Polliket

and whiplashed each time. How none of the demolition crew were seriously injured remains a miracle. These were steel brick lined chimneys and must have weighed many hundreds of tons.

Demolition of the 'A' station was also a major challenge as the 11kV switchboard for the 132/11kV substation was in the basement. This was preserved in operation until 1985 when it was replaced by a new 18 panel vacuum switchboard in a new switchroom adjacent to the 132/11kV transformers.

By the end of 1982, all 33kV feeders had been transferred from Groups 1, 3 and 4 to either the new Brimsdown NTL or existing Group 2 switch panels. Group 3 was first to be demolished with the adjacent cooling towers at the end of 1979. A new study of 33kV loading at Brimsdown led to a decision to take out of commission the two 45 MVA old 132/33Transformers in addition to the two 20MVA units decommissioned under the original Brimsdown North scheme.

Work commenced in 1984 to establish the new 18 panel vacuum (Brush) 11kV switchboard for Brimsdown South. This was also to accommodate the 11kV circuits of Brimsdown Factory 33/11kV substation, which was to be decommissioned, having been commissioned in the early 1950s.

In March 1985, a major fire broke out in the new switchroom whilst jointing work was in progress transferring the 1 sq in "Milliken" 11kV single core cables of the second 30MVA grid transformer to the new switchboard. All supplies were lost including those to Enfield Rolling Mills (Delta Enfield).

The Fire Brigade extinguished the fire with some difficulty as it was not possible to make the switchboard dead, despite the tripping of the two main 132kV infeeds, and a number of circuits were running open but energised from other sources.

When the fire brigade arrived they had no foam or gas facilities, only water! The fire was raging by then so there was no time for lengthy consideration of alternatives if the switchboard was to be saved from permanent extinction. The firemen were instructed to operate with minimum water pressure and an engineer directed from the door of the switchroom what they could and could not spray. Hardly in accord with HV Safety Rules! The fire was extinguished but not without considerable damage to the switchboard (mainly from smoke deposits on insulating surfaces and multicores).

At 13:30 the fire was put out and there was a visitation of directors from Delta Enfield (just across the road in Mill Marsh Lane) that if their electrical furnaces were to be saved, supply would need to be restored by no later than midnight.

Somehow, this deadline was reached by recommissioning the least damaged half of the switch panel by four minutes before midnight. There was a continuous crackle of discharge from the re-energised section which would probably not have sustained an AC Pressure Test!!

Some of the BT-H QF 11kV OCB moving portions, which were 250 MVA rated, were recovered from the old Brimsdown "A" 11kV switchboard and used to uprate the 150MVA QF switchgear at Chantry Lane substation (Hatfield) to 250MVA rating, allowing the 11kV Bus Section OCB to run normally closed.

In 1986 the last of the remaining "old" 132/33kV Grid Transformers, T3B 60MVA, at Brimsdown Control was decommissioned leaving all the 33kV load at Brimsdown, some 146 MVA at peak, on the two 90MVA units at Brimsdown North. The Group 2 switchgear stayed in commission, the six 33kV interconnectors with Palmers Green 132/33kV substation allowing load transfer in the event of loss of one of the Brimsdown North transformers.

With the decommissioning of Brimsdown Factory 33/11kV substation, the two 30MVA 132/11kV transformers at Brimsdown South had a peak 11kV load of 28MVA. The four remaining modern Grid transformers at Brimsdown were now really earning their keep. Although copper losses increased, decommissioning of the five old 132/33kV high iron loss units reduced total iron losses by some 70%.

Two new 33kV feeders were laid in 1989 to connect Lonsdale Drive and North Enfield 33/11kV s/stns to Palmers Green Grid. The project was justified more by the need to replace the fault-prone 33kV feeders with ageing insulation from Brimsdown to North Enfield than to relieve 33kV load at Brimsdown. However, the effect of the load transfer reduced the Brimsdown North 33kV load to about 117 MVA, the cyclic rating of each of the 90MVA transformers.

In 1991 the 33kV Controls for Group 2 were finally transferred from the old B

Station Control Room to the Group 2 Relay Room allowing the National Grid Company, new owners of the Brimsdown site, to demolish the building for further development of the site, beyond that carried out by Douglas Construction from 1986.

Group 2 (Brimsdown Control) was demolished in 1998 (with "B" Station Control Room) to allow the construction of a new Gas Fired Combined Cycle Gas Turbine Power Station. Group 2 switchgear was replaced by an extension to the Brimsdown North 33kV switchboard.

However, no gas turbines were installed at Brimsdown. Later the bulk of the site was sold for commercial use. By 12th March 1986 the site had been cleared and Douglas Construction were preparing to erect a distribution warehouse for Sainsbury's. With cables criss-crossing the site and in the knowledge that some of the switchyards were still in use the construction company did not have an easy time. They were given plans which alleged to show the cable routes but they found many other underground obstacles, not knowing what they were because they had not been given a plan of the site as it had been with the power station buildings and structures. The legacy of Northmet lived on.

Stevenage

The station was erected in Walkern Road by the Stevenage Electric Light & Power Co Ltd in March 1923 and was originally equipped with one 100hp semi-diesel engine direct coupled to a 60kW dynamo at 550 volts with static balancer and a 350 Ah 270 cell battery. Supply on the DC 250/500volt three wire system commenced on 27th July 1923 but in September 1923 a further unit was erected consisting of a 150 HP ABC semi–diesel engine direct coupled to a 100kW 550 volt ACEC dynamo with static balancer.

At the end of 1924. after Northmet had obtained control of the Stevenage Company a Sulzer 95kW Diesel set with two DC generators was transferred from St Albans. During 1925 two 125kW BT-H rotary converters were also transferred from St Albans[32]. In February 1926 the Stevenage Company commenced to take bulk supply from Northmet and the DC voltage reduced to

---

[32] Northmet Monthly Bulletin 6/26 Item 62

240. The station was closed down when the DC to AC changeover was completed in 1929.

Neasden (the one that got away)[33]

When London Transport was formed in 1933, it inherited three power stations, the Underground Group's Lots Road (Chelsea), the Metropolitan Railway's Neasden and Greenwich, acquired with the LCC tramways. Lots Road and Neasden generated at $33^1/_3$Hz, Greenwich at 25Hz. Traction power was also taken from local electricity suppliers for the outer reaches of the Piccadilly line and for much of the non-LCC tramways.

Most of the equipment in these three power stations was old and it was recognised that eventual conversion to the standard 50Hz system would be necessary. However, with all the substations operating at lower frequencies this was not a change which could be accomplished overnight. Various options were considered, the security of supply in the event of failure always being paramount.

On 5th June 1936, Frank Pick, London Transport's Vice Chairman, wrote to his Electrical Engineer, J H Millan: "I saw Mr Donaldson the other day .... I propose to make him an offer to take over Neasden Power Station ..... [it] will be transferred, with staff complete to the North Metropolitan Company and the North Metropolitan Company will pay rent for the station. Mr Donaldson agrees that the station should be worth about £250,000 to him, therefore the interest and sinking fund on £250,000 worth of capital will be borne wholly by the North Metropolitan Company. The interest and sinking fund upon the balance of the power station changes, as represented by the rent, will have to be borne by the [London Transport] Board and will be represented by a charge for current.

"The Board will enter into an agreement with the North Metropolitan Company for a supply of current from the Station. Thee will be an undertaking by the North Metropolitan Company to maintain in existence plant capable of supplying to the [LT] Board a certain number of kilowatts at any time at $33^1/_3$ cycles and this obligation will continue for, say, a period of 10 years during which time the [LT] Board will have to deal with the conversion of its Lots Road Power Station to 50 cycles.

---

[33] LT Group Archive ref LT12/377 (LPTB file 843/2)

"The contract for the purchase of current will have to extend over a period of, say, 40 years ...... to maintain the charge at a reasonably low level ..... It almost looks as if we ought to be able to secure our current supply at a price of, say, 0.25d or 0.26d, coal being 20/-d per ton ....

"The North Metropolitan Company will be entitled to commence the replacement of plant not required in respect of the guaranteed supply to the [LT] Board and will build alongside the $33^1/_3$ cycle station a 50 cycle station. After 10 years the North Metropolitan Company will be entitled to convert the whole station to 50 cycles and the [LT] Board will have to take its supply on the 50 cycle basis."

It would have been necessary to take in the Metropolitan Railway sports ground for coal storage or cooling towers. Pick went on to ask Millan to work out the scheme and concluded: "The matter must, I think, be pushed ahead with dispatch".

Donaldson wrote to Pick on the same day, referring to their meeting on the 3rd June and the proposal by LPTB on 9th May 1935[34]. The "Central Electricity Board have found themselves to be liable to be short of plant in the Western area [of London] in about 3 years' time and have come to the conclusion (which we had reached many years ago) that a larger station in the west of London was desirable even if it could not have the advantage of a riverside situation." With regard to Neasden, he continues: "..there is very little in the station which would be of use to us, in fact broadly speaking, merely the site, the sidings, the buildings and the boiler plant with the possibilities of the larger condensers and, for part time only, the wooden condensing towers....

"The operation of the better plant at $33^1/_3$ cycles would appear to be quite reasonable .... and the Northmet Company is quite prepared to operate the station for a definite period." This depended on the circumstances and Donaldson pointed out that the existing boiler plant was by no means capable of dealing with all the machines then installed.

On the 11th June the LPTB Estates office sent Pick a copy of the plans of the 3½ acres of land let to the Neasden Village Welfare Association for a recreation ground used "somewhat extensively" by children living on the Neasden Estate.

---

[34] No documentary record of this proposal can be found.

The memo noted that there was no other space in which these children could play and that the land had been provided following many complaints of children using the roads as a playground. There was also another 4½ acres acquired from the Metropolitan Country Estates for extending the power station. This was let to British Oxygen as a sports ground until 1939 although the agreement could be terminated at 28 days notice.

London Transport's Engineering Committee met on 15th June and discussed the proposals. It was decided[35] to have further meetings with Northmet with a view to leasing the power station to Northmet for 40 years with an option to sell or renew at that time. Northmet could take possession on, say, 1st July 1937, LT would convert their substations to 50Hz over 10 years, Northmet would be contracted to supply up to 180 million units per annum and Northmet would be obliged to retain reserve $33^1/_3$ Hz plant (capacity to be agreed) to cover emergencies at Lots Road.

The Commercial Manager commented on 3rd July that the 'Electricity Board', presumably meaning the Central Electricity Board, would only give their blessing to the scheme if the cost of coal at Neasden were the same as at Brimsdown. However coal was 2/- dearer at Neasden. The LNE and LMS railways agreed to a reduction in order to keep the business and LT would contribute 3d per ton as their share of the transportation cost over the Metropolitan line. Pick replied that he did not see why the rates should be the same!

The Parliamentary Officer reported that the North Metropolitan Electric Power Supply Company's last Bill had included a measure enabling them to purchase Neasden power station but he pointed out that there could be potential problems over the employment rights of staff transferred.

At the beginning of October a memo to Pick from the Comptroller and Accountant's office concluded, from a detailed analysis of the proposals, that LT would be effectively giving Northmet the power station free, although LT would be paying Northmet less per unit than their present generation costs.

Pick still wanted to go ahead and the Staff, Stores and Accounts Committee agreed that a Mr C Latham, an independent accountant, be appointed to conduct

---

[35] Minute 2800 in LT Group Archive LT12/377

the final negotiations on behalf of the LPTB. At the estates meeting in November it was decided to inform British Oxygen Company of the possibility that their sports ground would be needed for power purposes but that no final decision would be taken until Spring 1937. On the same day, Pick, sounding slightly tetchy, was writing to his Electrical Engineers asking what Donaldson's plans were.

Having met Donaldson, The Electrical Engineer reported that Donaldson would develop the station to supply at 33kV 50Hz for distribution purposes and connect, as required, to CEB. The existing plant would be removed and high pressure turbines and boilers would be installed. Transformers would supply one section of the existing 11kV busbars at 50Hz for LPTB requirements, increasing with time, as required. This would be done by installing three 54MW turboalternators with boilers in three stages over 10 years. The Electrical Engineer pointed out that if Northmet did take over the power station it might be necessary for LT to accelerate the conversion to 50Hz. This might lead to a small increase in costs to cover security of supply during frequency changeover but the takeover by Northmet would make no material difference.

This is the last direct reference that can be found to Northmet taking over Neasden power station. It seems that the deal fell through. By March 1937, the Engineering Committee had "decided to postpone, for the time being the commencement of the conversion for operation at 50 cycles of Lots Road and Neasden generating stations." During 1939 22kV tie lines were installed between Lots Road and Neasden and Neasden to Greenwich. When Neasden power station finally closed on 21st July 1968 it was the last station in Britain generating at $33^1/_3$Hz.

Rye House

In 1942 a site of approximately 90 acres was acquired by the Station Company in the Urban District of Hoddesdon for a proposed new generating station and on 2nd July 1945 the Central Electricity Board notified Northmet of the proposal under Section 6 of the 1926 Act for the construction of a new station on the site to be known as the Rye House Generating Station.

On 30th November 1945 application was made to the Electricity Commissioners for their consent under Section 11 of the 1919 Act and a copy of the application was sent on the same day to the Hoddesdon UDC in accordance with the Town & Country Planning Acts.

At about the same time the Northmet Company deposited a Bill in Parliament to authorise that Company to take on lease and operate the Rye House Station. However, on account of the objections lodged by the Hertfordshire County Council and the Local Authority against the erection of the Station, the Electricity Commissioners and the Minister of Town and Country Planning decided to hold a joint Local Inquiry on 26/27th March 1946. The result was that the consent of both parties was given on 22nd June subject to certain conditions and the Northmet Bill received Royal Assert on 6th November 1946.

The building was engineered by Northmet's building department with Sir Giles Gilbert Scott advising on architectural design. Lying low in the Lea Valley, Rye House suffered from the high water table and this was a big problem during construction requiring continual use of pumps[36]. The main civil engineering contractor was Walter Lawrence and Son Ltd

The station was designed initially for six 30MW turbo-alternators but only four units were installed, leaving the building with a temporary end wall. Northmet's 'belt and braces' security of supply philosophy resulted in double-busbar, double circuit breaker 33kV switchgear using BT-H JB427 OCBs. The 3kV works power QF361 switchboards were also double busbar.

Each of the four Richardsons Westgarth steam turbines was supplied by a Babcock & Wilcox single drum high head boiler providing up to 350,000 pounds of steam per hour at 650psi and 875 degrees Fahrenheit. Each of the turbines drove a 2MW generator for station supplies as well as the main Parsons generator. There were also four 45MVA transformers supplying the 132kV National Grid.

The station was designed to be coal-fired, there being seven acres of storage for 85,000 tons at 12 feet depth. Coal arrived by rail from the East Midlands and was handled by tipplers, conveyors and four pulverising mills for each boiler. Three-stage Lodge-Cotterell electrostatic precipitators were fitted to the exhaust, dust being removed as a slurry to disused gravel pits. Ash was removed dry by road or rail.

---

[36] PC C J Knight

10: **Rye House Power Station** [*CEGB*]

Rye House had some 4½ miles of railway tracks, Unlike Brimsdown and Taylors Lane, the station shunting was done by conventional steam locomotive rather than a fireless type.

Cooling water was taken from the River Lee as required to supplement the water circulated through the cooling towers.

Generation commenced in December 1951. No 2 unit was commissioned in March 1952, No 3 in May 1953 and the fourth unit in December 1953.

Around 1967, two 70MVA Gas Turbine Generators were installed for peak lopping duty at Rye House, equipped with Rolls Royce RB211 jet engines. They were connected to the 132kV Bus Bar and were prohibitively expensive to run.

In 1981 CEGB decided to decommission the Power Station[37]. Rye House did not represent anything like as complex a task as Brimsdown because the power station, 33kV outdoor switch yard and the 132kV substation (including four 45 MVA 132/33kV Grid transformers) were geographically quite separate.

The first task was to "de-bank" the 45MVA transformers which were connected as two pairs, restricting the firm capacity to about 120MVA. The 33kV peak load level at Rye House at this time was about 130MVA. To avoid installing more 132kV switchgear, the decision was made to bank two of the 45MVA transformers with the Welwyn/Hatfield 132kV circuits. This scheme involved one of the earliest uses of polymeric 132kV single core cables.

Two 18MVA 132/25kV Single Phase Railway Supply transformers were commissioned in 1982 to replace the existing 33/6.6kV units to allow the upgrading of the traction feeds to 25kV on the Liverpool Street to Bishops Stortford and Cambridge line.

This further complicated the banking arrangements on existing 132kV circuits at Rye House. Bill Murphy, who was Deputy Chief Planning Engineer at HQ, had an aversion to 132kV circuit breakers; he never seemed prepared to buy new ones. There was now one Welwyn/Hatfield circuit with a local 45MVA transformer and a Railway Traction transformer banked to it. Switching out this circuit for maintenance took a great deal of time.

---
[37] PC G Mackenzie

By 1981, the gas turbines were about as redundant as the four 30MVA steam sets. Why their 132kV air break circuit breakers were not used for the debanking project in not known but it may have been some strange quirk of ownership.

In 1984 Eastern Electricity took over responsibility from the then Transmission District of the CEGB for maintenance of the 132kV air blast switchgear and the grid and railway transformers and their connections. The power station staff had been responsible, until 1981, for maintenance of the 33kV switchgear.

Without wishing to denigrate either party, one could not say that either had distinguished themselves with the thoroughness and endeavour of carrying out their maintenance responsibilities. Multicore cables associated with the 33kV switchgear were generally in a very poor state with VIR insulation flaking away in terminal boxes.

Soon after the generating sets were decommissioned, a decision was made to run the four 45MVA grid transformers in parallel to maximum firm capacity. Being rather nervous about the implications of a 33kV busbar fault on the raft, it was decided to test and maintain thoroughly the obsolescent Busbar Protection which worked on the "rough balance" principle. The bus zone relays were found to be virtually seized up and it was highly unlikely that they would have worked before the maintenance rendered them serviceable again.

The 33kV connections from each of the 45MVA grid transformers to the switchyard were oil pressure cables each about 400m long. The Transmission District staff had long taken the view that it was pointless trying to locate and repair the numerous leaks on these cables so emergency pressure tanks were in continuous use and needed to be replenished regularly. It was of great surprise that British Waterways, or their equivalent of the time, did not make a fuss over pollution of the water table in the vicinity. Certainly Pirelli Cables or BICC were making a lot of money pumping oil into the cables. Eastern Electricity quickly undertook some checks of the oil terminations in the basement of the switchyard which was continually under water and difficult to access, and managed to reduce the leakage from each cable by a significant amount. The CEGB had tried to say that the lead sheaths on these cables were porous.

The 45MVA transformers had slow speed tap changers, which again had seen infrequent maintenance so it was probably fortunate that tap changing was non-automatic, being carried out manually (and infrequently!) from the power station Control Room.

So that the Control Room could be de-manned on closure of the power station, Automatic Voltage Control equipment was installed for the four units using one of the earliest microprocessor based AVC systems. Although this included a load drop compensation compounding facility, there was concern not to put too much duty onto the slow speed tap changers and the 33kV bus bars were run at constant voltage.

In 1986, a scheme was justified to replace the outdoor 33kV BT-H Switchgear with a new SF6 insulated indoor switchboard manufactured by South Wales/Hawker Siddeley Switchgear Ltd. The new switch house was located in the 132kV substation adjacent to the 45MVA Grid transformers.

The new switch house occupied about 10% of the space of the old switch yard. The comparison with the old switch yard was amazing, the age gap being about 35 years.

The concrete support structures of the switch yard were spalling badly, the typical cause being poor construction with reinforcing bars too close to the surface of the concrete. The insulation of the multicore cables had also deteriorated.

The two relay houses were permanently damp, the height of the water table and the close proximity of the River Lee ensuring that the basement of the houses were permanently under water. Relay surfaces had a virtually permanent covering of moisture which caused verdigris to form on copper connection surfaces.

The BT-H 33kV switch gear was still in robust condition but because maintenance of this equipment had not been the highest priority for the power station staff, tripping mechanisms occasionally failed to operate in the required time.

By 1990, the 33kV peak load at Rye House was in excess of 150MVA and the firm capacity of the four x 45MVA Grid transformers, was 160MVA on a cyclic basis.

Modification carried out at West Hertford and Much Hadham 33/11kV substations provided a little relief by transferring about 5MW of load to Welwyn and Bishops Stortford.

Further relief was provided by installing a second 90MVA transformer at West Harlow Grid (removed from Hornsey Grid) in 1991. This permitted a second 33kV underground cable to be laid from West Harlow to North Harlow 33/11kV substation thus relieving Rye House 33kV by a further 25MVA.

CHAPTER 4
THE SOUTHERN UNDERTAKINGS

BARNET

The Distribution Company commenced DC supplies for street lighting on 31st August 1900 from the generating station in Tapster Street (see chapter on Generation). The High Street was lit by 14 Verity enclosed arc lamps, arranged two pairs in series at 230 volts, and two sets of five in series at 460 volts. There were also two 100 cp and 129 16 cp incandescent lamps.

The Verity arc lamps gave a considerable amount of trouble from the time of their installation and, at the end of 1901, they were changed for Jandus enclosed arcs. In 1907 four extra posts were erected and two series of 9 Excello flame arc lamps replaced the Jandus arcs. The Excello arc lamps were at a later date replaced by vacuum and gas-filled lamps. By 1926 there were 167 lamps in service, most of them switched on only half the night. The all night lamps, and some of the twelve 500 watt lamps had individual time switches, the other 150 or so were switched by hand.

From May 1905 bulk supply at 11kV was taken from the Supply Company and during 1906 and 1907 the Hart battery was removed from the generating station and the battery room was turned into No 2 EHT switch room. BT-H 11kV cell type switchgear was erected and one 300kW 500rpm 10kV AC to 560/480 volt DC Bruce Peebles La Cour converter (the first built for this voltage) was installed. The two 50kW and the two 100kW steam sets were scrapped.

In 1908 a second 300kW Bruce Peebles La Cour converter was added, bringing the total installed capacity of the substation up to 800kW and in 1909 the Babcock & Wilcox boiler was transferred to Hertford. The two dry back boilers were broken up for scrap. The old boiler house was demolished, and rebuilt as a battery room, in which a Tudor battery of 800 Ah capacity was installed.

In 1910 a 36kW 1000 rpm Holmes booster was installed, a second, similar, booster being added several years later.

During 1911 and 1912 further extensions to the HV switchgear were rendered necessary in order to give supply to the Dental Works extension, East Barnet Valley and Hadley. For this purpose Ferranti switchgear was transferred from Maynards' Substation and the old Imperial Works Substation and two 50kVA 10kV to 3kV Brush transformers were transferred from Tramway Avenue, Edmonton.

In 1917 Tylor and Sons factory (later Standard Telephones & Cables Ltd) was built at New Southgate. The extensions cost approximately £5000 to which cost Messrs Tylor & Sons contributed. Supply was given by running two EHV feeders from the Barnet substation to the railway bridge, New Southgate, cutting in one of the Finchley–Wood Green feeders, and jointing straight through. The Substation at the factory was equipped with BT-H cell type switchgear for the EHV side and Reyrolle oil switches on the LV side and three 250kVA BET oil-cooled transformers.

A 140kVA dry type BIH condenser was installed at this factory in 1918, this being the first condenser to be connected to the Northmet system. It was divided into two sections, the smaller section being one–third, and the larger section two–thirds of the total capacity. Each section could be independently controlled.

During 1923 and 1924 further extensions to the High Barnet substation were made. Two 500kVA 10kV/3kV transformers were installed for the AC supply, BT-H cell type switchgear was erected for the transformers, Reyrolle ironclad HV switchgear for the main 11kV trunk feeders and Ferguson & Pailin Switchgear for the HV supply. A 500kW 1,000 RPM 10.25kV AC to 490 or 545 volts DC Mather & Platt rotary converter and a 560kVA 10,250/363 volt BET transformer were also installed.

In 1925 supply was given to Totteridge, HV supply being taken overhead from Arkley and Mays Lane. In the same year, Northmet lit the Barnet Badminton Club court[1] with two lines of eight 60W lamps placed either side of the net. The two centre lamps of each line were fitted with reflectors but the others were bare. The Club Secretary reported that this installation was "excellent".

In 1926 a 33kV feeder was laid direct from Brimsdown and outdoor type switchgear and transformers were erected for its control. The 30kV supply was

---

[1] Northmet Monthly Bulletin No 1 Item 6 2/12/1925

taken to the Reyrolle ironclad EHV switchgear in the substation through a bank of 30/10kV transformers of 3,000kVA capacity, with provision for later extension to Potters Bar and the northern area. A further 500kVA 11/3kV transformer was installed in 1926 for the AC supply.

On 20th July 1926 two 970kVA BET auto-transformer regulators were commissioned, resulting in a considerable improvement in the voltage.

Tapster Street retained its DC convertors until the trolleybuses finished. Around 1974 an intermediate floor was put into the switchroom for the telecommunications equipment which allowed the final transfer of Northmet system control from Northmet House to Millfield (Brentwood).

SOUTHGATE[2]

The ELO for the supply of electricity in Southgate was originally obtained by the Urban District Council in 1904. They procrastinated so long that it had become an encumbrance and a penalty clause was likely to be invoked if they did not provide directly, or indirectly, a supply of electricity to their residents. They therefore wanted to make the transfer to Northmet with the minimum of fuss and publicity. They published their intention, as required, in the local press but only in the Barnet Press, which had a very limited circulation in a small part of Southgate. Unfortunately for the Council, the notice was spotted by a new resident who realised the implications and got the Winchmore Hill Residents Association to call a meeting. They objected to the Board of Trade, causing quite a stir at the time. Eventually, however, the Order was transferred to Northmet in an Agreement dated 2nd August 1910 and Northmet supplies commenced in March 1911[3].

In order to give a supply to Southgate it was necessary to lay a main between Wood Green and Enfield. A temporary substation was erected in Queen's Avenue (Winchmore Hill), into which 11kV mains were laid. From this substation 3kV feeders were laid to Aldermans Hill, where an underground substation was commissioned in January 1912 and equipped with Berry series

---

[2] Much of this information comes from Northmet Monthly Bulletin 3/27, March 1927
[3] Gillam G *Bulletin of the Enfield Archeological Society* No.123, Dec 1991

gear similar to that installed at Tottenham. This substation was superseded in November 1924 by the Palmers Green Substation.

Offices were attached to the Queens Avenue building, and a showroom was opened at 29 Broadway, Winchmore Hill, in 1911 (until 1925). In 1913 another showroom was opened at 27 The Market, Green Lanes, Palmers Green[2].

The LV network in the Palmers Green district was somewhat unusual in that it consisted of two main 4-core distributors in Aldermans Hill and Fox Lane, the connecting roads having single phase cables only. Presumably this arrangement was to save money by using cheaper cables. However, it was not entirely satisfactory, and by the late 1920s was superseded by the standard 4-core cable system.

One of the first consumers to be connected was Marion & Co, photographic plate manufacturers. A substation was commissioned at their premises in June 1911, being fed by a spur from the Queen's Avenue - Aldermans Hill 3kV feeder, a feeder pillar having been placed at the junction of Green Lanes and Hoppers Road for this purpose. Marion's substation was completely destroyed in the early hours of 9th October 1920 by a disastrous fire, which started in an adjoining building, caused by the spontaneous combustion of straw used for packing.

The cables were immediately diverted, a storage shelter was used as a substation and temporarily equipped, supply being restored in 34½ hours. At that time the whole of Old Southgate was supplied from Marion's substation, and all the Consumers in this district were, in consequence, shut down for this period.

A substation at Hedge Lane was put into commission in February 1913 and supply was given to James Bruton & Sons' enamelled iron works on the last day of 1913.

Demand for supply at Grange Park, Enfield, led to a kiosk being erected in October 1913. For convenience of supply, this neighbourhood was treated as part of Southgate.

Supply was given in June 1915 to the French Cleaning & Dyeing Co Ltd and to the dye works of W S Simpson & Co but no new distribution substations were built in Southgate during the Great War. The next commissioned was for the supply of current to charge the three electric dust collection vehicles of the UDC at Barrowell Green, Winchmore Hill, in October 1920. The had UDC built a dust destructor at Barrowell Green in 1909 and rebuilt it in 1935. The idea was that the rubbish would be burnt to heat the adjacent municipal open-air swimming pool but if the wind was in the wrong direction the swimmers got a soft coating of ash.

Refuse collection in Southgate was by three electric vehicles and five horse vans. Northmet had, of course, great hopes for the electric vehicles which were said to collect rubbish at a cost of 9/6.7d per ton, against the horse vans which cost 10/9.2d per ton. The longest runs were done by the electric vehicles. In the event the electric vehicles were replaced by Scammell mechanical horses which ferried semi-trailer refuse vans to streets where the horses waited patiently to pull them up and down while the dustmen collected the rubbish[4]. The horses were not retired until after the Second World war.

The early 1920s was a period of rapid growth in Palmers Green and Southgate for the Company. Supply was given to W M Still & Sons Ltd manufacturers of gas mantles from 5th May 1920. There is no record of the irony of that situation being recognised by either Northmet or the Gas Company. Another temporary substation was put into commission in April 1921, this time at New Southgate, the permanent substation being erected in September 1923.

In July 1921 supply was commenced to the Edmonton Cooperative Society on the Oakthorpe Estate between the North Circular Road and Pymmes Brook. The Society was taken over by the London Co–operative Society Ltd, in April 1925, by which time the maximum demand was over 80kVA.

In October 1921 a substation was erected at Bourne Hill followed in November 1923 by one at Eversley Park.

The Alderman's Hill substation was replaced in November 1924 by a substation at the rear of the new showroom in Palmers Green. This substation was supplied direct from the Enfield - Wood Green 11kV feeder, and equipped with transformers of 1500kVA capacity.

---

[4] Author's personal recollection

In January 1925 a substation was put into commission at Bowes Park. This consisted of one 200kVA outdoor type transformer connected to the HV feeder with an LV feeder pillar to take care of the low voltage supply from the transformer.

In April 1926 supply was given to the Mayfield Laundry at Chequers Way (then called Blind Lane) off North Circular Road, the demand from the laundry being just over 40kVA.

In 1927 an agreement was made with the London Hosiery Factory, whose premises were being built in Bounds Green Road at the junction with the new North Circular Road. The factory covered over an acre of land, for the production of knitted underwear.

To Northmet, in its developing years, every load, however small, was important. There were two large cinemas in Palmers Green, the Palmadium and the Queens' Hall (later just known as 'The Queens'). The Palmadium was built just after the First World War and was, at the time, the largest cinema in London. It was originally designed to hold 3,000 people although the seating was slightly reduced to meet the Middlesex County Council Regulations. At Winchmore Hill, the Capitol cinema and theatre was opened in 1929, seating 2,500, being 'specially designed for talking films'. The Capitol closed in 1959, the Palmadium in 1961 and the Queens in 1967.

Public Lighting was another important source of revenue. The load from one individual lamp was insignificant but as a whole public lighting was all-important and, in a way, publicised the benefits of electricity. The part of Green Lanes which lay in Southgate was lit from end to end from 30th January 1913. On that date 210 lamps were put into service, arranged two on a span on Barrow suspensions from the tramway overhead wires, the first application of this method by Northmet. The installation was inspected by a meeting of local authorities on 19th February 1913[5].

The lamps were originally 60 watt vacuum but were changed to 100 watt gas-filled on 1st October 1925. Half of the lamps were lit for half the night, and the other half for all the night, control being by timeswitches. There were in addition

---

[5] Northmet leaflet, 1913

three lamps on single suspensions. It is said[6] that the lamps were so located that they could be changed from the upper deck of an open top tram although pictures of the installation show the lamp suspensions to be too far outside the tram tracks for this to have taken place. In later years the incandescent lamps were changed to mercury vapour and, later still, after the end of the trolleybuses, sodium lamps were erected on new lighting columns.

Besides the lighting of Green Lanes, an Agreement was entered into in December 1926 to supply nine 300 watt gas-filled all-night lamps on separate posts on the North Circular Road between Green Lanes and the Cambridge Arterial Road, and these were lit from 7th March, 1927.

After the First World War the Southgate undertaking led in the number of Consumers connected, though Wembley was close behind. By 1927, there were nearly 6,000 consumers, and approximately 12,000 houses in this rapidly growing district. The Units sold during that year amounted to approximately 3½ million.

11: Former Palmers Green showrooms and offices [Author]

[6] by the Foreman Public Lighting Attendant to the Author in 1956.

The original Southgate showroom was at 27 The Market, Palmers Green, latterly Lloyds Bank, 369 Green Lanes. It was replaced by the new, purpose-built, showroom at 286 Green Lanes (on the corner of Lodge Drive) on 14th October, 1925. The oak-panelled Manager's office at the rear of the showroom gave rise to a story that the study of the former house on the site might have been incorporated into the new building, but this is unlikely in view of the construction of the building and its similarity to other Northmet offices built around the same time. The new up-to-date showroom brought an increase in the sales turnover from £14,067 in 1924 to £23,017 in 1926, the corresponding profit figures being £836 and £1700.

With the coming of the Tube railway to Southgate, Southgate Circus was rebuilt and a showroom was opened in 1934. It was later moved to a new location a few doors away and finally closed in 1991.

In the early 1930s Southgate was included in the plans for the formation of the North Middlesex (No 4) Distribution Area of the London & Home Counties Joint Electricity District. This scheme, which would have involved the takeover of much of Northmet's undertaking, would have meant the local authorities buying out the company and transferring their rights to the proposed JEA. Southgate District Council appointed two representatives to confer with other authorities (Edmonton, Enfield and Tottenham) and with Lord Ashfield. Other local authorities were also invited to a conference[7]. However, no record can be found of any conference until one held on 19th March 1937 where it was suggested that supply in the area could be afforded jointly but not necessarily by the JEA[8].

Eventually the threat of the formation of the JEA receded.

After nationalisation, Southgate became part of the Wood Green District.

ENFIELD[9]

Supply in Enfield commenced on the 20th September 1906 by the North Metropolitan Electrical Power Distribution Company Ltd, 10kV underground

---

[7] Enfield District Council Minute 677 (vol 73) 5th June 1935.
[8] Enfield District Council Minute 2891 (vol 74) 23rd March 1937.
[9] Based on Northmet Monthly Bulletin 8/26, October 1926

mains being laid by the British Insulated & Helsby Cables Ltd, from Brimsdown to the substation in Ladysmith Road via Brimsdown railway station, Green Street, Hertford Road and Southbury Road. Only direct current was supplied to the consumers; 240 volts for lighting and 480 volts for motors larger than 2 HP. The official inauguration took place on the 16th February 1907 and, by this time, 15½ miles of mains had been laid and 50 consumers connected up.

The original installation at the substation consisted of:

two 125kW 10.000/400 volt, 50 Hz, 3-phase, type ABT air cooled transformers, manufactured by the General Electric Company of the United States.

two 100kW motor generator sets, consisting of 150 HP 400 volt AC motors direct connected to 100kW 480/550 volt DC generators, manufactured by the British Thomson-Houston Company.

one 250 cell 860 ampere hour capacity Tudor accumulator.

The 550V supplies were for the Metropolitan Electric Tramways and the trolleybuses which later replaced them.

The Substation was built by Mr Albert Monk, and was originally lit by means of seven Luna Nernst lamps. The title 'Enfield Electricity Works' appeared in the stonework of the original building.

The original Enfield electricity offices were attached to the works in Ladysmith Road. An exhibition was held at the works on 18th February 1907 to 'encourage a still more general use of electricity for domestic and industrial power purposes'[10]. In November 1914 a showroom was opened at 5 Church street on the corner of Burleigh Way, Enfield Town.

Changes and additions were made to the electrical equipment from time to time, as follows:-

In 1909 a 300kW 500 RPM, 11kV AC to 480/560 volts DC La Cour converter was installed.

---

[10] Northmet souvenir booklet *The Enfield Electricity Works* 1907.

In 1920 a 250kW 750 RPM rotary converter, previously at Wood Green was added and in 1923 a similar machine was transferred from Finchley Traction Substation.

In 1925 the two original 100kW motor generator sets were removed and stored at Finchley, being replaced by another 250kW motor generator from Wood Green. The original GE single–phase transformers were replaced by BET transformers with a LV star point tapping switch to give the necessary regulation for traction and lighting. Two transformers with Reyrolle HV switchgear were installed to supply the first portion of the 3kV 0.1 sq in HV ring main. Changeover of consumers to AC started in 1925 and was complete by 1934 except for a small area around Ladysmith Road and a few consumers in Enfield Town plus, of course, the traction supplies.

Distribution was carried out by means of four feeders laid solid in concrete troughing. The original layout, though slightly modified by reducing the length of certain feeders, and by relaying the original Ponders End feeder to the centre of the town, sufficed for 20 years for the needs of the central district without adding to the distributors.

In 1910 additions were made in the Bush Hill Park area, the greater portion being laid with two or four core cable, suitable for Northmet standard 3 phase AC distribution. In October 1922 it was transferred to the Edmonton AC supply.

In 1914 supply was given to the Enfield Wash area by means of two 0.05 sq in EHV feeders, between Green Street and Elmhurst Road Substations, to a standard four core 3-phase network. This was subsequently extended to join up with the supply in Waltham Cross.

In 1919 a distributor was laid from the Green Street Substation to Cedar Road, thus starting a standard 4–wire network in the Enfield Highway area.

In 1923 the whole of the Ponders End area was changed over from DC to 3–phase 4 wire AC working, which required all distributors to be relaid. The original distributors were recovered as work proceeded. This changeover necessitated the exchange of about 25 DC motors, the majority of which were 480 volt, for suitable 3 phase motors. The exchange was carried out 'without any material inconvenience to the power consumers'. One exception was a woodworking factory, where an open type AC motor was supplied, and which tended to become choked with sawdust etc. The difficulty was overcome by the substitution of an enclosed ventilated motor (the DC motor previously used was of the open type). The other exception was a dynamo at the Ponders End Picture Theatre for which a special motor had to be built by Messrs Newton of Taunton to fit on the existing bed plate.

There was particular difficulty in changing over Hobart sausage making machines from DC to AC. The makers contended that it was impossible to make a satisfactory job by changing the motor only, and that completely new machines were necessary. This made the cost of the exchange somewhat excessive. The price for four new machines amounted to £200, while credit for the old machines of £100 was allowed by Hobarts, making the nett cost to Northmet £100 including all costs. As the motors were single phase the existing wiring was suitable.

In 1923, the company was given the contract to wire 250 houses in course of erection by H G Stacey at Bush Hill Park and, in order to demonstrate to the district the many domestic uses of electricity, the company fitted one of the houses on the estate with electrical apparatus[11]. "Electricity House" was at 178 Village Road (opposite St. Stephen's Church). The showhouse is described in Chapter 8.

In 1925 it was decided to change the Bycullah area west of the Great Northern Railway from 3-wire DC to 3-wire AC single phase working. This was accomplished by erecting a Substation at Drapers Road, quite close to the position of the original feeder pillar, and installing 3 to 6 phase transformers. This allowed the area to be divided into three equal and separate portions taken across the opposite points of the 6 phase transformers, the result being three independent single phase networks with a common neutral.

A small portion of the northern end of the Ridgeway was changed over to the standard 3-phase 4-wire system and fed from a substation about 200 yards north of Chase Farm Schools. A considerable number of consumers had DC fans which had to be exchanged for AC. A number of charging boards for motor car and wireless batteries had to be replaced at Northmet expense by rectifiers, the majority of which were of the BT-H 'Tungar' or Phillips manufacture.

---

[11] *Electrical Review* vol 95, p54 (11/7/1924)

A few small motors also had to be exchanged for single phase, arrangements being made with Messrs Bates & Windibank to exchange the DC for Parkinson AC motors. Northmet was a little uncertain as to the attitude which the consumers would adopt in regard to the single phase commutator type motors, but 12 months' experience showed that the consumers were quite satisfied, and, if anything, preferred them to the DC motors. From the Northmet point of view a satisfactory feature of this type of motor was the good power factor from light load to overload.

A similar change-over took place in the Bush Hill Park Area in 1927, the area being divided into three portions, each fed by a 0.2 sq in feeder terminating in a feeder pillar, supply being taken from a modified substation in Lincoln Road, adjacent to the Great Eastern Railway level crossing.

Early in 1926 an agreement was negotiated for supply to the Enfield Workhouse. A substation was built and equipped with two 50kVA transformers, this substation also being used to supply a small 3–phase 4–wire local network.

By 1930 the showroom at 5 Church St had become too small and another site in Church Street was purchased and, after delays and negotiations with Enfield Council[12] a shop with offices on two floors above was opened in 1934. By this time there were 30,000 consumers in the Enfield undertaking[13].

As with other Northmet purpose-built showrooms at this time, there was a model kitchen on the ground floor where the latest cookers and other kitchen appliances were displayed and cookery demonstrations were given at 2.30pm every Thursday. The building was heated by a hot water storage system and sand-filled tubular radiators[14]. Behind the building was an appliance repair workshop, a garage for servicing company vehicles and a stores where wiremen (electricians) could get the materials for house wiring or connecting cookers and other appliances.

Supply commenced in December 1906 to Ediswans, the first 'Act' power consumer to be connected to the Company's mains. The factory had been set up in a former jute factory in 1881 as a joint venture by former rivals Edison and

---

[12] Enfield District Council Minutes 519 & 1774 (vol 71) 13th June & 15th November 1933.
[13] Gillam G *Bulletin of the Enfield Archeological Society* No.123, Dec 1991.
[14] Northmet booklet *Enfield Electricity* 1934

Swan. Although locally electricity supply was a slow starter, the demand for electric lighting was phenomenal. D'Oyley Carte installed hundreds of lamps in his new Savoy Theatre and it was not long before the Mansion House and the Royal Academy had the new electric light.

The Ediswan factory produced 5000 lamps a day using glass bulbs blown on site. A 1000HP steam engine drove the line shafting for the machines until electricity took over. Before this, in 1904, the factory had produced the world's first thermionic valve to the design of Ambrose Fleming. Britain's first radio valve production line started in the factory in 1916 and in 1930 they started to make cathode ray tubes, becoming the country's first television tube factory in 1936[15]. The Ediswan site was sold for redevelopment in 1970.

By 31st December 1925 there were 31 power consumers in Enfield with a total connected load of 7391kW receiving supply, the largest of these being -

	TOTAL CONNECTED LOAD IN kW
Enfield Cable Works	2235
Enfield Rolling Mills	1258
Edison Swan Electric Co.	1100
Corticine Floor Covering Co.	431
United Flexible Metallic Tubing Co.	367
Cosmos Lamp Works.	317

The Enfield Rolling Mills took supply mid-1926. They had the largest rolling mills in the South of England, having purchased the site of the old London Foundry Co. They installed, among others, a 1200 HP motor which had a considerable overload capacity, and was the largest sized motor on Northmet mains. It operated at a power factor between 0.95 lagging and 0.95 leading with the assistance of BIC condensers.

In 1930 Enfield Council realised that they had the power to purchase Northmet's Enfield undertaking in 1932 and this made Northmet reconsider the expenditure on changeover from DC to AC. The Council formed an Electricity Undertaking (Purchase Rights) Sub-Committee and appointed W C C Hawtayne as technical

---

[15] Enfield Archeological Society *Research Report No. 2: Industrial Archeology in Enfield* 1971

advisor. Following his report, the Council agreed to reimburse the company if the purchase took place[16]. In January 1931, the Council agreed to give to Northmet the statutory two years notice to buy the undertaking from Northmet on 19th January 1933[17] although negotiations with the London & Home Counties Joint Electricity Authority suggest that there might never have been any intention for the Council to run the undertaking themselves. The scheme became mixed up with the general discussions by the Local Authorities in the area over the government's proposals for a Joint Electricity Authorities[18].

A conference held in Southgate on 18th March 1937 resolved that "the London & Home Counties Joint Electricity Authority be asked to prepare a draft scheme on the lines of that embodied in the Colne Valley and Northwood Electricity Act 1936 for the undertakings of the North Metropolitan Electric Power Supply Company in the North Middlesex (No 4) Distribution Area, and including the part of the Company's statutory undertaking for the supply of power and street lighting in the area at present not subject to purchase rights, without prejudice to the question of the body which should operate such a scheme, and to which the undertakings in the area should be eventually transferred under the scheme."

It was further resolved that each of the local authorities be asked to submit their views to the JEA. The Enfield and Edmonton District Councils had voted against the resolutions so the Enfield decided that they had no objections to the

---

[16] Enfield District Council minute 784 (vol 68), 22/7/1930.
[17] Enfield District Council minute 1843 (vol 68), 19/1/1931.
[18] Enfield District Council Minutes 521 (vol 71), 13/6/1933; 695 (vol 72), 12/6/1934; 677 (vol 73), 5/6/1935; 2891 (vol 74), 23/3/1937. See also Chapter 2.

preparation of the draft scheme but reserved the right to dissent from it when prepared[19].

Eventually the threat of the JEA disappeared, the matter was dropped and, in the event, the purchase of the undertaking was never completed.

During the early 1930s further changeovers from DC to AC had to be agreed by the District Council as they might be involved in paying for them if the undertaking was taken over. In June 1935 formal consent was given to the conversion of Essex Road and of the area between Southbury Road and Lincoln Road on the west side of the Great Cambridge Road.

The Church Street showrooms closed in 1970 and office staff moved to new premises in Carterhatch Lane where they were joined by staff from Edmonton, Hornsey and Wood Green. The Carterhatch offices were finally closed by privatised Eastern Electricity in 1999.

EDMONTON

Edmonton District Council were granted a provisional Electric Lighting Order in 1902 and commissioned reports from Mr B Hammond and Mr W C C Hawtayne. In his report Mr Hammond said that the undertaking would not be dependent upon electric lighting only, as the neighbourhood was ideal for a first-class motive power business. He referred to the large factories already established in the district, the bulk of which might be relied upon as users of electrical energy.

---

[19] Enfield District Council Minute 2845 (vol 74) 18/3/37.

The extent of the area for which the supply was to be given would permit the use of the low tension direct current system. Mr Hammond recommended that, at the outset cables should be laid in certain streets, which would give a total of 6,200 yds of distributing mains. This would probably ensure consumers whose total demand would be equivalent to 15,000 8cp lamps. He estimated the maximum load at 300kW, including 15kW for public lighting and 55kW as motor load.

Mr Hawtayne, in his report, noted the working-class character of the district, and said that if arrangements could be made with one of the several companies who undertook the wiring of premises on the easy payment system and, if slot meters were to be adopted, he had very little doubt that within a few years 17,000 to 20,000 lamps of 8cp their equivalent would be connected. He recommended the adoption of the three-phase alternating current system, and estimated the capital expenditure, if the Council provide their own power station, at £33,000, provision being made for generating plant of an aggregate of 375kW. Nothing was included in either scheme for public street lighting. A large profit, the reports added, should not be expected[20].

Edmonton UDC transferred its Order to Northmet for £2800[21] and supply commenced in July 1907 from a transformer substation in Church Lane, Tottenham. There is a possibility that there was an earlier street lighting installation along Hertford Road, Church Street, Victoria Road and Angel Road. If so, the electricity supplier was probably the Tottenham & Edmonton Gas Light and Coke Co which had powers to produce and distribute electricity under the Tottenham & Edmonton Gas Act, 1898[22].

Northmet electricity offices were set up in 1908 at 89 Fore Street, Edmonton, but by 1912/3, they had moved to 387 Fore Street, Town Hall Buildings. As part of the wave of new Northmet buildings in the 1930s a new purpose-built showroom with offices above was constructed at 305 Fore Street[23] where they remained until the 1970s when a shop was opened in the newly built precinct at Edmonton Green. The Fore Street offices had closed in 1965 when Edmonton District was merged with Enfield.

---

[20] Electrical Review vol 52, p 870 22/5/1903
[21] Electrical Review vol 59 p134 27.7.1906
[22] Gillam G *Enfield Archeological Society Bulletin* No.123 Dec 1991
[23] Electrical Review vol 108, p1002 12/6/1932

TOTTENHAM UNDERTAKING[24]

The Order for supply in the district of Tottenham was given to the Supply Company in 1900. Supply was first given temporarily to the Tottenham Urban District Council Offices in 1906 by means of a gas engine and dynamo installed in the Town Hall.

With the above exception the system has always been alternating current, and supply was originally made from Edmonton in 1907 via the Fore Street East and West Distributors. These, at the commencement, were laid as far as Bruce Grove, and the drop in pressure, due to the long length of mains, was rectified by the temporary installation of a BT-H induction regulator in the premises of the Acme Electric Company (then situated at the junction of the Tottenham and Edmonton boundaries). This state of affairs continued until a temporary substation was erected, on the site of the later Church Lane Substation, and supply commenced from the Edmonton - Tottenham HV trunk main in December 1908.

The first Consumer to be connected was the Baptist Chapel on the 4th October 1907, followed shortly afterward by Wallace Bros (fishmongers), Coombes (outfitters), and Whartons (clothiers), all on the High Road.

The steady development of the load from 1907 to 1926 can be seen from the following list, which gives the various substations which were erected over that period.

"ACT" SUBSTATIONS.

Maynards (superseded by Vale Rd)	May 1908
Fountayne Road	Jan 1909
Hale	July 1910
Vale Road	May 1911
Duncan Tuckers	Oct 1912
West Road	May 1920
Tottenham Traction (South Grove)	April 1922

---

[24]Based on Northmet Monthly Bulletin 10/26, December 1926

"ORDER" SUBSTATIONS.

Town Hall	Aug 1908
Palace	Aug 1908
Chessums	Oct 1908
Church Lane	Dec 1908
Boundary Road (temporary kiosk)	May 1909
Green Lanes	June 1909
North Eastern Fever Hospital	July 1909
Seven Sisters Road	Feb 1910
Trumans	June 1911
Tariff Road	July 1911
London Emery Works	Aug 1913
Cornwall Road	Sept 1913
Schnurmann's Kiosk	Nov 1913
Rangemoor	June 1917
Dowsett Avenue	July 1917
Boundary Road (or Crawley Road)	Jan 1918
Paxton Road	Dec 1918
LGOC Garage	Dec 1920
St Anne's Road	July 1922
Rowleys	June 1923
South Grove (Tottenham Traction)	Jan 1924
Prince of Wales's Hospital	Feb 1925
White Hart Lane	Aug 1925
Klinger's (now dismantled)	Feb 1925

These were followed by "Act" Substations at Gestetners and Ferry Lane, and "Order" Substations at High Cross, Lealand Road, and Devonshire Hill.

The substations at Fountayne Road and the Hale were originally fed from the Order supply via Church Lane at 3kV. In 1910 they were reconnected to the trunk mains via Wood Green - Vale Road and subsequently through West Road to Brimsdown via Ponders End.

The substations at Green Lanes and Seven Sisters Road were 6kV substations, originally equipped with Berry series gear. This gear consisted of a small transformer with its windings connected in series with other transformers of a much larger capacity. When the load on the substation was too great to be dealt with by the smaller transformer its windings were short circuited by means of a switch controlled by a suitable relay, leaving the larger transformer to deal with the increased load. Tests on the gear showed that the saving in light load losses justified the increased cost of the equipment but the character of the load on these two substations changed so the gear was subsequently removed in favour of standard Northmet equipment.

The important power Consumers in Tottenham included:-

	Approximate Demand in kVA
Millington & Sons, stationers	300
Prestwich & Co, manufacturers of motors for motorcycles	300
Gestetner Ltd, manufacturers of cyclostyle duplicators	280
Maynards Ltd, confectioners	200
Flatau & Co Ltd, boot manufacturers	200
Weber & Phillips Ltd, boot manufacturers	120

The last two were the largest boot factories in England south of Northamptonshire. Another power load was that obtained from the manufacture of pianos and piano parts. There were seven piano factories and several piano part manufacturers including John Clark & Co who had a foundry where the iron piano frames were designed and cast.

The Albion Sewing Cotton Co Ltd had a medium sized mill where cotton was mercerised.

Several of the larger power Consumers, including Klingers, moved away from the district during 1925, but the connected load in motors nevertheless increased owing to new consumers being added and existing consumers taking additional load. By 1925, the connected load in the district was over 6MW, shared almost equally between the 89 'Act' consumers and the 356 consumers supplied under Electric Lighting Orders.

In the main streets the early public lighting was by means of arc lamps, the first lamps being put into lighting on 12th December 1908. The Oliver, Davy & Gilbert types were considered but it was decided to standardise on the Oliver magazine type and 110 of these 400 watt flame arc lamps were erected in the High Road, Seven Sisters Road, Green Lanes and Lordship Lane. At the request of the Council 10 Davy Arcs, of the four carbon long hour burning type were erected in Bruce Grove. The guaranteed power factor for these arc lamps was not achieved, and the deficiency was overcome by the use of condensers manufactured by the BIH Co. It is believed that this was the first occasion when they were used commercially for such an application.

Incandescent lamps were first substituted for Arc Lamps on 27th June 1923, and complete changeover to 240 volt incandescent lighting was effected by 27th March 1925. In the High Road, Green Lanes, Seven Sisters Road, Bruce Grove and part of West Green Road 500 watt lamps were used, and in Lordship Lane 300 watt, the lamps in each case being gas filled and fitted in Benjamin Reflectors.

The swan necks used for the arc lamps were retained, and the reflectors were designed with a heavy boss in order to utilise the original contact gear made by the London Electric Co. The lighting of the side streets, however, had commenced in 1919 with 120–100 watt gas filled lamps on Harp Fittings made by the Pontifex Co, to our design.

Prior to the First World War the load was largely industrial. From a residential point of view property was in the hands of weak landlords and many houses were vacant. It was only after the War that any impression was made on the side streets, the residents being now more settled.

A feature of the Tottenham Undertaking in the 1920s was the very large revenue obtained from entertainments, there being many cinemas, dance halls, billiard halls, etc., in the district.

Tottenham was an important source of revenue from Council housing. At the end of 1926 an order was received for wiring 110 new houses west of White Hart Lane, under a 'free' wiring scheme whereby the Council paid 6d per house per week. There were 82 seven room Parlour Type houses, and 28 six room Non-parlour type. The tenants paid 1/3d per week for lighting in the case of the Parlour type house and 1/2d per week for the Non-parlour type. The Council collecting these payments and remitted them to Northmet quarterly (less 5%, to cover the cost of collection).

Tottenham district eventually merged with Edmonton before being moved to Carterhatch Lane with the other southern districts.

WOOD GREEN

Electricity supply commenced in Wood Green in 1913, the powers granted to the local authority in 1902 being transferred not to Northmet but to the Tottenham District Light Heat and Power Co. That company installed gas-engine driven generators at Watsons Rd[25] and supplied DC in the Wood Green Area until 31st December 1932. Gas for the generator engines was stored in a gas-holder nearby. Northmet took over 5,300 consumers, the Tottenham company having changed its name in 1928 to the Tottenham & District Gas Co[26].

12: **Northmet temporary showroom at Wood Green Underground station, 20th June 1933** [*London Transport Museum*]

---

[25] H W Morrison *A brief account of the Tottenham & District Gas Company's first 100 years, 1847–1947* Pub T&DGC, 1947.

[26] *TEE-GEE NEWS* (House magazine of the Tottenham & District Gas Co), Centenary number, winter 1947.

The gas company had had its offices in High Road, Tottenham but outgrew them and in 1930 acquired the old Freemasons' School building at 658 Lordship Lane, Wood Green. A new wing was added and the building renamed Woodall House after the Chairman of the company. In more recent time the building has become Wood Green Crown Court[27].

Until their own new showroom and offices were opened in Station Road, Wood Green, Northmet had a temporary showroom in the concourse of the newly-opened Wood Green Piccadilly Line station[28]. The new Station Road offices had Northmet badges and slogans cast into the fabric of the building where they could still be seen in 1999 in spite of change of ownership. After nationalisation the Wood Green offices also accommodated staff from Southgate.

Wood Green was seriously affected by the cold winters in the early 1950s when domestic heating loads led to overheating of cables and switchgear, particularly in the streets off the High Road, where the pavements were kept clear of snow in winter by the heating effect of the cables beneath. Emergency remedial work in difficult conditions followed. At this time there were still some homes which did not have mains electricity but it is not known whether this was the result of a deliberate policy towards their electricity business by the former Tottenham company.

In the 1970s further mergers of district undertakings took place and the offices in Station Road were relinquished, staff moving to Carterhatch Lane, Enfield.

---

[27] PC K R Lambert, former EGB employee.
[28] See photographs in LT Museum archive.

CHAPTER 5: THE WESTERN AREA

KINGSBURY & HENDON UNDERTAKINGS[1].

Supply in Kingsbury started on 25th December 1910 chiefly on account of an order for public lighting which Northmet received from the Kingsbury UDC. The Council were most anxious for Northmet to take over the Order which they held for supply in the district, stating they would give Northmet some public lighting and assuring them that practically everyone would come on supply.

The most prominent part in the negotiations was played by Jose Diaz, a brother of a former President of Mexico, who was the then Chairman of the Council with full powers to act on its behalf. In spite of the Council's assurances, it was not until May 1924 that there was a total of 100 consumers in Kingsbury. Mr Diaz himself never had his house wired and Northmet only obtained payment for his service charge (about 25/–) from his Executors after his death.

Following the commencement of supply from Colin Deep (an annex to the Hendon traction substation) at 415V, the next substation to be erected was in February 1913 at Slough Lane (Green Man). Colin Deep was also used to give bulk supply to the Hendon Electric Supply Co who distributed to their own consumers. In October 1914 Thrupp & Maberly (motor body builders) took supply, a substation being built at their premises, which were later occupied by Lampson Paragon, who made paper bags.

In June 1917 the Barninghams (later known as Kingsbury South) Substation was put into commission. Messrs Barningham, aeroplane builders, afterwards went into liquidation, their premises being taken over by the Kingsbury Engineering Co, who made small motor cars and scooters. They in turn went out of business and the premises lay dormant for some time, before being divided amongst Bentley Motors (motor car repair shop), Van Den Plas (builders of high class motor car bodies), Donne & Willans (who made the framework for motor car hoods), Power Equipment Co (switchgear manufacturers), Fry's Metal Works foundry (chiefly cast iron and aluminium) and the Ajax Motor Works.

---

[1] The Outline of the following comes from Northmet Monthly Bulletin 4/27, April 1927

In August 1917 Northmet gave supply under their own Act to the Aircraft Manufacturing Co. An 11kV substation was erected and equipped with four 250 kVA transformers. The premises were left vacant for some time after the aircraft company went into liquidation and later the Daimler Co, who had a financial interest in the estate, commenced manufacturing motor car bodies in one of the bays. The project was abandoned, however, after 6 months, and the work transferred to Coventry.

The Winter Tennis Club then took over this particular section but they soon went into liquidation, and the Daimler Co again took possession. Part of the premises were occupied by Daimler Hire Ltd, and another part by the Daimler Co Ltd, first as a storage for cars, and afterwards for manufacturing and repair work.

Beardmore Motors took over the old canteen as a repair depot for their taxis and cars. Other blocks were occupied by Windovers Ltd (high class motor car body builders) and The Phoenix Telephone & Electric Works Ltd (manufacturers of telephones, accessories and wireless outfits). The largest shed (which was really built by the Government and rented to the Aircraft Co) was occupied by General Motors.

All five of these last mentioned Companies started taking supply in 1923, By 1926 maximum demands varied from 26kVA for Beardmore to 300kVA for General Motors.

Blackbird (Chalk Hill) Substation was built in April 1924 primarily for the Chalk Hill Estate, which was already receiving supply from the existing Wembley mains. A feeder was taken from Willesden to the Blackbird Substation and then on to Hendon. Mains were also laid from the Substation to the British Empire Exhibition, and from there to the British Oxygen Co.

Supply in Edgware commenced in August 1912, but progress in the district was comparatively slow until the underground railway was extended from Golders Green in August 1924. By the end of 1923 after over 11 years of working, the consumers had reached the total of only 219. But in 1924 there was an addition of 56 consumers and in 1925 the new connections totalled 162. Early in 1926 Northmet started to combine the returns for certain districts. Edgware was included in those for Hendon Rural which makes it difficult to see how the separate areas developed from then on.

Manns' Road substation was commissioned in August 1912. It was designed for 11kV, though the system up to then had been 3kV. Conversion to 11kV was carried out in 1927 by the installation of outdoor type transformers. In September 1926 the Buckingham Road Substation was erected to relieve Manns' Road, and also to interconnect between Stanmore and Edgware supply.

Supply in Stanmore & Harrow Weald was started in November 1924 with the erection of a substation at The Hare in Harrow Weald, which contained transformation to 3kV as well as to LV. A 3kV substation was put into commission at the same time at Old Church Lane in Stanmore and other substations were erected at Bamford's Corner in Harrow Weald in February 1925 and at Aborcorn Arms in Stanmore in Tune 1925.

In October 1926 the Bentley Priory Substation was commissioned for supply to the Air Ministry. They had taken over an old mansion for use as their London headquarters and this later became Bomber Command. The Northmet service was initially used for lighting only.

In 1927 an extension was laid to give supply to the Royal National Orthopaedic Hospital at Brockley Hill, Stanmore. The initial load was only about 50kVA, being used for the new hospital extension. About the same time supply was given to Sir John Fitzgerald's model dairy farm in Stanmore where an electric milking machine was in use.

Supply to Elstree and Borehamwood district was commenced in April 1926, when the Firs Substation was put into commission. This was designed as a 22kV substation although it operated initially at 11kV. A consumer of outstanding importance in the early days was the British National Pictures Ltd. Again a 22kV substation was installed which operated at 11kV for the time being. Direct current was used for the arc lighting in the studio and Northmet supplied two 250 kVA 6kV AC to 220V DC La Cour motor-converters purchased from the Aberdeen Corporation, which were re-wound for 415 volts AC and 3-wire working. The load was naturally very peaky and the supply agreement was, in consequence, arranged on a weekly basis. The demand typically varied from 190kVA one week to 600kVA another.

Although now forgotten, Wellington & Ward were, in the 1920s a major manufacturer of photographic plates and papers. The Coal Strike was largely responsible for this company coming on supply in August, 1926, owing to their fuel supplies running short. Northmet sold them a 50kW Rotary Converter ex Brimsdown to augment their 100 volt DC plant and about 30 HP of AC motors were also connected.

Messrs. Cambi's former Hat Factory at Boreham Wood was purchased by the Keystone Knitting Mills who took an initial load of about 30 HP of motors and 21kW of lighting. The latter included thirty 450 watt, 1200 cp mercury vapour lamps, made by the Hewittic Electric Co. Northmet got the order for the complete electrical equipment to the value of approximately £900.

A small showroom was opened at Bank Parade, Edgware in 1913, which during the Great War was used only for the display of apparatus in the window, the premises being given up after the War. This was superseded by a rented showroom which was opened on 29th September 1925, and was given up in 1927 when the new showroom opened as part of the Tube Station complex.

13: Edgware showroom, October 1937 [*London Transport Museum*]

The Hendon Urban District Council were originally the authorised distributors of electric current in Hendon but they transferred their Order to the Hendon Electric Supply Company[2]. This Company was registered on 27th June 1907 for the purpose of taking over the Hendon Electric Lighting Orders. The original Order of 1899 was granted to the Electrical & General Engineering Company and was transferred by that Company under an indenture dated 11th September 1899 to the Hendon UDC. That transfer was confirmed by the Hendon Electric Lighting Order 1899 Amendment Order 1905. Under the Amendment Order the Council were empowered to transfer the Orders to Messrs Crompton & Co Ltd. and this transfer was effected by an indenture dated 6th June 1904. On 2nd November 1902 Crompton & Co. entered into an agreement with the Electric Supply Corporation to transfer, inter alia, their rights, obligations and liabilities in pursuance of negotiations then proceeding between Crompton & Co and the Hendon UDC in connection with the Hendon Orders and this agreement was subsequently altered, modified and extended by subsequent agreements.

Under an agreement dated 25th July 1907 between the Electric Supply Corporation, Crompton & Co and the Hendon Electric Supply Co, it was agreed that the Hendon Orders should not be transferred to the Electric Supply Corporation but to the Hendon Company which had then been incorporated.

Northmet entered into an agreement for bulk supply in July 1907. Supply was first given at 3kV at Brent Street Substation in January 1908. On 1st August 1908 Crompton & Co. obtained the Hendon Electric Lighting Order (Amendment Order) 1908 under which they were empowered to transfer the 1899 to 1908 Orders to the Hendon Company and the transfer was effected by Deed dated 28th July 1909.

Northmet erected other bulk supply substations at Colin Deep in October 1910 and Child's Hill in August 1921. The maximum demand in 1926 was 5,512 kW and the consumption approximately 10,500,000 units, making Hendon the next largest Northmet bulk supply user after Willesden UDC.

Originally the Electric Supply Corporation held a controlling interest in the Hendon Company and provided services such as Head Office accommodation and accountancy work until the Northmet assumed control in 1938. The Hendon

---

[2] Outline of the History of the Northmet Power Company by E T Kingsbury and E Boys, 1946

Undertaking was vested in The Northmet Company on September 30, 1939 by their Act of that year and the Hendon Company went into voluntary liquidation; the final winding up resolution being passed on 6th December 1939.

WESTERN AREA & WEMBLEY UNDERTAKING[3].

It was not until early in 1914 that a programme was drawn up for the development of the Western Area by laying a 0.2 sq in cable from Willesden Power Station via Wembley and Wealdstone to Pinner. It was thought at the time that the Company had but little chance of being able to obtain an Order for supply to Harrow and, consequently, the Sheepcote Road route on the eastern foot of Harrow Hill was followed.

The order for supply in Wembley had been obtained by Wembley Urban District Council in 1906, and was transferred by them to the North Metropolitan Electrical Power Distribution Co Ltd, in 1907. The Board of Trade gave notice to revoke the order as from the 30th March 1912, but the Wembley Council purchased it five days prior to that date. Northmet supplied Wembley under its own 'Act' powers, the Wembley UDC giving their consent, in an Agreement dated 18th May 1914, to Northmet supplying current in their district. Supply in Wealdstone was also given under Northmet's own Acts. Pinner was developed by the Colne Valley Electric Supply Co Ltd, one of the National Electric Construction Co's undertakings.

Supply to Wembley commenced in October 1914, to Pinner at Christmas 1914, and to Wealdstone in April 1915. The Northmet trunk main was laid into Wembley at the outbreak of the Great War.

David Allen's printing works were taken over by Waterlow Bros on behalf of the Government for the national printing of food cards etc, and, shortly after the end of the First World War, His Majesty's Office of Works, Stationery Department (from which the name 'Hemstonery' was derived) took over the Factory entirely. The two 150 kW steam driven sets were replaced by two 250 kW Bruce Peebles motor converters, supplying a 3–wire 400 volt DC system. Northmet obtained the sales order, at a good profit, for the motor converters and switchboard, which

---

[3] From Northmet Monthly Bulletin 2/27, February 1927

were in the works proper some distance from the substation. The Power House chimney, which was used under the old steam conditions, was felled in 1925.

The Western Trunk was, at this time, being operated at 3kV from Wembley, and an 11kV substation was hurriedly put into commission, being replaced in January 1919. The load averaged approximately 200 kVA in 1927 with the consumption about 375,000 units per annum.

Bulk supply was given by Northmet to Pinner from the Love Lane Substation with 3kV feeders to a number of kiosks around the vicinity, the distribution system being 3-phase 4-wire 173 volts giving 100 volts for lighting.

The Northwood system was 3-wire DC and was changed over to a static supply using the usual 6-phase connection with the old mid-wire connected to the star point of the transformers. Apart from Northwood Hospital, only one 3kV static substation (on a large butcher's premises) was found necessary to deal with the changeover of the power load, which was of course small, the remaining motors being single phase.

Eastcote was fed from Northwood at 3kV, later upgraded to 10kV and connected with Ruislip, which also took supply from the District Railway.

For some years Wealdstone was supplied at 3kV from Wembley, from a temporary portable substation building at Cecil Road, erected in April 1915. The permanent substation was put into commission in November 1920, the switchboard being erected by Northmet from gear which was originally purchased under the 1914 programme. However many parts had been utilised for war factories, making the task somewhat difficult. This substation had LV transformers only and fed into the town feeder pillar with two 0.2 sq in cables.

Wealdstone was a valuable source of revenue from the start, the shops in the High Street availing themselves very quickly of the electricity supply. From the point of view of capital involved the revenue from this little Undertaking was, in fact, extraordinarily high.

In 1927 the power load was represented by:-

Ingall, Parsons, Clive, a coffin factory. They supplemented a wood refuse suction plant with Northmet power, and installed a 50 kW rotary converter ex Brimsdown. They were later supplied at 3kV from the new Kenton Lane Substation.

The Hamilton Brush Factory also supplemented their wood refuse plant by log sawing motors, and a small motor generator set.

C B Horton's factory next door had a varied existence, doing very useful War work when run by Renoplex Company, being taken over later by Sydbie and used as a Glass Factory. Afterwards they went into liquidation, and the premises were used as a small toy factory.

The Wealdstone Sewage Farm was connected in 1926 and took power for two 15 HV vertical Blacketons pumps with automatic starting gear from the Wealdstone - Hendon overhead line. This line was carried across country some three miles in 1922 to connect the Hendon group of feeders with the Western Trunk, in order to give a standby supply.

It was a fortunate happening that although the Western Trunk had been fed for eight years without a breakdown, this overhead line, within three months of its erection, saved the situation when a fault was experienced in the Willesden – Wembley cable.

In November 1919 an Agreement for bulk supply was entered into with the Harrow Electric Light & Power Company and supply was commenced in December 1920. This was at a time when their available steam plant was becoming insufficient for their requirements. The Sheepcote Substation was looped in on the Wembley – Wealdstone 0.2 sq in trunk, and two 0.025 sq in feeders were laid up the Harrow Hill to their West Street generating station, which became a substation with three 250 kW BT-H rotary converters. The plant later consisted of these machines, together with two 500 kW and one 1,000kW Bruce Peebles motor converters.

Towards the end of 1926 the load passed the safe limit of one 0.025 sq in cable and an additional 0.1 sq in feeder was, in consequence, laid up Harrow Hill, terminating in a Reyrolle feeder switchboard belonging to the Company, and supplying the usual BT-H truck type switchboard, which was their property, modified for supplying converting apparatus only.

Supply to Wembley was given in 1914 at 3kV from Willesden from a portable substation at Chaplin Road. 3kV feeders were laid to Geipel & Co, Alperton, a kiosk at Deadmans Hill, Wembley Hill, and a substation at Wembley Park. The substation proper was erected for the Company at Chaplin Road by BT-H in November 1920. A new HV feeder to the Fiat Motor Works was laid shortly afterwards, which feeder at a later date also supplied the Aster Engineering Company.

The first large development arose from the British Oxygen Company being enticed into the District at North Wembley in March 1918, with Hooper and Co's Aircraft Factory being erected alongside. To deal with the load thus created the 3kV ring main was completed between Wembley Park Substation and the Fiat Motor Substation and substations were erected in these two large factories.

During the last six months of the Great War the British Oxygen Company put down a second oxygen plant, which, as a temporary measure, Northmet supplied from five 100kVA transformers housed in a substation. The windows and doors of the substation were taken out and filled with expanded metal in order to allow the necessary ventilation.

A 0.05 sq in split conductor, 10kV feeder was laid from Chaplin Road to take over this load in 1919, and the General Electric Co. took over the Hooper Aircraft Factory in 1923. These consumers were fed from the British Oxygen Substation which supplied a 3kV system on the GEC site, two substations, the property of that company, being erected, and a portion of the old Hoopers' substation being taken over by them as a third substation.

The British Empire Exhibition of 1924-25 was a valuable experience for Northmet although they did not supply all of the load. An Exhibition power station was built in order that manufacturers' plant could be seen in actual operation[4]. In this power station three 1,500 kW 6.6kV turbo generators were installed, and three substations were erected by the Exhibition Authorities.

Northmet equipped a Type 1 Substation to deal with the normal load of the Exhibition, this substation containing four 500 kVA 11,000/415 volt 3-phase transformers, and a cell type 11kV switchboard which was constructed from

---

[4] Northmet Monthly Bulletin 2/26 Item 34 Feb 1926

loose apparatus purchased from the BT-H Co. This Substation was purchased by the Exhibition Authorities.

Supply to Wembley Stadium, which was first required for the Cup Final in 1923, was given independently of the rest of the Exhibition, and a separate and distinct substation, supplied from the Wembley local 3kV mains was installed. This substation, which remained in use after the Exhibition closed, was equipped with three 50kVA transformers, with an additional 100kVA during the Exhibition period.

In the second year, 1925, the Exhibition Power Station was abandoned and supply was afforded by Northmet entirely, two further substations, known respectively as the 'Main' and 'East' substations, being erected.

The three substations previously erected by the Exhibition Authorities were for 3 kV. The experience gained enabled Northmet to use 11kV substations only, thus obviating the use of 3kV.

The "Main" Substation, which was erected in the substation portion of the old Exhibition Power Station, was equipped with five 500 kVA 11,000/415 volt three phase transformers and a Reyrolle armour-clad switchboard for the 11 kV side.

In the "East" Substation four similar transformers were installed, as well as Reyrolle switchgear for the control of the HV side.

In both the "Main" and "East" Substations, the switchgear for the control of the low pressure side consisted of steel framework with Ferguson Pailin Oil Switches mounted above the transformers, and was constructed by us from loose apparatus purchased from the aforesaid and other manufacturers.

To afford the additional supply to the Exhibition during 1925 Northmet laid a new 0.2 sq in feeder from the Willesden Power House to the "East" substation, and a 0.1 sq in feeder between the "East" and "Main" substations.

Metering for the supplies from these two substations was carried out at 11kV by a special panel installed between the incoming feeder from Willesden and the transformer and outgoing feeder circuits on the switchboard in the "East" substation.

The cable system in the grounds consisted very largely of paper insulated cables in ducts, but practically all the street lighting was carried out in cab-tyre simply dug into the ground. Although a fair number of faults were experienced it was remarkable how it stood up for two years.

The greatest load density was in the amusement park, largely by reason of the great illumination required rather than from power considerations. Power taken by the Racers was approximately 100kW, the majority of the other power driven amusements taking from 15 to 50 HP.

In the Palace of Engineering the load during the first year, with its engineering exhibits, was about 1000kW This was reduced in the second year to about 200kW.

The Stadium, an oval ground 750ft x 400ft, was illuminated from 32 reflectors, the total load being 98kW. Coloured arc lamp projectors, giving streamer lighting effects from above the Stadium were staffed by the RAF and run from an 80kW motor generator set installed in the Stadium Substation.

The charging of the Railodoks and Electric Launches was done at night time from a 460 volt 3 wire DC network supplied from rotary converters in the first year and a 150 kW motor generator in the second year. This also supplied a few exhibits in the Amusement Park. It was further split into a 5-wire system with balancers for the battery charging itself.

There were four 50 HP Refrigerating Plants running at a very good load factor. One of these was used mainly for supplying restaurants with ice, the others being for the frozen exhibits.

The Neon Pylons, the load on which was approximately 10kW, appear to have given a fair amount of trouble. The use of coloured gelatine screens was abandoned owing to their not standing the weather, and eventually strips of coloured glass to reduce the cost of replacements were fitted to most of the flood lights. These strips were about 2" wide and after their adoption there were very few breakages due to heat and weather conditions. The outdoor strip lighting does not appear to have given much trouble.

In the Palaces of Housing and Transport the general illumination was approximately 200 watts per 625 sq ft and was obtained from Benjamin reflectors placed at a height of approximately 30ft. In the centre bays every 25ft of the 80ft span was illuminated by two 500 watt lamps placed at a height of 40ft and one 1000 watt at a height of 50ft.

A typical summer day load in the exhibition was 2200kW maintained with slight variation until darkness, when the demand rapidly rose to 4500kW, tailing off after 10 o'clock and falling very rapidly at 11.30 pm, leaving a general night load of just under 1000kW. When the Exhibition was closed the lighting load stood at the somewhat unaccountably high figure of about 500 kW

In 1925 the total maximum demand including the Stadium was approximately 5,500 kW and the total consumption slightly over 6,200,000 units.

The opportunity was taken to link up the British Oxygen Company with the British Empire Exhibition Substation via a new EHV Substation at the GEC works which supplied their own group of substations with 3kV current. These substations fed respectively the Glass Works (a subsidiary to the company's Leamington Glass Works), the Union Works (which were really the old Hoopers Aircraft Factory) and the GEC 'Hurst' research laboratories.

In 1926 the British Oxygen Co's load occasionally reached 575kVA with two 200 HP compressors and a 100kW Rotary Converter for a Hydrogen plant. The GEC load was 625kVA and growing.

The growth of Sudbury is interesting history. It was made possible by a small crate manufacturer who required supply, and for whom nearly a mile of 0.025 sq in HV cable was laid along Harrow Road, a substation being erected on his premises. Although this consumer failed two years after receiving supply, the ground was prepared for the domestic development of the neighbourhood. In 1918 a branch feeder was laid from Alperton to near Sudbury for the Blake Explosive Leading Factory which, after the Great War, became Sudbury Golf Club. The substation on the golf course was replaced by another substation at Clifford Road erected in October 1926.

The HV feeder to Geipels, cable manufacturers, which was laid in 1914 opened up Alperton, and it rapidly became a power district, a substation being erected at the bottom of Ealing Rood in June 1918 supplying Caribonum Glass Works, Rennie Forbes Fertilizer Works and the Wooller Motor Cycle Works, later the famous Glacier Metal factory.

The HV system was then extended to Mepsted and Heywood and the British Dynamo Works (later Anglo Abrasive Works), and supplied the Wembley Sewage Farm. The Standard Tyre & Rubber Company, took supply in January 1920, and the additional load from one or two other smaller concerns, necessitated a second 0.05 HV cable to Alperton.

The growth of this load and the widening of Ealing Road and formation of the Sudbury Spur encroaching on the site of the HV substation made it advisable to supply Alperton at 10kV. A substation was erected and fed from Chaplin Road. This was, at a later date, connected to the Taylors Lane through the future Standard Telephones and Cables Company's site south of the Stonebridge Park Power Station which then supplied the Bakerloo Line.

The Kenton area of Wembley was the last to develop. Supply was laid to the large Northwick Estate, fed from the Wealdstone Overhead line from a temporary substation and HV line to Kenton. Development was remarkably rapid and, after various intermediary stages were passed through a substation was looped into the overhead line. This substation took the place of a temporary substation and fed substations at Kenton Lane, Gooseacre Lane and Oxen Park Avenue at Preston. This was on the route of a 3kV feeder between Wembley Park and Kenton which had also been serving the district for some time in readiness for the final substation at Kenton Lane.

The area fed from this group mingles with the Wealdstone District to such an extent that for this and other reasons the Wembley and Wealdstone Undertakings were merged in 1926 as one district for operational and statistical purposes.

In 1922, as the result of a sample Harp fitting being tried in the Ealing Road, an agreement was concluded for lighting the Harrow Road by means of 47 - 100 watt gas-filled lamps suspended in Wardle fittings and 34 - 100 Watt vacuum lamps which were changed to gasfilled in 1923, and also for lighting the Ealing Road by 22 - 100 watt gasfilled lamps in Harp Fittings, and the local

National Housing Estate by 20 similar lamps. The ordinary gas lamp was replaced in each case except for the Housing Estate where new lamps were provided, and in that area only the fittings were paid for by the Council.

In 1924 the British Empire Exhibition made it desirable to increase the lighting for the Harrow Road, and a total of 38 - 100 watt, 36 - 500 watt and 40 - 300 watt lamps in Wardle fittings were installed. A steady increase in the side street lighting resulted in there being 523 Harp Fittings installed which were all 100 watt gasfilled but later 200 watt gasfilled lamps were installed in the Ealing Road.

At Wealdstone, too, as the result of a trial, 38 - 100 watt gasfilled lamps in Harp Fittings in the High Street were installed to replace gas lighting in 1922, and 35 of these were increased to 200 watt in 1924 and lit all night. A steady increase in the number of side street lamps resulted in 89 lamps being in lighting at the end of 1926. There was a tendency to convert all side street lighting to electric but, in the mid-20s, some of the poorer side streets had no cable so this was not possible.

The Company opened a Showroom in 1915 at 3 Neeld Parade, this being rented from Callow & Wright, one of the first building estates in the District. The flat above was taken over for office purposes several years later but became too small for the requirements of the district. A new Showroom was built nearer Wembley Bakerloo Station in the Harrow Road and opened in 1927.

HARROW

The Harrow Electric Light and Power Co Ltd was registered on July 5, 1895 and in October of the same year obtained by transfer from the local authority, the Harrow Electric Lighting Order 1894. A further Order for a portion of Wealdstone which had been added to Harrow was granted to the local authority in 1900 and transferred to the Harrow Company in April 1901. In 1911 the Harrow Company were granted an Order for another portion of Wealdstone. In July 1933 the Northmet Company obtained control of the Harrow Company. The Urban District of Harrow was considerably extended by the Middlesex Review Order 1934 and the Council became the purchasing authority for all these Orders.

The tenure of the undertaking under the 1894 and 1900 Orders expired on 14th October 1937 and there was no provision for any extension beyond that date but the undertaking under the 1911 Order was not purchasable until 1953 unless the local authority were authorised by Order to supply prior to that date. In 1936 it was agreed with the local authority that the Northmet should take over the distribution rights of the Harrow Company and that Company be wound up. To give effect to the arrangements with the Council it was necessary to promote an Act of Parliament and this received Royal Assent on 10th June 1937. By this Act the Harrow Orders undertaking was transferred to the Company until 1st January 1951 or any subsequent tenth year. The final winding up resolution of the Harrow Company was passed in March 1938.

CHAPTER 6
THE NORTHERN UNDERTAKINGS

ST ALBANS DISTRICT[1]

At the end of the 19th Century, the City of St Albans had a population of about 16,000 in an area of 4.22 sq miles. The City Council had only a very small staff and no access to technical advice. Water and gas were supplied by two private companies and the City had no public tramway system. One of the corporation's most important functions was sewage treatment and refuse disposal. The St Albans Urban Sanitary Authority and the City Council's General Purposes Sub-Committee considered electricity supply as early as 1897. They invited representatives of Edmundson's and other companies to meet them and they also sought advice from other local authorities such as Bedford, Croydon and Shrewsbury, who had experience of electricity supply. The St Albans Gas Co said that they were willing to apply for a Provisional Order and construct and operate an electricity supply system in the City.

On 7th September 1897 the Committee recommended the Council to apply for a Provisional Order. The Hertfordshire County Council objected (as they did for any electricity or tramway order) to protect their interests in roads and bridges, but a compromise was reached with them. A Provisional Order was made in 1898 by the Board of Trade under the Electric Lighting Acts, 1882 and 1888.

The Order specified the streets in which cables had to be laid within two years but instead of getting on with the job there was a period of indecision. In the end the Council employed a consultant (Alfred Miskin) to report. His report was mainly projections of investment, running costs and income but without any real justification for the basis of his figures. He mentioned the North Metropolitan Electric Power Supply Co but his report contained no specific recommendation as to who should implement the Order. However, the minutes of his meeting with

---

[1] From a booklet *St Albans Electricity* published in 1934 and kindly lent by Miss Marion Thody, and Northmet Monthly Bulletin 1/27. The information has been further expanded by Messrs Bill Killick and Eric Wright. The 'City' here refers to the City of St Albans, there was also a Rural District and the boundaries of both changed as the built-up area expanded. Further information about the power station at St Albans is contained in chapter 3.

the Committee record his recommendation to transfer the Order to a private company.

Indecision continued until, on 9th October 1900, the Council decided to seek offers. Three were received; Northmet Power Distribution Co, British Shuckert Electric Co and the St Albans Gas Co. Another consultant, Robert Hammond, was employed and he recommended (in March 1901) that the Council retain the Order and work it themselves. In the event, the £33,000 capital investment was considered too much for the Council and they followed up the Northmet offer on 11th June. There followed protracted negotiations about the Council's right to purchase the undertaking after 16 years and each 7 years subsequently. There was also concern about the Company's plans to take supply in bulk from the Northmet Power Supply Co. A municipal election in the meantime did not help either.

As the time limit to lay cables had expired, the Board of Trade pressed the Council to act. They did this by again seeking offers. One was from a Northmet subsidiary, the St Albans and District Electric Supply Co Ltd (which was not registered until 7th November 1903 and was legally owned by the British Electric Traction Co Ltd (BET), Northmet's owners). A third consulting engineer, MacGregor Duncan, visited Hertford on the Council's behalf and reported favourably that "..,the Company are well qualified to to give an entirely satisfactory service."

At last, on 26th September 1905, the Provisional Order was transferred to the St Albans Company.

Meanwhile, in 1904 the St Albans Company applied for a Provisional Order for supply in the Rural District around the City itself. That Order was granted in 1905 and, again, cables had to be laid in certain streets within two years. That year BET reorganised its holdings and the Northmet Power Supply Co held all the shares and took complete control of both the St Albans Company and the Northmet Distribution Company.

After Northmet took over the Electric Lighting Orders, there was agreement on 3rd May 1907 that the company would burn the whole of the City's refuse. It was incumbent, therefore, on Northmet to obtain a site for their works which would be suitable for the purposes of generating Electricity and yet would be as near as possible to the centre of the town, not only to cut down the length of the feeder mains, but also because it was desirable to have the Refuse Destructor as near as possible to the town itself.

After considerable difficulty a site was secured in the Camp Field, which was then in the Rural District of St Albans. A piece of land one acre in extent was bought from the late General William Booth. The Salvation Army established a musical instrument factory and printing works adjacent to the Great Northern Railway branch line, opposite the generating station. As part of the deal, Northmet contracted to supply electricity and steam for heating the building. The new power station doorway had a ELECTRICITY WORKS carved in the lintel.

Before electricity supply commenced, the St Albans Company applied to transfer its powers to the Northmet Distribution Co. This transfer was made in March 1908 so the St Albans Company never actually supplied any electricity.

When electricity supply began on 26th September 1908, St Albans seemed a long way from the main Northmet Power Stations and, for an isolated station of small size, direct current was much easier to operate, more particularly as batteries could be used for storage purposes. As soon, however, as bulk supply became available from other stations, a changeover was made to AC. At the same time the pressure was raised from 230 to 240 volts, which was the standard introduced by Northmet in 1906 and became the national standard for over 90 years.

For some years the whole of the electricity supply to the City and district was furnished by means of the refuse of the City, but as demand grew the conditions became rather difficult and the staff were from time to time constrained to go out into the road to see if another refuse cart was in sight as steam was getting low!

End of	1909	1919	1929	1934
No. of Consumers	135	619	2621	6150
Units Sold	100,848	516984	2632346	7300000
Average Price per unit	3.66d	4.09d	2.981d	2.02d

The first AC consumer to be connected in St Albans was the New Barnes Mill in 1916. A substation was erected at their premises, which was fed from a 3kV cable laid from the Power Station, supply being given by a motor-alternator, a step-up transformer, 2 miles of 3kV cable and a step-down transformer. All AC service was given by this means until December 1922 when supply was taken from Luton Corporation. When the Electrical Apparatus Co factory was built in June 1920 the one and only 3kV network path box was jointed to the New Barnes cable and extended to their premises. In 1922 a 3kV cable was laid, at the same time as the Luton link, from the Power Station to the Corporation Depot (dust destructor works) in Sandridge Road, where a substation was erected.

A mercury arc rectifier substation was put into commission at the showroom in Market Place in January 1923 to augment the supply in the centre of the Town, a 3kV feeder being laid from the power station via Victoria Street into the Showroom. This cable was continued in 1925 via Dagnall Street to Harley Street, in order to give supply to the printing works of Messrs Fisher Knight & Co.

In 1924 high voltage connections were made between St Albans and Brimsdown via Hertford and Hatfield. Later a direct connection was made with Taylors Lane, Willesden. After this the independent plant at St Albans ceased to be big enough for the job and being far from economical, was entirely removed. Generation had ceased on 31st December 1929.

The former Engine Room then housed two rotary converters (each of them being larger than the largest generator previously installed) for the remaining DC supplies. There was also a mercury converter which was the second of its type to be introduced into this country. The remainder of the space was used for storage. The old Destructor House was converted into a switch room and a substation.

The ground at the back, part of which was originally occupied by two wooden cooling towers for cooling the turbine condensing water, was been made into tennis courts for the use of the Staff, while the chimney was taken down at some considerable expense as, in the opinion of the Company, it did not add to the amenities of the neighbourhood and had become unnecessary.

St Albans was linked to Hatfield in 1925 and, at the same time, a 3kV cable was laid to Hill End where a substation was erected in April. That June the HV main at the Electrical Apparatus Co was extended to Highfield Hall, about 1½ miles distant and in November supply was given to the St Albans Hosiery Mills. A substation was erected at their premises, the Sandridge Road HV cable being looped in. In December 1925 a rotary converter substation was equipped at the

International Rubber Manufacturing Co's works, in order that these consumers could be supplied with AC and, at the same time, maintain their DC.

Two substations were installed in July 1926, one at the Power House, mainly to supply the Breakspear estate of about 100 houses valued at £800 to £900 each. The other was at the GPO wireless station (which received messages from the continental service), the cables from Hill End being extended across Oaklands for this purpose. The Marshalswick estate of quality housing was also started in 1926 requiring a new substation. Also in 1926 a 0.1 sq in 3kV cable was laid from the power house, along the Great Northern Railway embankment, London Road, Old London Road and Pageant Road to Saracen's Head Yard and thence via the Cloisters to the Showroom Substation. A substation was erected in Saracen's Head Yard, equipped with two outdoor 3-phase and 2 indoor 6-phase Transformers, the latter being used for the changeover from DC to AC in the centre of the town enabling use to made of the existing 3-wire DC distributors.

By 1927 all new business of any magnitude was being supplied with alternating current. Small LV networks were run from the substations and existing DC consumers in outlying districts were being changed over to AC where possible. A large part of the revenue was derived from an industrial power load of nearly 1000kW. There were no very large consumers, but the industries were many and varied, including motor tyres and rubber goods, musical instrument repairs, printing, electric meters and switchgear, flour mills, hosiery mills, raincoat and clothing manufacture, electrical fittings and equipment, refuse destruction, wireless receiving station, deep well tool and boring machinery (heavy engineering), gravel pits, saw mills and manufacture of boot and shoes, hats, cardboard boxes, silk, brushes, bricks, notebooks, buttons and buckles and mineral water as well as engineering works, dairy farming and laundries.

The following figures show the growth of the undertaking. The demand and consumption increased from 148kW and 10,700 units in 1908, to 1,844kW and over 2,500,000 units in 1926. The number of Consumers was 67 at the end of 1908 and 1,641 at the end of 1926. The Sales Turnover increased from £218 in 1918 to approximately £5,500 in 1928.

The 'Act' mains laid up to the end of 1926 amounted approximately to 10 miles HV and one mile DC, and the 'Order' mains to 34 miles.

In 1927 the largest power Consumers consisted of -

	Approximate Maximum Demand.
International Rubber Co.	240kW
Salvation Army Printing Works	130kW
New Barnes Mill	80kVA
Electrical Apparatus Co	50kVA
Nicholsons Raincoat Co.	45kW
W. 0. Peake, Ltd.	45kW
Brushes, Ltd.	41kW
St Albans Corporation Depot	40kVA

St Albans was one City where electric street lighting was not an early consumer. Street lights were all gas until 1933 when Northmet won the contract by competitive tender. There had, however been earlier installations of market lighting in 1923 and the first traffic signals in 1931.

14: **Ivy House, St Albans, 2000** [*M A Friswell*]

As mentioned above, when Northmet first started in St Albans their offices were in the Camp and they had no showroom; in fact showrooms in those days were unknown. On the last day of 1915 however, the Company opened a showroom at 6, Market Place, St Albans. This showroom was well situated but it became far too small for the amount of business. In addition, the office accommodation was still far from adequate. Under the circumstances, therefore, the Northmet decided to make a move and took over Ivy House. Ivy House had been built by Edward Strong (a stonemason at St Paul's Cathedral) in the early part of the 18th Century and later became the residence for many years of the Debenham family.

The Company endeavoured to alter as little as possible the features of this charming old house. What alterations were made were reckoned, at the time, to be improvements, such as removing the chimneys and generally opening up the front. The northern side which was always very poor and was not visible normally from the road, was also improved and an extension built behind with matching bricks.

During this process part of the ivy, from which the house took its name, had to be destroyed but where possible it was allowed to grow again. Northmet boasted that 'the amenities of the district will not be in the least worsened by our activities'.

Inside the building changes were made but, here again, they were reckoned to be improvements, opening up the beauty of the old staircase (designed by Wrenn) and enabling the full value of the rooms to be obtained.

The entrance from St Peter's Street was intended for public use and led into the entrance hall of the original house. The features of the entrance hall were very little altered. The two rooms on either side were opened up to the entrance hall through archways and were used as showrooms for displaying domestic electrical fittings and apparatus.

On the first floor a comfortable lounge was provided for the public to meet Northmet staff away from the main showroom. Leading from the lounge was a demonstration kitchen where all types of electric cookers, washers, refrigerators and other kitchen equipment were on view. Demonstrations of electric cooking were given on alternate Wednesdays at 11 am and 2.30 pm for the benefit of those interested, whether they were electricity users or not.

Contrary to the usual practice, the display window was entirely detached from the showroom proper, the window actually facing on to St. Peter's Close. It was been arranged in this manner to avoid interfering with the architectural features of the old building.

There was a cashier's grille at the rear of the right hand showroom on entering the hall.

In the basement of the building were stores, while in the extension there was an up-to-date workshop where consumers' apparatus was repaired.

The building was heated by means of an electric hot water storage system. In a large tank in the basement were electric heaters which were switched on during the night only.

Northmet hoped that this new showroom would enable residents to come and see for themselves the many applications of electricity, have them demonstrated and learn the cost of running before purchasing apparatus. Residents were welcome, whether they planned to make a purchase or not. The staff offered advice or help on any electrical question.

STEVENAGE

The Stevenage Electric Light and Power Co Ltd was registered in February 1923 and was granted its Order in 1924. Northmet purchased the whole of the share capital of the Stevenage Company in 1924 and Sir James Devonshire and Mr E Boys were appointed Directors in place of the two original Directors who resigned. The Order was transferred to the Northmet Company in November 1927 and the Stevenage Company was wound up. Mr S T Drake, who was one of the founders of the company, became District Superintendent at Stevenage until his untimely death at the age of 60 in 1943[2].

---

[2] *Electrical Review* 15/10/1943 and *The Electrician* 22/10/1943

HERTFORD[3]

Although Hertford was one of the first areas of Northmet to have a supply of electricity, the start was really rather slow following the local Corporation obtaining an Electric Lighting Order in 1891. Having set up an electric lighting committee, the Council proposed initially that electricity should be generated from three 70 horse power gas engines supplied by a Dowson gas generator (a system used at Morecambe, Lancashire). There would be 2kV to 100V transformers in 2ft by 4ft by 2ft deep pits supplying ½"x¼" copper conductors mounted on insulators in 6" glazed earthenware pipes. A consultant recommended forcing dry air through the pipes as was done at Newcastle upon Tyne. The power station and 1½ miles of mains to supply up to 1500 consumers was to have cost £4900. The total running cost would be £838 or, with depreciation charges, just less than £1000 per annum[4].

There were arguments and counter-arguments, consultants employed and reports considered. This 'lost' the lighting of the Post Office and the Barracks to gas[5]. The Council considered a quotation from the Brush Electrical Engineering Co but the terms were not acceptable[6].

By 1898 still nothing was done and the Council discussed the possible disposal of its ELO to the Municipal Electric Supply Co who proposed a DC system of distribution[7]. Finally, on 25th August 1899 the ELO was transferred to the North Metropolitan Electricity Distribution Co for £345. Before supply commenced, the North Metropolitan Electricity Supply Co appeared on the scene and Hertford Council became worried that the Supply Co might use the power station to supply other authorities in bulk and could exercise its powers to construct tramways[8].

Eventually Electricity supply commenced in Hertford in 1901, the local power station supplying DC. Fore Street and other thoroughfares were lit by arc lamps,

---

[3] This section is based on *Outline of the History of the Northmet Power Company* by E T Kingsbury and E Boys, 1946 and *Centenary of the Bishop' Stortford Epping and District Gas Company, 1835-1935* published by Northmet, 1935. Additional material supplied by Alfred Phillips, George Sibley, Bill Killick and N F Smith.
[4] *Herts Mercury* 11/10/1893
[5] *Herts Mercury* 12/9/1894
[6] *Herts Mercury* 6/4/1895
[7] *Herts Mercury* 13/8/1898
[8] *Herts Mercury* 24/2/1900

the posts also being fitted with incandescent lamps which were switched on after 11pm. Large buildings fitted with electric lighting included the infirmary, Christ's Hospital Girls School and the covered market[9]. The excitement moved one person to write[10]:

"The City Fathers had an invitation
From Barnet, not so many days ago,
To visit their Electric Lighting Station,
Which the Directors would be pleased to show.

"Half a score or more of them attended
To solve the mysteries of Electric Light,
And see that if in Hertford could be mended
The scant illumination of its streets at night.

"It took some time of hot and weary walking
To reach the place where electricity was made,
And courteous officials 'midst much talking
The machinery most willingly displayed.

"The engines very steadily were working
In form and manner very scientific,
The wheels and spindles not a moment shirking
Revolving with a speed that looked terrific.

"The Civic Fathers with their minds enquiring
Evinced much wisdom in their search for knowledge
And questions asked which proved their zeal untiring
to supplement what they ne'er learnt at college.

"And to improve their early education
Were told of 'dynamos' and 'energy' and 'power'
And all that's necessary for an 'installation'
'acids' and 'storage', meters for an hour.

[9] Leaflet: *Electric Light and Power* in Hertford Museum
[10] *Herts Mercury* ? September 1901

"The 'volts' and 'units' occupied attention,
'Electric currents', 'candle power' and 'switches'
'Amps' and other terms I need not mention,
Were quite enough to drive away the witches.

"And in the streets the lighting was inspected
On columns low containing 'incandescent'
And high above the 'arc' lights were erected
To show their brightness in each road and crescent.

"The City Fathers had to now decide
That their inspection had been true and thorough,
Having then their inner wants supplied
Dispersed in safety to their ancient borough."

The Corporation made a comparison of gas and electric lighting, considering three scenarios, one with 28 lamps would cost £1/7/2½d for gas and £2/2/- for electricity, one of 52 lamps would be £2/15/6d for gas and £3/10/- for electricity and a third of 50 lamps lit for shorter periods would be 14/8½d for gas and £1/5/- for electricity[11]. The figures were prepared for the Council by John J Steinitz, Chief Engineer, The Electric Power Distribution Co.

In 1925 negotiations commenced for a new showroom and substation opposite the War Memorial in Parliament Square[12]. By 1926, work was under way on a feeder from Brimsdown to Hertford via Cuffley to provide a direct link with future extension to Royston[13].

Conversion to AC was completed by 1926 except for two printing works; Simpsons and Stephen Austin. The two works were adjacent and were supplied from a mercury arc rectifier at the rear of the new Hertford District Office[14] in Parliament Square.

In 1927 there was a fire at the Hertford showroom and Northmet paid the Fire Brigade £5 for attending[15]. About the same time, there were worries about

---

[11] Hertford Corporation Papers vol X, paper 10/1901
[12] Minutes of Northmet Management meetings Item 30 11/3/1925
[13] Resident Engineers' Meeting min 447 12/4/1926
[14] PC W Killick
[15] Northmet Management meetings Item 554 26/1/1927

security of tenure, presumably because of the possibility of the Council purchasing the undertaking.

When the office was occupied in 1930, there were five statutory undertakings, all of whose statistics were separately recorded. With the absorption of Bishops Stortford there was some reorganisation and Bishops Stortford became part of Hertford District. The Resident Engineer about this time was Mr C R Marshall. There had been two branch offices (and showrooms) at Hoddesdon and Ware. each was supervised by an Assistant Engineer, Mr Rouse (later Mr Winder) at Hoddesdon and Mr R A Voit at Ware. Later Mr Voit returned to the Hertford office as Senior Assistant Engineer.

The rapid expansion of the network and the increase in business in the Hertford district during the 1930s led to the appointment of six young 'qualified' assistant engineers; Bill Smeed (son of the company's architect), George Burrell, E T A Webb, L A Tuttiett, the son of A H Watson and Ronald Gregory (son of H W Gregory). There were also two specialist advisors on the use of electricity in agriculture; A H Rankine and W C LePage. Although they were based in the Hertford sales office, they worked throughout the company's rural area.

The sales function was very important. To determine where the effort should be targeted, the office boy[16] in the Sales office compiled a 'non-consumers' register by comparing the voters' lists with the consumer record cards.

In the Hoddesdon office, as well as domestic and commercial sales, much of the business was electrical installations in factories in the Rye House area, the glasshouses of the nurserymen and gravel extraction in the Lea and Stort valleys.

BISHOPS STORTFORD
Northmet; Gas Supplier

The Bishops Stortford, Epping and District Gas Company was established in the year 1834, first producing gas on 27th August 1835. The gasworks were in Anchor Lane, the coal being brought from Durham by water and discharged from barges on the River Stort Navigation alongside the gasworks. The company was registered in 1871 as the Bishop's Stortford and District Gas Co Ltd. and incorporated by Special Act in 1904; it was reincorporated as the Bishops

---
[16] PC Mr W Killick

Stortford, Harlow and Epping Gas and Electricity Company by Special Act in 1910 on the acquisition of five other gas undertakings making it one of the largest pre-nationalisation gas companies, covering approximately 310 square miles.

The 1910 Act authorised the Gas Company to supply electricity in Bishops Stortford but the Great War intervened and it was not until December 1919 that a supply was available from a gas engine and batteries installed at the gasworks. The DC cable ran up South Street and North Street to the College, but there were relatively few electricity consumers. The statutory electricity area was 15 square miles and included the Urban District of Bishops Stortford.

Early in 1921, the half-yearly meeting of the gas company was dominated by problems with controlled prices falling following the War[17] and coal was being advertised at the reduced price of 47/- per ton. Later in the year there was an issue of 7% redeemable debenture stock[18]. Negotiations were started for a takeover. Northmet only wanted to acquire the electricity business but the then Directors of the Bishops Stortford Company would only consider an offer for the combined undertaking. So Northmet became, albeit reluctantly, a gas supplier. Control by Northmet enabled the gasworks at Bishops Stortford and Epping to be reconstructed 'on the most modern lines'. Naturally, the electrical installation at the new gas works was done by Northmet electricians. The other five small gasworks were closed down.

Northmet may not have wanted to be gas suppliers but, typically, they seemed to have entered into the business with enthusiasm. Quite apart from the refurbishment of the two gasworks, they built new offices and stores and a 'handsome' showroom in South Street. Although they were supplying both gas and electricity the stated company policy was that the competitive services of gas and electricity should each stand on its own merits. The Gas Company's directors included the familiar names of Lord Ashfield (Chairman and MD) and Sir James Devonshire. Captain Donaldson was Assistant to the Managing Director and Evelyn Boys was the Company Secretary.

Having taken over the Bishops Stortford electricity business, Northmet commenced a supply of AC power which gradually replaced the limited DC

---
[17] Herts & Essex Advertiser 26/2/1921
[18] Herts & Essex Advertiser 9/7/1921

service previously available. In 1921, the White Horse Inn, in North street, Bishops Stortford, was purchased by the gas company and later a substation was commissioned in the yard by Basbow Lane. From this Northmet gave electricity supply to the gas company. When control of the electricity undertaking passed to Northmet, plans were made to use the old inn for showrooms and offices.

The building was a timber-framed structure which probably dated from before 1500. Although mentioned in early records as the White Horse Inn, it seems that over the years various owners had also followed trades such as tanner, ironmonger, grocer and leather seller. The adjoining land was used for a market, its nature changing over the years, sheep in the early days and poultry by the 1860s. It had also been used as HQ for volunteer forces (including storage of ammunition) and as a practice hall by the town band[19].

In 1932 these historic premises were converted for Northmet. It appears that the timber frame building was jacked up while new foundations and damp courses were inserted. The interior was sympathetically renovated with exposed beams and the outside was plaster finished with pargeting. The ground floor became a well-equipped showroom with offices upstairs. In the process of renovation an old staircase was uncovered. Some examples of stained glass can still be seen. Although the glass appears to be hand-made, there is some dispute about its age. Behind the building was a yard which ran back to Basbow Lane and contained stores for mains and contracting departments, a small workshop built to typical Northmet design for appliance repairs and pre-sales assembly and two small wooden barns. One of these was used for larger electrical and contracting materials and was still called the 'slaughter house' twenty years later. There was also a vehicle maintenance bay, an area for storing drums of underground cable and parking for a couple of lorries and a few vans (in Northmet blue livery).

The bicycle shed was essential, bicycles being the main form of transport for the electricians, for which they were paid 3/6 a week. The main high and low voltage substation was in the back yard. It was equipped with BT-H and Crompton Parkinson switchgear, hand operated and very dangerous. Under lightning or fault conditions the oil got hot, smoke poured out all over. The small substation building was later converted to offices.

---

[19] Talk by Mr W J Killick to the Bishops Stortford Local History Society, 11/9/1981

15: The *White Horse* at Bishops Stortford before conversion to Northmet electricity offices and showrooms [*W Killick collection*]

16: A happy occassion! The official opening of Bishops Stortford offices in the former *White Horse* [*W Killick collection*]

The Herts & Essex Obesrver Year Book, Directory & Almanack, 1938

ANY HEAT
YOU WANT WHEN YOU WANT IT

With Gas you can get Exact Heat—there's no need to be always on the watch.

The New Automatic Oven Control does your Oven Cookery for you.

You can put a whole dinner in the oven, leave it, and take it out—perfectly cooked.

EASIEST - CHEAPEST - QUICKEST
—THAT'S GAS COOKING.

Instal a
"REGULO" controlled GAS COOKER
and take a burden off the housewife's shoulders.

Hire Purchase Terms if desired.

Call and inspect them at—
THE GAS SHOWROOMS
45/47, South Street, Bishop's Stortford.
Phone 395—6.

17: Gas advertising: note the ring and bar logo with the addition of two flaming torches [*Bishops Stortford Library*]

The gas company's electricity business had been very low key, but under Northmet the numbers of staff increased, as did the number of consumers. Initially there was no Resident Engineer at Bishops Stortford, the Engineer in Charge being Mr Beddoe (ex Royal Navy), who later went to the Admiralty and served in South Africa, being replaced by Mr Vigar. The senior engineer at the time, who had previously run the old Bishops Stortford Gas Company was Mr W E Knocker. He was 'taken over' by Northmet and was seconded to Hertford District for six months to learn the Northmet way of working. It was he who operated the low and high voltage system which Bishops Stortford covered. He was reported as being a very nice gentleman with a rather 'old fashioned' manner, preferring his own flask of China tea to the usual office brew. He drove a Morris two seater soft top convertible; the junior staff sat in the dicky!. Unfortunately he had a bad impediment in his speech causing problems with communications.

As the business grew, W Hatton Ward became Resident Engineer and remained for many years.

The number of electricians was increased to six. They would go out to the villages to install meters, etc. One of the installation inspectors, Vincent Royce, was tall, fair headed, smoked a Sherlock Holmes pipe, had plus fours and tweed jacket and never carried anything. Villagers greeted him with hand-shaking and called him Sir. Tea, cakes, home-made wine, you name it, they had it! They were treated like conquering heroes for bringing light and heat from wires across the skies. One electrician was asked to go and live in one of the outlying villages, using his lodgings as a base. This was in order to follow up the mains department and install lighting and a few power points in the cottages to replace the old oil lamps, candles and, occasionally, gas lights. The curious term 'no gases' to indicate that the electrician had not blanked off any gas points, was still in use well into the 50s. Electricians who had moved into villages to do this work were given time and travelling expenses from home to their depots long after the villages had been wired and the separate districts amalgamated and moved to Harlow.

Supply was provided from Brimsdown power station by 11 kV overhead lines via Sawbridgeworth. Two 11kV feeders from Much Hadham 33 kV substation. Three feeders came into Thorley Junction controlled by Crompton Parkinson TAP switchgear which was adequate for the low fault levels then but later became under-rated. During thunderstorms the electrician cycled out there, about two miles, and stood by with fuses ready to replace on instructions via a public telephone box half a mile away. When the engineer was in sight he waved his white hanky, the switchgear was racked down, the HT oil fuses replaced and the OCB closed with a silent prayer, hoping that there was no sustained fault on the system. Later Engineers did all the operations on switchgear and had the use of cars. There was still no radio and all operations had to be notified using the GPO telephone.

The former Gas & Electric Company had employed one cable jointer, Mr D G Lodge, who lived at Elsenham and cycled into work each day. He had a gang of four, a mate and two labourers. They operated with a hand cart which they pulled over the Bishops Stortford area. He was well known because of his long association with the early introduction of electricity to the rich areas of Bishops Stortford. He always insisted that he worked in and around Bishops Stortford High Street on Thursday, market day. He would meet all his pals in the public houses (of which at that time there were many). Working on live low voltage cables was a hazardous job, needing full faculties and a clear head. Gregory's most dangerous moments came after drinking Benskin's best bitter, the pubs being open all day on market day!

In the early days of Northmet at Bishops Stortford, a lorry was hired as required for deliveries, &c. Local delivery was by hand cart or cycle. The Bishops Stortford showroom had a bicycle with a sidecar and a small third wheel, and the showroom boy hand delivered fires, bulbs, lamp standards, kettles, irons, etc. The boy was a trainee electrician who had to spend a period in the showroom as part of his training. Apart from his delivery tasks he had to make tea and coffee for the entire building and run errands for everyone. This Northmet idea carried on into nationalisation.

Later on in the 30s, the undertaking had its own lorry and a petrol filling plant was installed at the gas works. Vehicles were filled up with benzene petrol and any coke or creosote tar which was needed was got from there. Employees could purchase coke at half price. Alf Phillips, who was probably the oldest established electrician, had a small Morris van to enable him to get to the outlying villages as rural electrification progressed.

In the early Northmet days there was a big programme of changeover from one system to the other. The replacement of appliances and light bulbs, etc, and meter service connections was a very costly exercise and took lots of manpower but it seems that it all went very smoothly.

In 1935 the electricity part of the business became an integrated part of Northmet's Hertford District and the gas business became the Bishops Stortford Epping and District Gas Company, still a subsidiary of Northmet. Meter reading and billing was on the Northmet system. The meter-reading books were sent to Northmet House and the bills sent out from there to the consumers.

The senior officers of Northmet were not people who hid themselves away in offices. Captain Donaldson, the Chief Engineer, made regular visits to Bishops Stortford, arriving in a silver Lanchester with a driver dressed in peaked cap, leggings, etc. Even allowing for a somewhat feudal attitude, they mostly seem to have been well-respected by the workforce. However there was one engineer called Busby who was said to be a terrible man. When he arrived at a time of crisis, following a big blow-out or fault (fairly common in those days), he would be red-faced, shouting and swearing at repair men and engineers alike[20]. (Busby is thought to have been the Mains Engineer from the Construction Department at New Southgate.)

In about 1935-36 the installation inspection and supply electricians, street lighting attendants and meter readers were all given blue serge uniform suits from bespoke tailors. A man came from London twice a year and measured up each person. Very smart they were. Other manual workers all had brown boiler suits or bib and brace overalls with the Northmet logo on the top pocket, two sets a year. At one stage soft shoes were issued for indoor house works'

Clearly it was not all grim seriousness in the thirties. There was a big fat electrician named 'Tubby' Emery. He had all the public house and brewery installation jobs so his mate became well-informed about beer, darts and free beer. He rode a 250 cc Matchless and was said to be often drunk at going home time (although it is unlikely that the works manager would have tolerated it). Like a horse his mate would point him towards home and hope for the best, later passing him on his bicycle. When working at Rayment's Brewery at Furneaux Pelham there was an issue of two pints of beer in the morning, two pints at dinner

---

[20] PC George Sibley

and one pint at teatime. Emery drunk his mate's as well as his own, so he was a merry chap!

The street lighting had been gas and George Sibley recalls that his father's cousin, Stan Sibley, was the Gas Lighter and scouted the area every night on his cycle with a ladder on his shoulder. Gas lighting was replaced during the late thirties. The main highways were then lit by the early blue mercury vapour system. The concrete standards were erected by hand with poles and ladders by a building firm from Ware, Fred Hitch and Company. They were also responsible for building Northmet showrooms offices and substations. They also laid miles of underground cable.

Northmet had a monopoly of all street lighting. Bishops Stortford had three attendants. All lamps were scouted each night on cycles and they had a wooden tower waggon on two wheels which they pushed. It had extended sections inside, pulled up by ropes. Lamps, large or small were replaced at night (now it is all daywork and lamps are left out for weeks).

The war came in 1939 and the staff went their different ways, although a few remained, being in reserved occupations. Northmet supported their absent employees. As well as half pay, no matter where they were in the world at Christmas they all got 100 Gold Tipped cigarettes and a commemorative booklet showing every service person and rank (dead or alive).

At the outbreak of war, the Bishops Stortford District covered some 70 square miles in area and included some parts of Ware RDC and Epping RDC. Most of the District was supplied at 11kV from the 33kV substation at Much Hadham. The area was still largely rural but there were several industrial consumers including the United Match Co in Bishops Stortford, Lawrence Joinery at Sawbridgeworth and Holbrook Machine Tools in Harlow. Call up into the armed forces meant that two Assistant Engineers (Watson and Ron Gregory) had to go leaving the Senior Assistant, George Burrell, and two Assistant Engineers, Mr Knocker and Mr Killick.

When office was closed, one of the telephone lines was switched through to the home of the Engineer on stand-by but George Burrell was a bachelor living at the *George Hotel* so he could not take part in this arrangement. This left the two remaining Assistant Engineers on stand-by alternate weeks. When they were out dealing with trouble, their wives had to act as local Northmet telephone operator.

Mr Knocker suffered from ill health and died in 1942 leaving only Bill Killick to deal with all out of hours work for much of the rest of the war. The arrangement only stopped after an irate farmer was extremely rude to Mrs Killick and Bill received an ultimatum from her on his return.

At the outbreak of war the Ministry of Supply moved some smaller workshops into the more rural areas and Bishops Stortford had a few military establishments. In 1942, when the USA joined the War, they sent their Construction Corps to build an airfield for their bombers and this required an 11kV supply. That airfield has now been developed into London's third airport, Stanstead.

Typical of many, George Sibley came home in 1945/46 and got his job back. He went to night school and moved on into engineering, eventually completing 46 years service with, as he recalls, "many happy and sad memories of those past and time spent but grateful to Northmet for the job I had and enjoyed. It was a privilege to serve with the many colleagues and many long gone".

After the 1939-45 war there was much reinforcement to catch up on and, with many coming back to work from the forces, Northmet took on lots of trainee men. At the advent of Harlow New Town, Eastern Electricity's Chairman, C T Melling visited. He was heard to say that "This New Town project will not get off the ground"!

It was, however, seen that the designated area was mostly in Bishops Stortford District with some in Hertford. The District boundary was adjusted and Bill Killick, as District Engineer, dealt with the early planning and negotiations for the electricity supply system.

It was some years later that the combined Hertford District moved offices to Harlow.

BEDFORDSHIRE, CAMBRIDGESHIRE & HUNTINGDONSHIRE[21]

In 1925 a Bill was deposited in Parliament having for its objects the incorporation of the Bedfordshire, Cambridgeshire and Huntingdonshire Electricity Company with powers (inter alia) to erect a Generating Station at Little Barford in the County of Bedford and to generate and distribute electricity for all purposes in any part of the area comprising the Counties of Bedford, Cambridge and Huntingdon and the Urban District of Newmarket.

The Act received Royal Assent on December 22, 1925 but three material changes were introduced into the Bill in its passage through Parliament. The area of supply was curtailed, a purchase clause exercisable at the expiration of 50 years was inserted and the provisions in regard to the acquisition of land and the erection of a generating station at Little Barford were excluded. These provisions in regard to the generating station were subsequently incorporated in a Special Order made by the Minister of Transport in 1928. From the commencement the BC&H Company was managed by the Northmet Company who had initiated the scheme, probably because it wanted another power station to the north of its own territory.

In accordance with its 1925 Act, the BC&H Company provided a supply of electricity in the northern part of Bedfordshire, practically the whole of Huntingdonshire, and most of Cambridgeshire excluding the Cambridge urban area. This area, of roughly 1,200 square miles, covered many types of countryside from marketing and general farming in the south and west, rich fen farming areas in the north-east, and the eastern area largely dominated by farming and the prosperous establishments associated with Newmarket, the well known centre of the horse racing and breeding industry.

Established towns and larger villages which were included in the area included (looking from the west at St Neots to the eastern boundary at Newmarket): St Neots, Gamlingay, Offord, Buckden, Brampton, Huntingdon, St Ives, Warboys, Ramsey, Chatteris, March, Sawston, Shepreth, Fulbourn, the Swaffhams, Ely, Littleport, Burwell, Soham, Fordham, Cheveley and Ashley, and Linton, whilst

---

[21] Based on *Recollections; A record of Memories and Experiences in St Neots and Other Places 1912-47* by E G Davies and *The Outline History of the Northmet Power Co* by Kingsbury & Boys

Newmarket, which had electricity supplies much earlier before 1900, was later transferred to the control of the BC&H Company.

In some of the towns, fairly large industrial factories already existed, being powered by their own generating plants, and these, together with many small establishments, quickly took advantage of the new electricity supply which undoubtedly accelerated the development of industry in a hitherto largely rural area.

The development was initially planned and operated by management, engineering and experienced supervisory construction staff transferred from the North London organisation who set up headquarters at St Neots in Huntingdonshire, where a house named 'Arbroath' was purchased in Avenue Road and used for a few years until a new building with offices and showrooms in the centre of St Neots was occupied in 1928. Town gas was used temporarily at 'Arbroath' at the outset until electricity supplies were provided in St Neots in 1926-27.

The engineering policy adopted in extending electricity supplies into the new area was that already successfully used in the North London area of the parent company, which consisted of a primary 33kV system feeding to a number of main substations at selected positions. From these a more extensive 11kV network radiated to feed to distribution transformer stations in the areas to be supplied. Low voltage supplies of 240/415 volts were provided by local distribution and services to consumers. This well-tested system undoubtedly provided a very secure initial background to the supply system in the new area.

The extensive use of underground cables in the North Metropolitan area was largely dictated by the intensive built-up and industrialised area and justified there by the revenue received. However, the very heavy costs of extended underground networks in the rural areas could not be matched by the initially very small revenue returns.

Initially the BC&H Company had to establish itself and set up the staff to carry out the large job of electrifying the area. The engineering section consisted of only three or four engineers with foremen and some linesmen, jointers and fitters, all having had considerable experience with the Northmet Company.

H J Smith, an engineer and manager with world-wide experience, became Manager of the BC&H Company on its inauguration in 1926 and retired in April 1940. A large gentleman with a similar attitude to all he undertook, he ruled his staff in a very forthright and strict manner and every member must have received his opinion of themselves in no uncertain terms at one time or another. Referred to as the 'Guvnor', everyone treated him with respect and recognised his ability to achieve results and the support he would always give if necessary. He was what present day people might describe as an 'old fashioned boss' and, like other Northmet managers it is not likely that he would have appreciated or taken kindly to labour relations as they were in the latter part of the 20th Century.

A regular duty shared by any junior available in the office was to make a quick response to a bellow of 'Boy!' from outside his office door, which meant that because of his generous stature, he required assistance in doing up his back braces buttons after a visit to his private toilet!

Mr Smith earned a reputation for imposing instant reprimands for mistakes or omissions by his staff and a regular practice of his was to 'sack' immediately anyone who displeased him but, after being sent home one day, the defaulter would have a messenger next day from the 'Guvnor' to reinstate him, with a warning not to let it happen again! One engineer responsible for arranging for transport to bring the overhead line gangs back to St Neots on Saturdays received this treatment once or twice because a delay in the transport had caused some doubt in the appearance of of a gang which included footballers who played for St Neots Football Club, of whom Mr Smith was a very staunch supporter.

A D Church, known as 'Uncle' by his staff, also came from Northmet in the late 1920s to assume control of the engineering departments of the new BC&H Company. This must have been a formidable task for a relatively young man who could only have been between 25 and 30 years of age at the time. He was a quiet man, in direct contrast to Mr H J Smith, and his reserved but very conscientious and meticulous nature made it more difficult for him to meet the often stringent demands made by the Manager.

Vernon Smith and his brother Dick (both sons of the Manager, H J Smith), although young men, were responsible for sections of the engineering work and also carried on a vigorous social life which entailed much tact and tolerance on Mr Church's part to shield them from the wrath of the 'Guvnor' and to ensure their continuing availability as very essential members of this small staff. Vernon, was in charge of the work of planning, surveying, construction and the maintenance of all the 11kV and the small amount of low voltage overhead lines existing or being erected in the area. The 33kV overhead lines were constructed by British Insulated Cables Ltd, but when they became part of the system, the maintenance of these also came under local control. Brother Dick supervised the underground network.

The overhead line section general foreman, Mr C W (Charlie) Sykes, was middle-aged, typically bluff Yorkshireman who also transferred from Northmet and was said to have been one of the most experienced overhead line construction experts in the country at the time.

On 1st July 1935 the BC&H Company was taken over by Edmundson's Electricity Corporation who already owned a number of supply organisations in rural areas including the adjacent East Anglian Electric Supply Company. This organisation had considerable experience in providing supplies in the smaller built-up and rural areas and, by the much more extensive use of overhead lines, particularly for low voltage systems, achieved a satisfactory balance of costs to revenue whilst the initial development was being carried out in early years.

Therefore, whilst many of the towns and villages which received electricity supplies prior to 1935 enjoyed underground networks with only small sections of overhead mains, subsequent schemes employed overhead lines almost exclusively, and no doubt this change ensured the continued extension of supplies to the remote areas. However, the initial costs of providing underground cables were not altogether wasted when, in later years amenity and conservation concerns initiated the replacement of overhead low voltage systems by underground cables at considerable expense.

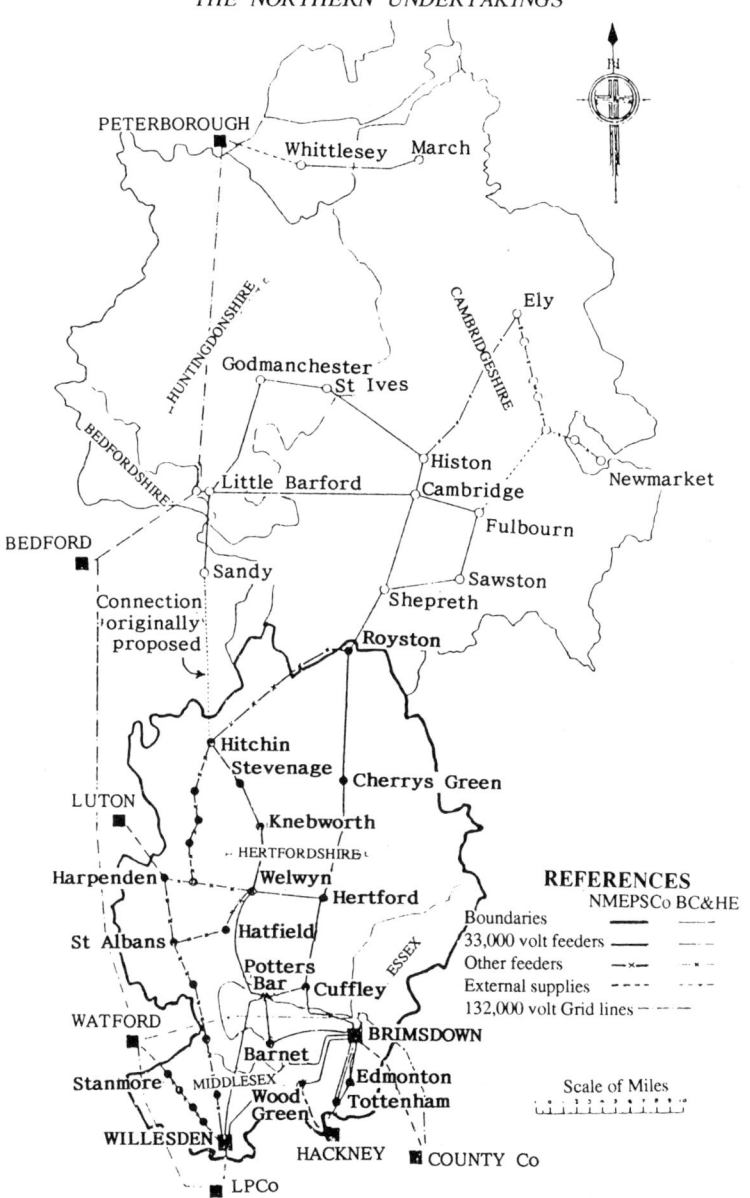

18: Northmet area of supply at its maximum extent in 1935 before BH&C was sold to Edmonsons [*O Elias collection*]

CHAPTER 7: HEAD OFFICES

The location of the Head Office of the Company changed from time to time according to changes in the financial control. On the formation of the Company in 1899 the Head Office was situated at Donington House, Norfolk Street, Strand, WC, the offices of the British Electric Traction Co Ltd, who were responsible for the promotion of the Company. It was here that meetings of directors and shareholders were normally held.

In 1905 a move was made to the City of London where offices in Evelyn House, 101 Finsbury Pavement were rented from Northmet's associated company, the Metropolitan Electric Tramways Limited.

In 1907 Northmet and the Metropolitan Electric Tramways Company joined the British Electrical Federation and on 1st December 1908 the office was moved to the newly opened headquarters of the Federation in Kingsway, London WC.

By 1913 the Engineer-in-Chief had his office at Manor House, Seven Sisters Road, a former North Metropolitan Tramways horse tram depot and stables. Some Northmet departments stayed there until the establishment of Northmet House.

Later the control of Northmet (and MET) passed to the Underground Electric Railways Company of London Ltd (UERL) and in 1915 the Head Office was moved to the Underground offices at Electric Railway House, Broadway, Westminster, London SW1. The UERL offices over St James's Park station had been enlarged in 1905, and four years later the District and tube companies' offices were grouped together and the premises named Electric Railway House, with reconstruction carried out by Harry W Ford. The old overall station roof was removed and steelwork erected to support a new building over the line. This preliminary work was completed when architects Albert Richardson PPRA FSA FRIBA (1880- 1964) and Charles Lovett Gill FRIBA (1880-1960) designed a further six-storey block built between 1922 and 1924 to occupy the space directly over the railway station.

When some adjacent property was acquired there was a move on 10th April 1924 to 55 Broadway, probably the best-known address of a transport headquarters in the world, but head office was moved again on 11th October 1926 to Broadway Buildings, Broadway, SW1 when site redevelopment began. All these were in reality offices in the same block of buildings, which were being rebuilt and extended[1].

The Underground Group was again outgrowing the existing premises, and wanted a modern and efficient office block. The architect, Charles Holden, was commissioned to produce designs, and for the first time the Underground gave him complete control over the planning. The building was to occupy a triangular corner site bounded by Broadway, Tothill and Palmer streets to the east of Electric Railway House, and would be named after its postal address: 55 Broadway. This was to be the centre of the Underground Group's transport empire but it was decided to bring together at some future time in one building elsewhere the Northmet Head Office, General Manager's Office and the Consumers' Accounts Office, then housed in separate premises considerable distances apart. A central department for dealing with the stores, meters and mains laying work had already been established at New Southgate, which was approximately the geographical centre of the Company's activities and it was considered in 1926 that the most suitable site for the new Head Office would be on the adjacent Arnos Grove Estate.

Difficulties were encountered in proceeding with the matter as the scheduling of the Estate under a Town Planning Scheme prevented the erection of office buildings. Negotiations were however opened with Lord Inverforth for the purchase of a mansion known as "Arnos Grove" at the northern end of the Estate. The Southgate Council having agreed to waive the Town Planning restrictions to the extent of allowing the mansion to be used as offices and the addition of a new wing, the property was purchased in 1928 and re-named "Northmet House".

Like all old buildings, the history of Northmet House is the history of its owners. An old map shows the landowners in the 14th century in what was later known as Southgate. The name Margery Arnold appears on a deed dated 1344. Who she was and what she did, we shall never know, but it gives us the origin of the name of what came to be called, Arnold's Estate.

---

[1] *Outline of the History of the Northmet Power Company* by E T Kingsbury and E Boys 1946; C S Smeeton *Metropolitan Electric Tramways*, pp194 & 202 LRTL 1984

Exactly when a house came to be built on the estate is difficult to establish, but it is known that, in 1610, Sir John Weld and his wife Lady Frances Weld made their home here. They both had close ties with the City. Sir John's father had been Lord Mayor of London in 1608 and his maternal grandfather and his brother-in-law also held this high office, in 1595 and 1631 respectively. Sir John built Southgate's first place of worship, The Weld Chapel, in 1615.

Lady Frances, who bore 4 sons and 5 daughters, continued to live at Arnolds after Sir John's death in 1622, but eventually sold out to Sir William Acton in 1645. It passed to Sir William's daughter and sole heiress in 1651 who, coincidentally, had married Sir Thomas Whitmore, a nephew of Lady Frances Weld. From Sir Thomas, the estate was handed down to his son, Sir William Whitmore, who sold out to Thomas Wolstenholme in 1699.

19: **Northmet House** [*Author*]

In 1720, James Colebrooke appears on the scene. He bought the Arnolds estate and decided the house was not up to standard. He had it demolished and set about building a new one to plans prepared by Sir Richard Naylor. The new building was scarcely under way when he died, and the ownership transferred to his son George, who was created a baronet by George II in 1759[3].

Sir George Colebrooke seemed determined to create a mansion of some distinction. He employed as his architect Sir Robert Taylor (1714-1788), Sheriff of London and Middlesex, who preceded Sir John Soane as architect to the Bank of England. The downstairs rooms facing West were particularly fine, the lofty reception room and the antechamber in period style, the drawing room having been redecorated in the Adam style, with fine plaster work and classical friezes, by Sir Robert Taylor.

The feature which strikes the visitor first of all, however, is the entrance hall, whose upper walls and ceilings were decorated in 1723 with the fine murals by the Italian artist, Gerrard Lanscroon. His signature appears in the bottom left hand corner of the East wall (on the first landing)[2]. By 1723 Lanscroon was a master in his own right, having been a pupil of Antonio Verrio, whom he assisted with the adornment of Windsor Castle for King Charles II and Hampton Court for King William III.

Although they suffered some damage during the alterations by Northmet, the paintings were generally preserved by the various owners of the property and can still be admired today. They were finally restored, in 1968, to their former glory with the help of a generous contribution by the London Borough of Enfield.

It is thought to have been around this time that Arnos Grove got its name. Apparently, the Italian craftsmen had difficulty in pronouncing the word Arnold's correctly, and referred to it as Arno's. Sir George Colebrooke heard it and decided on the name for his new house, Arno's Grove. Early paintings of the house are captioned Arno's Grove, with the apostrophe, but this was later omitted.

Although the estate was not so extensive then as it eventually became under the Walkers' control, it must have been a beautiful scene, with the new house set in a

---

[2] *Northmet House, a History of the House and its Owners and a Description of the Lanscroon Murals* Unpublished text, ref JBA/VES dated 1/10/69, Author unknown

prime position overlooking a picturesque valley in which, at that time, both the New River and Pymmes Brook flowed.

In 1762, Sir George Colebrooke sold the estate to Sir Abraham Hume. Sir William Mayne (later Lord Newhaven) who apparently added extensions to the North and South and the apse or porch on the West and re-named it "Arnos Grove". James Brown was a subsequent owner until, in 1777, Isaac Walker arrived to start a new era in the house's history. Isaac (1725-1804) was a successful wholesale linen draper whose sister had married into the Taylor family. The estate passed eventually to Isaac's son John and, in 1853, Isaac Walker (the second) inherited Arnos Grove.

Isaac (the second) had married Sophia, sister of Donnithorne Taylor, and had joined the board of Harford & Taylor in 1816, when the brewery company became known as Taylor Walker. He already possessed and was living at Southgate House with his family but, before he could make the move to his new home, he died in October 1853 at the age of 59. His bereaved wife, Sophia, and family of 12, had to make the move without him and the eldest son, John, became head of the household.

By this time the Walkers had begun to acquire land whenever possible. The reasons were plain. The family had untold wealth and resources. The acquisition of land then, as now, was a good investment, but there were other considerations too. They wanted the area to remain as it was, a relatively quiet and unspoilt backwater, and the buying up of land was their way of ensuring that the developers would be kept at bay. It was a sort of 'private green belt policy'. As a result development came later than it would otherwise have done, postponing the inevitable. The large house called Minchenden on Southgate Green was purchased in 1853, the house was demolished and the grounds added to the Arnos Grove Estate[3].

The Walkers were famous as a cricketing family and a plaque commemorating their residence, particularly the seven brothers famous in the cricket world, is on the East wall of the house, on the left of the main entrance. Cricket was not their only contribution to local life, however, for the first Boys' School in the district was built by them in 1812 and they maintained it until 1868, the building being in use until 1886, when it was finally demolished. Meanwhile, they had built in

---

[3] pp 124-126 *Southgate, A Glimpse into the Past* A Dumayne, 1987. ISBN 0 9512286 09

1840 another School for Girls and Infants, on which site the present Walker Primary School stands today. They also provided the land and the main financial support for Christ Church on The Green when it was built in approximately 1850.

The eldest of the cricketing brothers was John Walker who was, among other things, the first Chairman of the Southgate Local Board of Health when the district was separated from Edmonton in 1881. However, it was the sixth brother, V E Walker, who in 1896 modernised the house and installed electric light, the first house in Southgate to have it. A picture of the house about this time shows a further addition in the shape of a large porch on the North door.

Throughout the 19th century the family had added to the Estate and when it was sold to Lord Inverforth in 1918 it extended over 300 acres. In 1928 he developed the land, except for 44 acres of parkland sold to Southgate UDC (Arnos Park), for housing and sold the house to the North Metropolitan Power Company. Although the interior of the old mansion might lead one to think that it is somewhat palatial and expensive for use as an office, the building was acquired at a price considerably less than it would have cost to erect a new building providing equal accommodation. A new wing corresponding in architecture with the main building was erected on the south side, the first section of which was completed in 1929 and the second section in 1932. Owing to the further expansion of the staff it was necessary in 1935 to add the first section of another wing on the north side and this necessitated the demolition of Walker's North porch, the materials from which were used for the new porch at the East door, latterly the main entrance[2].

Not all Headquarters functions moved to Northmet House immediately. There were still some staff in offices shared with other members of the Underground Group, for example the accounts department at Manor House in the former tram stables, more recently used as offices by London Transport[4]. Some of the other administrative functions remained at 55 Broadway, the weekly 'pay-run' to outside staff being based there[5].

It was said that when Northmet House was taken over in 1928, the move from Manor House was carried out by taking the furniture, etc, on the trams to the

---

[4] PC c1960: Mr H Cook, Draftsman at Northmet House.
[5] PC c1955: Mr Travers, Construction dept, New Southgate.

Triangle, Palmers Green and then up Aldermans Hill by steam lorry. The story is probably apocryphal but it does illustrate the close links that Northmet had with the other enterprises within the Underground Group.

By the end of 1930, a new south wing had been added to the original building and both the *Electrical Times* and the *Electrical Review* reported[6] that all the Headquarters departments had moved in. The Secretarial department, under Evelyn Boys, was on the first floor of the old building and on the ground and first floors of the new wing. The drawing offices of the engineering and architectural departments were on the second floor of the new wing.

All the consumers' accounts were centralised at Northmet House, the forms being filled in and calculated mechanically, and were also printed on the premises. As the *Electrical Times* put it: "There are all kinds of weird and wonderful electrically operated machines for assisting the officials in making sure that the consumer is charged that which is duly owing by him and no more".

The basement of Northmet House housed the staff canteens and hot water came from a 440kW electric storage system, powered overnight with a short boost at midday.

---

[6] *Electrical Review*, p820, 14/11/1930 and *Electrical Times*, p879, 20/11/1930.

HEAD OFFICES 151

20: **Lighting globe at Northmet House, said to be from the 1924-25 British Empire Exhibition at Wembley** [*Author*]

The distinctive lighting globes on the entrance gates of Northmet House and on some concrete pillars in the grounds came from the 1924 Wembley British Empire Exhibition. Most survived well for many years although some have recently been replaced by very undistinguished spheres. Northmet also bought the AC/DC rotary converter from the Exhibition's Neverstop Railway and installed it at Wood Green where it ran until the trolleybuses were withdrawn in 1963.

During the second world war, Northmet House had firewatch duties carried out by control room staff. There was a good view up the Lea Valley from the flat roof to spot where incendiary bombs fell. It was also convenient from the Company's point of view to establish points of damage to the distribution system although perhaps not the type of remote control that they would have liked. For these duties the staff received a ration of one pound of tea and four pounds of sugar each month. The ration continued right up to the reorganisation of the sub-areas in 1976 when the new Group management would not sanction payment for the rations on the grounds that the staff could no longer perform these duties at Northmet House.

As the control centre for the company and later the sub-area, the telephone exchange was manned out of hours to take calls from the public. The exchange was called 'Walker' after the former owners of the house, so if anyone asked for the name of the operator, he would always say "Walker".

The control room was on the top floor of Northmet House and when it was pointed out that there was no fire escape, the management solution was to fit a sling device. The escapee was meant to don the harness and throw himself from the window, the device allowing him to descend gently before being wound up for the next escapee[7].

A highlight of the Northmet House year was the children's Christmas party, fondly remembered by those who attended[8]. The children were not the only people who had parties at Christmas. In those days before drink-driving was seen as a problem, the last working day before Christmas was the scene of high jinks and much merriment. This could be quite frustrating for those who had a job to do, as when a fault occurred at Wood Green on Christmas Eve,1960. The only

---

[7] PC Jenkins RW
[8] PC Mrs E Davies (c1966)

mains drawings were in the draughtsmen's office at Northmet House and they were too busy enjoying the drink to be able to help. In spite of the party problems the power was eventually restored in time for Christmas Day. The last Northmet House party of all was on Friday 4th October 1974 when a capacity crowd said a final farewell to the building[9].

A change of ownership to Northmet House had occurred in 1948 when the Electricity Supply Industry was nationalised and the area supplied by the Company taken-over by the new Eastern Electricity Board. The building became their administrative centre for the Northmet Sub-Area which was largely the old Company area with the addition of the District Council undertakings.

For many years Northmet House continued to perform its pre-nationalisation functions. Before computerisation, a large accounts staff was needed to prepare all the bills for the sub-area. Seating was arranged so that all the staff faced one way with the supervisor(s) behind them. Talking amongst staff was frowned on although provided staff were discreet they could manage to hold a conversation with a neighbour and, of course, there would be trips to the store-room to look up old records[10].

In the 1930s men were expected to wear suits on weekdays but were allowed to wear sports jackets and grey flannels on Saturday mornings. It was many years after the second world war before the strict dress code was relaxed. It was only on very hot days that a message would come down from the Chief Accountant that gentlemen might remove their jackets. However, this only applied in their own office. When leaving the office and especially if crossing the upper gallery to the other wing, jacket and tie had to be in place. It was feared that a consumer calling at the enquiry desk might see someone incorrectly dressed[11]. Ladies would never, of course, wear trousers!

Northmet House was purchased by the Legal & General Assurance Society Ltd in 1975 although Eastern Electricity's new control room at Millfield, near Brentwood, was not ready and Northmet Control remained as lodgers until 4th September 1978.

---

[9] *Northmet Sports Association Club Review* September 1974
[10] PC G Gillam, former clerk at Northmet House.

One night during this period, a telephone call appeared to come from the now-empty planning office. There was no-one there so one of the Control Engineers set out with the caretaker and his dog to find the phantom caller. On reaching the the historic hall in the centre of the building, the dog refused to go through it. He was dragged through by his master and promptly made a puddle on the floor. Did he see something the humans did not? Unfortunately for a good ghost story, the mundane explanation was two bare wires touching a metal filing cabinet[11].

More recently it became an up-market old people's home; Southgate House Close Care apartments. The rooms were all en-suite with some fully self contained apartments for those who could still look after themselves. The old Board Room became the restaurant and a swimming pool was built into the basement[12].

APPENDIX: THE LANSCROON MURALS; A Description

The subject, the *Triumph and Apotheosis of Julius Caesar*, is typical of those used for such decoration in the age of the Grand Manner. Ascending the staircase one passes a number of columns and then you see before you on the North wall Caesar returning to Rome in triumph from foreign wars. Unfortunately, Northmet added a doorway at the expense of Caesar and his chariot but four horses and their grooms can be seen attended by Roman Senators bearing fasces (axes and bundles of wood, their signs of authority), the procession being led by an Officer wearing a laurel wreath. Above, a winged cherub trumpets Caesar's entry, which is witnessed by several spectators, including slaves and flower-sellers.

The procession continues to the left along the landing (West wall). The scene is dominated at the top centre by Diana, Goddess of Hunting, who symbolises Caesar's military prowess represented by the spoils of war, crowns, sceptres, coins and other treasures, borne on a litter by men burning incense. People can be seen standing on the parapets and at the windows of the buildings in the background (including the Pantheon as it became, only after Caesar's death! The procession includes several women (possibly sat for by the ladies of the

---

[11] PC Fase E
[12] PC Dawes C

Colebrooke family as was the custom of the time) carrying musical instruments and bearing sprigs of laurel and baskets of fruit.

21: **Details from the Lanscroon mural at Northmet House** [*D Willis*]

Continuing to the left, the South wall represents an allegorical subject in a large gilt frame. The nine Muses are shown extolling the virtues of Caesar, who is seated on a cloud at the top left. He is wreathed and holds a golden lyre, with the Muses grouped beneath him on the ground. The Muse on the left plays a stringed instrument and has books, scrolls and maps at her feet. The next, who can be identified as Urania, reclines on a globe and holds a pair of dividers. A seated Muse wearing thonged sandals and bracelet, with flowers in her hair, studies a scroll of paper. Above her another holds a caduceus and has one arm uplifted towards Caesar, a fifth, probably Clio, holds a writing tablet, whilst another above bears an astrolobe and holds a telescope to her right eye. On the right a seventh, possibly Terpsichore, is seated at a table-like instrument with a keyboard (perhaps a primitive organ). An eighth Muse, perhaps Euterpe, holds a flute and the ninth Muse holds a quill out towards Caesar, alluding, no doubt, to his written works. In the bottom right hand corner are three cherubs, one writing on a scroll, another holding what appears to be a magnifying glass to his eye and the third seems to be singing or reading to Terpsichore.

This leads one naturally to look up and behold Caesar dressed as a soldier and wearing a laurel wreath ascending to heaven through the open dome with the assistance of the winged, bearded figure of Time to the welcoming arms of Jupiter, King of the Gods, with his Queen, Juno at his side and accompanied by their symbols, an eagle and a peacock respectively. The scene is framed by the balustrade of the dome around which are various figures symbolising aspects of his life and character, including Mars, God of War, Venus, Goddess of' Love, Minerva, Goddess of Wisdom, Diana again, Mercury, the Messenger of the Gods and Ganymede, their cup-bearer, Hercules, Bacchus, Zephyus, the West Wind; and various cherubs.

The coving between ceiling and walls is elaborately decorated with birds, flowers and fruit and in opposite corners are crests and shields. Described in heraldic terms the crests have "on a torse Or and Gules, a wyvern Or, tongued and tailed gules, holding an escutcheon of the last" and the shields bear the Arms of the Colebrooke family, or rather the heir George, who became a Baronet, and his wife, described as "Colebrooke Gules a lion rampant Ermine, crowned with a mural crown Or, on a chief Or, three martlets Azure, impaling Hudson (his wife); partly chevronwise embattled Or and Azure three martlets counterchanging"[13].

---

[13] *Northmet House, a History of the House and its Owners and a Description of the Lanscroon Murals* Unpublished text, ref JBA/VES dated 1.10.69, Author unknown

CHAPTER 8
SHOWROOMS
EXHIBITIONS AND DEMONSTRATORS

From the early days of Northmet, every effort was made to develop the electrical load through the sale and use of electrical apparatus. The first showroom was opened as something of an experiment at Edmonton in 1911[1].

It was said that the sole function of the showroom and its staff was to assist consumers and non-consumers in every possible way. The Company never missed an opportunity to educate the public in such a way that the demand for electricity would increase. Showrooms were seen as a means to that end and no doubt readers will make their own comparisons with the facilities offered by the re-privatised electricity companies at the end of the 20th Century.

Showrooms were generally in the main offices of the local undertaking, usually in a good location on the high street. All had large illuminated NORTHMET signs which, in the 1930s tended to be similar in style to the UNDERGROUND signs used by UERL. The showroom windows were designed with ample dressing space and most of the showrooms contained a model kitchen and rooms for the demonstration of apparatus and fittings under conditions of normal use.

At St Albans, the company opened a shop in Market Place in 1915 to hire apparatus to consumers. A brass property label with the company's full name was fixed to all apparatus which, at that time, was Direct Current. In the window of the shop was a cutout model house with all the windows lit by electricity.

By 1934 new premises were taken at Ivy House, St Peters Street and fitted out in typical Northmet style. The front of the building was retained and became the showrooms, the cashiers office, demonstration kitchen and manager's office. A new front door was fitted with NORTHMET written vertically on each pillar. The large neon NORTHMET signs were fitted outside the mains office and above the show window at the side. A workshop was built on the back of the house for use by electricians to repair consumers' apparatus.

---

[1] The *Electrical Review* vol 107 p93 18/7/1930

At the back of the house was the remains of the lawn with a greenhouse fitted with electric heating and an electric lawnmower used by the gardeners who also tended substation gardens.

The rooms were very large and panelled and the staircase (by Wrenn) had a large stained glass window. Showcases contained table lamps, toasters, irons and electric clocks. Some cookers were on show and there were more in the kitchen upstairs. To complete the picture, there were carpets on the floor, display tables, arm chairs and two fireplaces with mirrors, Berry electric fires and the chiming clocks. The ceilings were very high and displayed the light fittings for sale. The cashiers desk, with a large grill, was in the next room. Earlier showrooms had cash chutes, the theory being that while the customer was waiting for his change he would have time to look around the showroom[2]. Two Smiths chiming clocks were used and ran to synchronous time throughout the war. Clocks by Temco were set by the makers at ten to two but those from Smiths were set at nine twenty three. Apart from the clocks everything was suitable for AC or DC.

To avoid danger from live flexes most apparatus had no switches except 2kW electric fires which had one switch and cookers which were connected to control panels. The usual question asked by the consumers, was does my house have AC or DC supply?

Typical showroom stock consisted of cookers by GEC, Jackson, Belling, Falkirk and Moffat. Some had solid hotplates, some had ring elements and there were a few with a transformer and exposed low voltage elements. Belling cookers for AC had an oven thermostat. Cooker panels also had a socket for an electric kettle. Kettles were, at first, brass with an element clamped to the base. The Bulpitt 'Swan' brand aluminium kettle had an immersed heater with a cutout which threw the plug out. There were also kettle saucepans and a universal kettle with a flat ground base suitable for both gas and electric. Prestcold refrigerators for AC were available filled with Freon gas and had to be commissioned by an electrician.

Hoover cleaners were the American design with a bayonet adaptor to plug into a lampholder. 'It Beats As It Sweeps as it Cleans', was protected by patent so other makers used two motors or followed the example of Electrolux which did not beat the carpet at all.

---

[2] Resident Engineers' Meeting Minute 543 7/5/1928

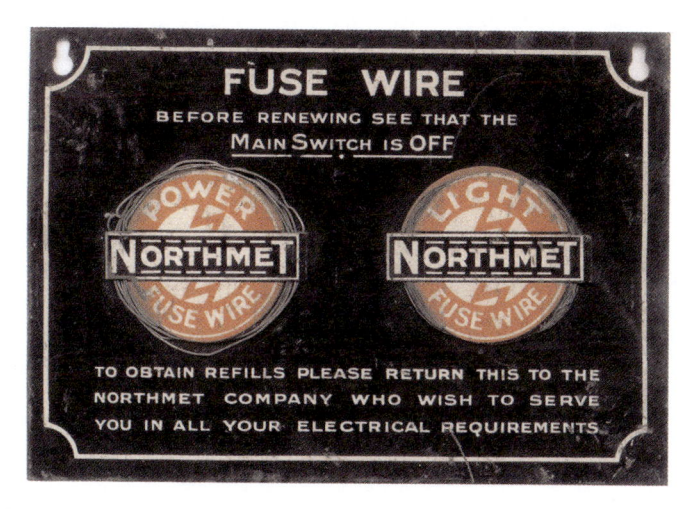

SHOWROOMS

22: Metal card for fusewire showing use of Northmet logo [*Author's collection*]

Irons and trouser presses were available, GEC Magnet irons for AC or DC and Morphy Richards for AC only with a thermostat. In 1925, the GEC Magnet electric iron sold for 16/- costing Northmet 12/- in small numbers or 10/- each if bought by the gross[3]. The bodies of Morphy Richards irons were either steel or porcelain. The latter came back broken but could only be replaced, not changed to steel, due to different construction of the sole plate.

Fires were by Belling, Falkirk or Hotpoint. There were also Berry fires which had imitation coal or wood with a flickering light. Lumps of coal were obtainable to fill in the spaces at the back of the grate. Table lamps were porcelain or wood, floor standards wood or metal, shades available as required. Other lighting fittings were wood or metal and had normal or flame lamps or imitation candles. From Czechoslovakia came glass bowl lights with hanging chains. Five and 15 amp fuse wire was available on a card or tin holder printed with the Northmet logo.

---

[3] Resident Engineer's Meeting Min 374, 18/6/1926

House wiring could be carried out by any contractor or the company or by the consumer himself. To purchase wiring material from the company meant a visit to the showrooms to enquire the retail price (all trading was retail). The price was obtained by the showroom assistant after a visit to the the Kardex which was a system of record cards used to keep track of the stock and prices. Payment was made to the cashier and then there was a visit to the stores at the works to collect.

To match the variety of socket outlets in use, plugs were 15 amp 3 pin and 2 pin, 5 amp 3 pin and 2 pin and 2 amp 3 pin. MK (Multi Kontact) produced the fully interlocked 15 amp 3 pin socket with the non standard earth pin so that the plug would not fit other makes of socket. All plugs had a slot so that the earth wire connection was visible. There were adaptors 15 to 5 amp both 2 and 3 pin with internal fuses. Lampholders were brass or plastic, ceiling roses were metal, also available with hooks for light fittings. Switches were metal or plastic. The action on some was so heavy that it was not unusual to hear the neighbours operate their light switches.

Apparatus brought back by consumers was either repaired at the showrooms or sent back to the makers. Kettles were freed of scale by boiling with Margo, which was not always cleaned properly. The Hoover representative called to overhaul cleaners at first in the workshop, later in the stores. After the central Apparatus Repair Department was set up at Wood Green most of the apparatus for repair was sent there rather than being repaired locally.

Returned repaired apparatus was put in the back of a 3 ton lorry or sent by a boy on a bicycle. The railway delivered from time to time, post came daily. Carter Paterson delivered and collected every day. If required, lamps could be ordered from BT-H at Watford and sent as a parcel on the London Transport bus. Sometimes it would be missed and the conductor would leave the parcel with the agent to be collected the next day. The cinemas in St Albans and Harpenden used the same bus six times a day for the newsreel which also went astray sometimes.

No packing material was supplied so boxes received were used to send apparatus away. If required a wooden crate would be requisitioned and sent away to a different supplier with a charge added in the hope that it would come back. Wrapping paper and string were supplied, also tie-on or sticky red and white labels.

Showroom assistants sold apparatus from the showrooms or from the stores. An account or cash sale was made out and the purchase parcelled to take away or to be delivered.

Unofficially the showroom stores changed lamps in the building, attended to fuses and plugs and fitted plugs to new apparatus for display in the showrooms. New cookers were assembled. The consumer could walk out of the door with his purchase fitted with a plug, all done up in the green wrapping paper and brown sticky tape with the Northmet logo.

A form was available for staff to purchase apparatus at cost price plus 5% for their own use at their address or as a gift to someone else. Later, purchase tax was added to everything. Collections were made for weddings and the senior clerk arranged for gifts to be purchased via the staff form.

Long service awards to staff were made with a certificate showing the number of years and a gift was made to the appropriate value at cost. It was a free choice, not restricted to electrical equipment. Additional awards were made at various times. This scheme was extended to the Eastern board and the CEGB for total years of service in the supply industry. Cases were known of employees adding cash to the awards to obtain something of greater value. This practice was frowned on and finally stopped. Certificates were made out for various number of years as required.

The Northmet staff rate which also applied to employees transferred to the Eastern Board was applied to power station staff transferred to the CEGB.

The works stores at Campfield Road, St Albans received material from Central Stores including all wiring materials and large apparatus came direct from the makers. As required, the showroom stores requisitioned loose wiring equipment and cookers from the works. This equipment included plug tops lampholders and wiring flex but not any fixed wiring. Portable apparatus, light fittings and lamps were ordered direct from the makers.

In the showroom stores stocks were held of lamps (25 40 60 75 100 150 watt clear), bayonet and Edison screw cap, coiled filament pearl, coiled coil filament pearl, 300 watt Giant Edison Screw cap, candle lamps of all types, plain, flame, clear, pearl, bayonet and small bayonet cap, 5 watt neon, ½ watt neon for cooker panels. 15 25 40 60 watt rough service, and 8, 16, 32cp carbon filament lamps. There were flame coloured lamps for Hotpoint heaters, ruby glass for Berry electric fires. Lamps were tested and the date stencilled on the cap. Consumers would bring a lamp back and say they had just bought it although, in fact it was usually some years old. Faulty lamps had a white flash inside and were returned for replacement. (Woolworths at Watford had to sell two kinds of lamps, Watford Corporation 200 volts and Bushey, Northmet, 240 volts.)

There were flexes 14/40 twisted in gold or brown, 40/36 or 70/36 3 core circular brown. Core colours were red, black and brown (earth). The stores kept spare hotplates for cookers. An electrician would take one to the consumer's house and change 100 porcelain beads from the old one before bringing it back to be rebuilt by the maker. Switches, control knobs, door springs and elements for cookers, elements for electric fires, Hoover and Hotpoint belts were all kept in stock. Hoover brushes "yes, carpet or motor?". These were the days before paper dust bags.

The above description of practices and procedures at St Albans is by Eric Wright who started, as did so many other men, as a showroom boy and rose to become an operational Engineer[4].

The showroom at Bishops Stortford was similarly part of the company's offices in an ancient building. The conversion work was carried out carefully although a minstrels' gallery, a feature of the inn disappeared in the process. Like St Albans, the showrooms were fitted out with all sorts of apparatus, large and small. Some of the upstairs rooms were also used as showrooms, concentrating on heating displays at the time the building opened. There was also the obligatory demonstration kitchen[5].

Where an undertaking was still small and could not justify a showroom, as at Hatfield in 1926, arrangements were made with a local shop for display space in the shop window. W A Guest of Church Street, Hatfield also allowed space for a table which could be used by Northmet staff, if required and took messages. They also sold lamps and small apparatus. The arrangement cost Northmet 13/6d per week[6].

---

[4] PC E Wright
[5] Contemporary report in the *Herts & Essex Advertiser*
[6] Northmet Monthly Bulletin 3/26 Item 51 March 1926

23: **Palmers Green Showroom** [*Electrical Times*]

In contrast to St Albans and Bishops Stortford, modern offices and showrooms were built at many other locations including Barnet, Enfield, Palmers Green, Potters Bar and Wood Green. Most had in imposing central entrance with display windows both sides for maximum impact. The window displays were generally changed every two weeks to maintain interest. One of the showroom staff also acted as cashier and customers could pay their accounts there. As at St Albans, most of the showrooms had local sales engineers and a stores.

When the Wood Green electricity undertaking was acquired from the Tottenham Gas Co, Northmet had no showroom or offices there. Until the new building in Station Road was completed Northmet had a temporary showroom in the surface building of the newly-opened Wood Green underground station[7].

Each showroom had shop assistants under the shop manager. The showroom girls were specially trained to deal with the sale of small apparatus and minor repairs. Junior sales staff could attend lectures once a week; these usually being

---

[7] *Technical Developments Introduced by the Northmet* ref JMD/MAY unpublished 2/11/1933

on early closing day[8]. At the more important showrooms there was also a demonstrator[9]. Marguerite Patten (née Hilda Brown) started with Northmet as a Junior Demonstrator in 1934 having already done a short cookery course. She was employed at Barnet showrooms, the manager being a Miss Enid Yetton. Miss Yetton's standards were very high, everything was spotlessly clean and whatever was done had to be 'just so'. She groomed her staff to a very high standard.

The young Miss Brown was on duty in the showroom to sell and demonstrate appliances. She was sent on a number of courses at Northern Polytechnic for laundry and cookery. She also had to go to people's homes after they had bought a cooker, &c, to demonstrate it. This was often in the evenings and sometimes the demonstrators could be taken advantage of to cook a full-blown evening meal. There were also evening demonstrations in halls to women's groups. Occasionally, a prospective customer currently living outside the area but planning to move in would contact Northmet. This could result in her being sent to some distant part of the country to make sure that the new customer would cook electrically.

The showroom had three or four sales assistants, a senior demonstrator and three junior demonstrators. There were also two outside sales people (one man and one woman) paid on commission. The District was run by the Resident Engineer, including the commercial and sales functions. Although treated well, Marguerite Patten got the impression that the gas industry prized their home economists more than the electricity companies did their demonstrators.

She left Northmet in the summer of 1937 and subsequent experience as Frigidaire's Senior Home Economist demonstrating all round the country showed her that Northmet had very high standards. Some demonstration rooms of other companies were poorly fitted or even dirty and unhygienic.

The Electrical Association for Women did great work in raising the profile of a career in electricity for women. One of the Association's leading lights was Vera Norvick although she was not a Northmet employee. She wrote that although many women and girls were entering the electrical industry, it could not be because the remuneration was on an exceptionally high level, "nor can electrical

---
[8] Resident Engineers' Meeting Minute 619 8/12/1930
[9] The *Electrical Review* vol xx p94 18/7/1930

work in any way be called a 'cushy' job; in many cases it has not even the attraction of a pension, for a large percentage of women engaged as demonstrators and showroom assistants are not included in superannuation schemes. Wherein, then, is its attraction?

"The work they have to do is not only varied, but it possesses constant human interest. Its manysidedness and the ebb and flow of material with which they have to deal give full chance for the development of the workers and in addition there is the interest of the technical side of the work."

The job could appeal to all sorts of women, the "cultured woman of the world, ... the homely woman" and "The attractive, good-looking 'womanly' woman finds a place, too. ... Junior posts are filled by girls whose interest in the first place lies in cookery as an art. ... There are, likewise, just a few with a real bent for engineering who, having qualified, are engaged in practical engineering and contracting work; there are, further, some budding engineers in training at the moment."

However, as far as is known, no woman ever became a Northmet engineer.

As well as showrooms, there were, from time to time, show houses fitted out for prospective residents to see what electricity had to offer. A typical example at Enfield was described in the *Electrical Review*[10].

Attention was drawn to the house by a large sign at the side, and a KFM sign in the porch for day and night use. The hours of opening were 10am to 7pm except Sundays. Attendants were present to explain the cost and convenience of the electrical apparatus. 'Electricity House' stayed open for over a year, closing on 29th August 1925[11].

In the hall there was a Crypto rectifier, and a Tungar rectifier for battery charging which was a great convenience for broadcast radio receiving apparatus, the low tension being supplied from a rechargeable accumulator. A transformer was fitted for operating all the bells in the house.

---
[10] The *Electrical review* Vol 95 p54 (11/7/1924)
[11] Northmet Management meeting item 188 18/8/1925

The drawing-room contained a Magicoal fire, which gave out a comforting glow. An alabaster bowl was used as a light diffuser. No house of the time was complete without its gramophone and radio outfit. The former was represented by an electrically-driven machine, by Electric Gramophones Ltd, and the latter was an Ediswan "Two Vee" set with a loud speaker.

In the dining-room was a three-light rise-and-fall pendant fitting with a silk flounce, and in this room there were many useful appliances, such as a Singer electric sewing machine, coffee percolator, tea infuser, toaster, table grill, and warming plate. A Metropolitan-Vickers electric fan was provided for hot weather, and for cold days a Belling fire fitted with hot cupboards. There was an electric clock on the mantelpiece, its speed regulated by Greenwich time from the power house. Statuettes with candle lamps and shades gave a pleasing effect on the mantelpiece.

The kitchen was fitted with a Falco cooker, the oven of which had a thermometer. The Steemkleen electric boiler and washing machine stood in a corner, and other household utensils were on view, ie, a 3-pint Xcel kettle, a 1kW Belling boiling ring, a 5-lb iron, and a Universal toaster.

On the landing were a Hoover suction sweeper and a bowl fire. The bathroom was fitted with a Bastian geyser, which was said to provide a supply of scalding hot water (which sounds rather dangerous) at any hour of the day or night. There was also a Belling Fixall 2kW fire finished in white enamel.

In the front bedroom was a two-light rise-and fall pendant over the dressing table, also a light over the bed, controlled by two way switching, whilst an Adjustolite clipped to the bed made a very suitable reading lamp. A hair-drier, curling-tongs heater, electric shaving mug, early morning tea set (with electric kettle) and Belling Derby fire were among the many conveniences on view in this room.

The nursery was provided with a Bastian & Allen non-luminous type of air warmer, being particularly suitable for children. An electric food warmer and BT–H Nitelight were also on view.

Another room on that floor was arranged as a showroom, with a number of fittings and appliances, one of the most novel and interesting being a BT-H toy transformer suitable for working tiny motors and apparatus from the lighting supply. Much of the apparatus on view was made by local firms, such as the lamps and radio apparatus by Edison Swan Electric Co, fires by Belling, switchplugs by MK Accessories Co, and electric fans and bowl fires made by Metropolitan-Vickers at the Cosmos Works,

From time to time apparatus was changed. It was all priced with labels and tickets. The furniture, floor coverings and curtains were supplied by Messrs Henry Haysons, of Palmers Green. With the exception of the cooker and other heating appliances, nearly all the apparatus used a very small amount of electricity, approximately 15 hours' use for one kWh being the average.

The object of the demonstration house was to show how economical and helpful electricity could be in a home where the income was very modest and, particularly, the servant problem had been most acute. It was a luxury home but it was also an economy home.

Other show houses were fitted out from time to time for periods lasting from a few weeks to several months, including those at Hoddesdon, Potters Bar, St Albans and Wembley. The Wembley house was reported as having average attendances of 60 to 100 people a day with up to 600 people one Saturday[12].

---

[12] Northmet monthly bulletin 2/27, item 119

24: **Mobile showroom** [*Author's collection*]

Mobile showrooms were also used. Probably the first one was a converted bus which was acquired by Northmet on 28th June 1929[13]. At a Resident Engineers' meeting[14] on 1st October 1930, Captain Donaldson said that it would generally visit places where Northmet were already supplying or were about to do so. Resident Engineers were expected to co-operate in the programme and act as advance publicity agents. Where electricity supply was available this was used for the apparatus in the van although where there was no supply the van was 'complete in itself for this purpose'. It therefore looks as if the petrol-electric vehicle had been chosen so that there was a ready supply of electricity available although the standard Tilling Stevens used 110V DC instead of Northmet's standard supply voltage of 240V AC.

At Hertford, Northmet also used a smaller flatbed lorry fitted out as a demonstration float[15].

Later trailer caravans were fitted out and taken to shows and exhibitions.

---

[13] It had belonged to the Birmingham & Midland Motor Omnibus Company (better known as 'Midland Red'). It was their A390, Reg no HA2272, with Tilling Stevens 'FS' chassis no 3310, assembled by BMMO at their Carlyle works in 1924. The chassis had petrol-electric drive, in which the petrol engine was coupled to an electric generator, the electricity being supplied to motors which drove the wheels.

Originally the bus was fitted with an open-top front entrance body (no BB341) with 22 seats on the upper deck and 29 on the lower. It had been withdrawn by BMMO on 27th November 1928 and the body is recorded as having been converted by Hayward & Co, Wolverhampton to single deck (30 seats) and fitted to another chassis.

The photograph, however, shows the lower deck of an original type of body with original cab design and front bulkhead pillar. The original ceiling/upper deck floor had a hump running front to back (on which the upstairs seats were mounted back to back, facing outwards) which gave sufficient headroom in the lower deck.

By 5th May 1937 the vehicle had passed to Robert Moore of Bull lane, Edmonton; three years later he had moved to Provident Park, Montague Rd, Edmonton. The vehicle was last noted at Mortimer Latimer in August 1963, owner unknown. It ended its days at Hunt's scrapyard at Molesworth, Cambridgeshire, where it was finally cut up in the late 1960s, parts of it passing to various preservationists

(Information from Ron Thomas, The Hill, Abberley, Worcester, WR6 6BY. Peter Jaques, 21 The Oaklands, Droitwich Spa, Worcs, WR9 8AD and Lloyd Penfold, 13 Benson Rd, Maypole, Birmingham, B14 4PH.
[14] Resident Engineers' Meeting 1/10/1930, minute 609
[15] The *Electrical Review* vol xx p93 18/7/1930

25: **Northmet stand at the Great Hertfordshire show** [*Electrical Review*]

26: **Northmet entry at the Barnet Hospital Carnival** [*Electrical Review*]

Northmet always exhibited at the local agricultural shows and trade exhibitions, sometimes using the mobile showroom as a basis for its stand. The quality was reflected in the frequency with which Northmet stands were awarded prizes for the best exhibits. Northmet were very keen to encourage farm use of electricity for dairy machinery and poultry brooders, &c. Miss Marion Thody who was a Demonstrator in the 1930s-1940s remembers[16] visiting farms with a salesman who would talk to the farmers while she talked to the wives, trying to persuade them to have electricity installed.

Northmet also strongly supported the annual North London exhibition held at Alexandra Palace with a large stand for cooking and heavy domestic apparatus and a smaller stand for fittings, smaller domestic apparatus and office accommodation[17].

27: Former Northmet offices at Bridgefoot, Ware [*Author*]

---

[16] PC Miss M Thody
[17] Northmet monthly bulletin 1/33 item 420 and bulletin 2/33 item 426

In 1933 Northmet had 31 showrooms and boasted that "as far as is known, no [other] electrical undertaking in the country has such a large number of showrooms"[18]. By nationalisation, Northmet had 40 showrooms:

7 High Street, Barnet   opened December 1928 (replacement)
North Street, Bishops Stortford   opened November 1932 (there were also gas showrooms in South Street)
61 Shenley Road, Borehamwood   opened October 1926
High Street, Buntingford   opened October 1927
180 High Street, Waltham Cross   opened September 1931
Station Road, Chingford   opened December 1924
Hall Lane, Chingford   opened October 1935
245 East Barnet Road   opened November 1933
192 Station Road, Edgware   opened 26th August 1927 (built as part of Northern Line station)
305 Fore Street, Edmonton   opened October 1932 (replacing two earlier shops)
40 Church Street, Enfield   opened November 1934 (replacement)
Colney Hatch Lane, Friern Barnet   opened February 1937
29a High Street, Harpenden   opened December 1925
29 Grand Parade, Green Lanes, Harringay   opened May 1935
4 College Road, Harrow   acquired October 1937
370 Northolt Road, Harrow   opened December 1935
393 High Road, Harrow Weald   opened December 1933
St Albans Road, Hatfield   opened February 1937
137/9 Brent Street, Hendon   acquired September 1937
9 Central Circus, Hendon   acquired September 1937
43 Golders Green Road, Hendon   acquired September 1937
19 The Broadway, Mill Hill   acquired September 1937
Parliament Square, Hertford   opened May 1929 (replacement)
98 High Street, Hoddesdon   opened December 1926
Kenton Road   opened June 1932
Kingsbury Road   opened October 1935
122 Alexandra Park Road, Muswell Hill   opened February 1933
Hatfield Road, Potters Bar   opened December 1931
Kneesworth Street, Royston   opened December 1927
St Peters Street, St Albans   opened September 1934 (replacement)

---

[18] *Technical Developments Introduced by the Northmet* Ref JMD/MAY unpublished 2/11/1933

286 Green Lanes, Palmers Green   opened September 1925 (replacing two earlier shops)
2 Station Parade, Southgate   opened November 1933
2 The Broadway, Winchmore Hill   opened December 1933
38 High Street, Stevenage   opened September 1931
312 High Road, Tottenham   opened August 1929
Bridgefoot, Ware   opened October 1939 (rebuilt on same site)
High Street, Old Welwyn   opened January 1927
71 High Road, Wembley   opened December 1927 (replacement)
High Road, Whetstone   opened June 1933
13-27 Station Road, Wood Green   opened September 1934

Many of these were new buildings replacing older showrooms, as indicated above, often on other sites. In 1953 a small showroom was opened at 703 Green Lanes, Winchmore Hill, close to the site of the earlier one. However, it did little business and closed around 1960.

Northmet's successor Eastern Electricity gradually reduced the number of showrooms until all closed. Many, however, are still recognisable by their architecture and, in the case of Wood Green, by the roundels and motifs on the building.

28:   Enamel advertisement now in London Transport Museum [*Author*]

29: Northmet logo in its most used form

30: Eastern Electricity application of the ring and bar logo which was disputed by London Transport

Prior to the late 1920's Northmet did not have a corporate badge or logo. By 1928, however, the Underground Group were in charge and the same circle and bar 'roundel' was adopted by Northmet as was used on the Underground. For Northmet it came in a number of versions, the commonest being 'Northmet' across the bar with 'Power' in the semicircle above and 'Light' below[19]. Another common use was with 'Use' above and 'Electricity' below and this was set as standard in 1931[20]. Both these variations had electric flashes above and below the central bar. The Bishops Stortford gas subsidiary had a more ornate version. Not only was the lettering more complicated with 'Gas' above and 'Electricity' below the title (in two lines) 'Bishop's Stortford Epping & District' but there was also a flaming torch at each end of the crossbar. The largest roundel of all must have been the one painted, pre-war, on a cooling tower at Brimsdown. Regrettably no clear photograph seems to have survived. The roundel became a registered design in 1934[21] reserved for use by London Transport, General Omnibuses, LT tramways, Green Line coaches, LT trolleybuses and AEC (the Associated Equipment Co). However, Northmet continued to use it until nationalisation and Eastern Electricity continued with their own version ('Eastern' above and 'Service' below 'Electricity'). However London Transport put pressure on EEB's use of the roundel and it ceased early in the 1950s[22].

As well as the roundel, Northmet's showrooms and offices had vertical internally illuminated signs with the slogan 'Use Northmet Electricity' or, if there was not enough room, just 'Use Electricity'. The lettering had enlarged initial and final characters with intermediate letters underlined and overscored as on contemporary Underground signs.

---

[19] p1149 *Electrical Times* vol 75 26/12 1929
[20] Resident Engineers' Meeting Minute 631 26/3/1931
[21] Minute Book UER4/1 in London Metropolitan Archive
[22] Further information on the Roundel can be found in a book by David Lawrence, to be published.

CHAPTER 9
COMMERCIAL, SALES & CONTRACTING

Northmet recognised that every load was important to them, not only from the sale of electricity but also as an advertisement and a means to attract yet more custom. In many cases Northmet was also the installation contractor.

Council house contracts were deemed very important. In 1925 there was a typical contract for 40 houses at Little Heath, Potters Bar[1]. Supply was by two underground cables to overhead conductors at the backs of the houses. The brackets and overhead gear were supplied by Tramway Supplies Ltd. There were two types of house; the 9 roomed 'Parlour' house and a 7-room non-parlour type. They were wired by Northmet at a cost to the Council of £7/4/0d and £6/6/0d respectively. The number of points [it is not clear if these are socket outlets or only lighting points] was the same as the number of rooms and the installed loads were 230W for the larger house and 170W for the smaller. Current limiters were fitted, set at 160W and 130W respectively. The tenants paid to the Council, a fixed sum of 1/10d or 1/9d each week, 90% of which was passed on to Northmet. A similar scheme was also under way at Hatfield about the same time.

It seems that current limiters became necessary as demand increased. The Church Street, Edmonton council houses had been supplied with electricity in 1921. The annual consumption rose steadily over the next four years. As the tenants were paying a fixed 1/3d a week, the net revenue per unit fell from 4.74d to 2.5d[2]. Current limiters were installed set at 180W.

Shop lighting was also seen as valuable, both for revenue and as an advertisement for the use of electricity. In 1925 Northmet took part in a campaign by the Electric Lighting Manufacturers' Association and there were a number of demonstrations to Northmet's own Resident Engineers, to Chambers of Trade and other traders associations[3]. This resulted in the lighting of several shops in Hertford being altered "to the advantage of the consumers" while Northmet had the benefit of sales of additional reflectors, lamps, &c.

---

[1] Northmet Monthly Bulletin No 1 Item 2 2/12/1925
[2] Northmet Monthly Bulletin No 1 Item 22 2/12/1925
[3] Northmet Monthly Bulletin No 1 Item 14 2/12/1925

In 1926 the Electrical Development Association and the Electric Lighting Manufacturers' Association held a campaign for better home lighting. Unfortunately no-one had anticipated the coal strike which led to general appeals for economy. The campaign included a competition which Northmet engineers felt they could endorse but were reluctant at that time to do much promotion other than showroom displays[4].

Churches were also lit by electricity and must have been a vast improvement. No wonder some reports give the results as 'magnificent'[5]. Electric heating was also tried in churches using tubular heaters[6]. By September 1926, there were 130 places of worship being supplied by Northmet and eight of these included electric heating[7]. Special 'Church rates' for the supply of electricity required generally only on Sundays continued until well after nationalisation.

Electric heating is a heavy consumer of electricity. Northmet clearly saw the value of heating but also the disadvantages. Its own offices were, of course, electrically heated. An early installation was at the 'Central Office', a building not clearly identified but probably at Manor House. The office was not easy to heat because of the large amounts of glass at the sides and in the roof[8]. The office was 50ft by 26ft by 12ft and was heated by 15 heating panels totalling 13.1kW. The panels gave an average increased temperature of 8 degrees over the previous electric heaters.

Similar panel heaters were also installed at the Barnet office although additional radiant heaters were used to top up in very cold weather. There were also 'private' installations including a 24-panel installation totalling 13.75kW at Hadley Wood where the customer was on an annual service rate so it was not possible to determine the actual electricity consumption. One wonders if Northmet actually lost money on some of these installations.

Northmet were also keen to capture what they saw as a useful load at farms. In 1925 it was reported[9] that "We have installed at Oakmere Dairy Farm, Potters Bar, belonging to Mr Down, an electrically operated hot water and steaming

---

[4] Resident Engineers' Meeting Minute 468 1/11/1926
[5] Northmet Monthly Bulletin No 1/26 item 28 Jan 1926
[6] Northmet Monthly Bulletin 6/26 Item 65 August 1926
[7] Northmet Monthly Bulletin 7/26 Item 69 September 1926
[8] Northmet Monthly Bulletin No 1/26 Item 25 Jan 1926
[9] Northmet Monthly Bulletin No 1 Item 3 2/12/1925

installation for the purpose of pasteurising, sterilising and washing, this being the first installation of its kind. The apparatus consists of a 10kW hand-controlled 15 gallon Nobbs boiler and a 2kW 30 gallon Nobbs calorifier with automatic control". The supplier was reported as having "considerable experience in electric farming" so although it might have been the first Northmet installation of its kind, there must have been others elsewhere. An 'all round' rate of 1d per unit was given for this load.

There were two specialist sales engineers who advised farmers and other agriculturalists on the use of electricity. Although based at Hertford, they operated throughout the company's rural area[10].

It was said that laundries would not adopt electric power because they had to have a boiler in any case and the little extra steam needed for an engine was of no consequence[11]. By 1926 Northmet had persuaded three laundries in Hertford and Ware to abandon their steam engines and install electric motors. This led, in addition, to the adoption of electric lighting.

Sewage works were early users of electricity, the first being at Edmonton in 1912[12]. Enfield was connected in 1921 followed by Wembley, Hertford, Cheshunt, Upshire, Harpenden and Wealdstone. The electricity was used to power screens, to pump sewage and clean water as well as compressors for aerators and pneumatic ejectors. The later installations incorporated automatic control for the electric motors.

Each year Northmet produced an illustrated calender which was distributed to each of its consumers, usually by a boy on a bicycle. There was also a *Historical Country* booklet describing a grand tour of the country served by the company. Other booklets were produced from time to time to mark the opening of a new District office or some other significant event.

It can sometimes be difficult in these times when everyone has electricity to look back to the early days of electricity supply and appreciate how few consumers there were. In 1926 there were less than 100 consumers in Hatfield[13]. In the more urban areas, East Barnet just reached 1000, Barnet had 1223, Edmonton

---

[10] PC W Killick
[11] Northmet Monthly Bulletin 2/26 item 39 Feb 1926
[12] Northmet Monthly Bulletin 4/26 Item 56 April 1926
[13] Northmet Monthly Bulletin 3/26 Item 51 March 1926

1290, St Albans 1409, Enfield 1489, Tottenham 2708 and Wembley 4296. Southgate topped the league with 4956[14] but Hertford, one of the earliest supply undertakings, could not even reach 1000.

The total number of Northmet consumers in 1928 was 99,300 and this rose rapidly until the Second World War:

	Consumers	Units sold
1929	117,500	199.7 million
1930	138,600	228.6 million
1931	161,700	259.9 million
1932	185,800	298.7 million
1933	218,700	352.5 million
1934	254,735	423.5 million
1935	296,606	495.2 million
1936	336,722	597.6 million
1937	375,067	690.8 million
1938	407,106	759.5 million
1939	419,493	832.6 million
1940	423,000	825.1 million
1941	433,900	931.4 million
1942	444.859	1002 million
1943	446,472	984 million
1944	433,037	1054 million
1945	436,958	1058 million
1946	448,827	1219 million
1947	459,745	1256 million

The addition of Finchley, Hitchin, Hornsey, Letchworth and Welwyn Garden City to the Northmet Sub-Area at nationalisation increased the area to 700 square miles, with a population of 1.5 million. There were initially 20 districts but these were gradually reduced until the district organisation was absorbed into the sub areas and Northmet was no more.

---

[14] Northmet Monthly Bulletin 3/26 Item 48 March 1926

CHAPTER 10: ORGANISATION

Like all companies Northmet's organisation changed over the years. Early documents list the Directors but how the company was organised is not at all clear.

Captain Donaldson was appointed Chief Engineer in 1920 in succession to E T Ruthven-Murray who had moved to Northmet with the acquisition of Willesden Power Station. As Chief Engineer he reported to the Chairman, Lord Ashfield. The Chief Engineer's Office was at Manor House in Seven Sisters Road, the building previously being a horse tram depot for the North Metropolitan Tramways. It continues in use today as offices for London Buses.

It seems that throughout Northmet's independent existence it was regarded as an engineering organisation. At local level, each undertaking had a Resident Engineer who was responsible for all the functions including commercial. Much of the discussion at Resident Engineers' meetings was about showrooms, displays, publicity, appliances, sales and other commercial matters as well as tariffs.

The undertakings were kept separate for accounting purposes (in case any local authority wanted to exercise its statutory purchase powers) but they gradually became merged into Districts for practical management purposes. The number of Districts changed over the years, increasing to start with and then, later on consolidating; a process which continued after nationalisation.

In 1925 the were 26 Districts[1]: Arkley, Barnet*, Broxbourne, Cheshunt*, Chingford*, East Barnet Valley, Edgware*, Edmonton*, Enfield*, Friern Barnet, Harpenden*, Harrow Weald, Hatfield, Hertford*, Hoddesdon, Kingsbury, Potters Bar*, St Albans*, Southgate*, Stanmore, Tottenham*, Totteridge, Waltham Abbey, Ware, Wealdstone and Wembley*. Stevenage* was in the process of takeover and Bishops Stortford was soon to follow. Districts market with an asterisk had their own Resident Engineers[2]. Hoddesdon and Ware were

---

[1] *The North Metropolitan Electric Power Supply Company: Its History in Brief* Pub Northmet, July 1925
[2] Minutes of Resident Engineers' Meetings.

administered from Hertford. There were also Resident Engineers for Brimsdown and Taylors Lane power stations and for the Northern Area.

In 1926 the titles District Engineer and Engineer-in-charge began to be used when Mr W R B Wood became Engineer-in-Charge at Chingford, his predecessor, Mr C R Marshall having moved to Hertford. Edgware, Harrow Weald, Stanmore and Elstree were linked to form Hendon Rural District with Mr F B Preston as Engineer-in-Charge under the supervision of Mr H W Gregory at Wembley[3].

At the same time Mr C A Sayer became Engineer-in-Charge of a new Welwyn Rural District (Welwyn Garden City not being supplied by Northmet) formed from Welwyn, Digswell, Harmer Green, Mardley Hill, Danesbury and Oaklands estates, Woolmer Green and Burnham Green.

Each District had a main office and often had sub-offices, perhaps with a sales representative or a works section.

Junior assistants were transferred between undertakings in order to widen their experience[4].

By the end of the 1920s there were a number of central departments, not part of the local undertakings. These included:

Construction Department
Motor Repair Section
Overhead Line Department
Meter Testing Station
Outside Department
Apparatus Repair Department

The Outside Department had three sections with a small shared administrative section under a Chief Clerk. The three sections were the Construction Department, the Meter Testing Laboratories (MTL) and the Central Stores. The Supervisor, Mr P K Davis succeeded Mr H S Selves who was Deputy Chief Engineer.

---
[3] Resident Engineers' Meetings min 441 12/4/1926
[4] Resident Engineers' Meetings minute 454 14/6/1926

The Construction Department dealt with the installation and maintenance of the underground and overhead transmission and distribution systems although the low voltage and 3kV systems in the Northern (country) districts were usually installed and maintained by the local staff.

An Overhead Line Engineer was first appointed in 1927; Mr N S Snelling was based at Hertford but came under the management of Mr H S Selves, the Superintendent of the Outside Department[5].

The Mains Engineer in the late 1930s was Mr J G Park. The underground cable section had a high voltage test van (equipped with a mercury arc rectifier) with which the assistant engineers pressure tested high voltage systems prior to commissioning. They also had fault locating equipment and were responsible for locating and repairing high voltage cable faults.

Pre-War the Construction Department had cable-laying gangs of some 20 to 30 labourers supervised by a Foreman with a Sketcher/timekeeper who recorded the location details for the drawing office at Northmet House. The labourers were probably mostly casual employees but many were employed continuously. The size of these gags seems large but it must be remembered that they had few mechanical aids. Roads had to be broken up by 'pins' and sledgehammers and high voltage cables, some 400yards long, were laid by hand. After the war many cables were laid by contractors under competitive tender although some direct labour gangs remained for a few years. Gradually more and more LV work was done by the Districts themselves.

The Construction Department had a foreman cable jointer and about 8 to 10 jointers all of whom were trained to joint cables up to 11kV and some to 33kV. They ran a 'school', latterly at Hertford, to train jointers for themselves and the Districts. All joints until after nationalisation were by plumbing lead sleeves and much of the training was in this technique. District jointers were generally trained and approved for work on LV and 3kV only.

Later Construction Engineers included Mr P A Ward and Mr W J Killick, who has helped with details of this account.

---

[5] Resident Engineers' Meeting Minute 475 3/1/1927

ORGANISATION

The Overhead Line section (OHL) of the Construction Department was based at Hertford, supervised by Mr R T Bayford and his assistant Mr R P Howe. The section shared an office with Hertford District stores on the site of the old power station in Mead Lane until 1931 when the stores moved to the new District offices. OHL were responsible, with District and development engineers for selecting the routes, surveying, designing and constructing all overhead lines up to 33kV although the Districts obtained the wayleaves where necessary. Sometimes the OHL linesmen worked under the supervision of engineers from the Districts.

The Meter Testing Laboratories (MTL) was also on the New Southgate site. Previously in the basement of 15 Friern Barnet Road, a victorian company-owned house, a new test station was erected at the rear in 1926. In 1937 a major rebuilding took place. No 15 was replaced by a new three storey building specially constructed to provide a facility which could comply with the new Electricity Supply (Meters) Act 1936. There were test rooms on the ground floor and a standards laboratory and workshops on the first floor. The clerical and administrative offices were atthe front of the building.

31: **Meter Testing Laboratories at New Southgate prior to closure in 1999**
[*Author*]

32: **G F Shotter, the first Meter Engineer** [*Electrical Review*]

The test station was set up by Mr G F Shotter assisted by Bill Saxby. George Shotter was a most friendly and approachable man, with a great sense of humour. He had many patents to his name and was held in high regard by other meter engineers. Mr Shotter's assistants were Frederick G Talbot and George P Mitchener. George Mitchener went into the RAF during the war and returned to find that Fred Talbot had been appointed as Shotter's right hand man. George Mitchener was relegated to a lower grading and took over responsibility for the general running of MTL[6]. After Mr Shotter's retirement it was Fred Talbot who was appointed Meter Engineer with George as his assistant. The resultant bitterness was fairly evident and there was at times an 'atmosphere' in the MTL office[7]. This lasted until Fred Talbot was appointed to Meter Engineer for Eastern Electricity at Wherstead.

Prior to nationalisation Shotter had worked very closely with the Sangamo Weston company at Enfield. Consequently most of Northmet's meters were

---

[6] PC F Greenwood
[7] Author's personal recollection.

Sangamo until after nationalisation when the Electricity Boards were expected to spread their orders more widely.

Meters were returned from the District undertakings to MTL when their certification expired after 5 years (initially, this was later extended to 25 years). They were cleaned and repaired as necessary before being tested in accordance with the legislation. At times MTL was severely stretched, for example on the occasion of the East Coast floods of 1953. Meters had to be found for whole areas which had suffered flood damage and MTL had to institute overtime and week-end working. Crates of meters would come into the yard, some meters half full of dirty water, others caked in mud and rust.

Over the years, the testing regime and the equipment used changed. In the earlier days it meant the tester having to maintain voltage and current settings while timing a set number of revolutions of the meter disc. Often 'boys' were used to control the settings. In later years more automatic equipment was installed. In the late 1950s a new building was constructed on the site of the old vehicle section and this housed the single phase lab, the standards lab, the polyphase lab and the workshops. The new test benches were of the latest design and the lab was considered the best in the country.

Before dispatch for further use, each batch was sampled in-house, being tested in the Standards Laboratory. A further sample was taken by the visiting Meter Examiner (who was treated like God because the slightest thing wrong could mean the re-working of hundreds of meters).

On the ground floor of the building was the Polyphase Laboratory. By the 1950s Charles Trottman was in charge and the work was changing from relatively simple two- and three-phase meters to Landis & Gyr 'Trivectors' which could be tested twenty at a time.

Direct Current meters were never subject to the same certification procedures and, as DC supplies died out, these meters were treated as special repair and testing jobs. Some incorporated mercury in their construction and there were special facilities for dealing with this (which were a long way short of modern Health & Safety requirements).

The Standards Laboratory was also responsible for the calibration of various instruments used by Northmet engineers including stop watches, voltmeters, ammeters, wattmeters and recording instruments. They also carried out high voltage tests on samples of transformer oil, rubber gloves and rubber mats.

In the basement were card records of every Northmet meter, hundreds of thousands and, after nationalisation, they probably reached over 1 million.

MTL had their own outside engineers who checked industrial metering installations on site (also not subject to Ministry Certification) and investigated those metering disputes which could not be settled at District level. Apart from Freddy Greenwood who joined from Sangamo Weston, most of the outside engineers graduated from other duties in MTL. In the 1950's Will Martin headed the section of four engineers, Frank Bonner came from Finchley. At various times, Dennis Burrows, Sid Herring, Frank Carter, Ted Major and Len Peveritt passed through the section, many leaving eventually to join the CEGB measurements section at Cockfosters. So many left this way that there was something of a dispute about poaching. It was said the at Cockfosters there were so many ex-Northmet people it was like a club[8].

The outside section tested large power metering of industrial consumers. Supplies up to 100kW demand were metered with Sangamo 3-phase 4-wire meters with a thermal kW demand meter which worked on the principle of heating a bulb of liquid which pushed up a float in a tube, the float remaining at the highest point until reset. This way it was possible to read the maximum demand during the month. Supplies over 100kW had a Hill-Shotter kVA demand meter with a rotating disc driving a pointer, reset every half hour by a timer. This was considered a very advanced technique for its day. All high current metering had current transformers with 5-amp secondary windings. High voltage metering also had to be supplied from Voltage Transformers.

After nationalisation, meter testing was rationalised leaving EEB stations only at New Southgate and Norwich. Eventually New Southgate was closed by the privatised company in 1999 because, by then, it was cheaper to buy new meters than reclaim and retest old ones.

---

[8] PC F Greenwood

The remaining part of the Outside Department was the Central Stores. They serviced Districts by a regular, usually weekly, delivery of stores and meters as requisitioned.

The Apparatus Repair Department (ARD) was at Ringslade Road, Wood Green. It was set up in 1938 at a time when the local undertakings were accumulating a large stock of second-hand cookers returned from hire-purchase. Local staff were unable to keep up with the reconditioning work which was better done at ARD because they had specialised facilities such as degreasing baths. Cookers were completely stripped down, components replaced as necessary before being rebuilt. An ARD-refurbished cooker really was as good as new.

ARD also dealt with the repair and renovation of other appliances although a few, such as Hoover vacuum cleaners, were the subject of arrangements with the manufacturers. Some small repairs were still done in local workshops, particularly in the rural Districts where transport costs were not justified.

A section of the Department also manufactured displays for showrooms and exhibitions.

The Department was presided over by a Superintendent who, in the mid-1950s was regarded as somewhat old school. One itinerant Student Apprentice who had spent some weeks their as part of his training was summoned into the office on his last morning. "Well", asked the Superintendent, "how have you got on?".
"I've enjoyed myself here",said the unsuspecting lad.
"You're not here to enjoy yourself, you're here to learn", was the reply. The student had to explain that he had found that the places he enjoyed most were those where he learnt most[9].

Adjacent to ARD a section was set up specially to test and approve new apparatus. Some appiance testing had been done pre-war at the meter testing laboratories, the only department capable of this work. Although designed by Northmet, it is believed that the appliance test department did not come into use until after nationalisation. A Mr Boysen was in charge of testing refrigerators, fires, irons, fans, vacuum cleaners, water heaters, light fittings, switches, fuses, control gear, paint sprayers, floor washers and polishers, pasteurisers, sterilisers, &c. Life tests on switches were carried out as well as flexing tests for electric

---

[9] Author's personal recollection

blankets[10]. The testing of new apparatus was later transferred to the Electricity Boards' test station at Leatherhead.

District offices,

Each Northmet undertaking had its own office, usually combined with a showroom. Great care was taken to impress the public. In later years many offices were built new to a common overall design but some offices, such as those at St Albans and Bishops Stortford, were adaptations of old buildings.

Initially it appears that each of Northmet's undertakings had a Resident Engineer but as electricity supply developed adjacent undertakings were merged to form local units. Many of the individual undertakings had a local office under the supervision of an Assistant Engineer. It is noticeable how Northmet was very much a company managed by Engineers.

In the late 1930s the Resident Engineers became District Superintendents and then, just before the outbreak of war, the company's area was divided into four Areas. The Area Superintendents were[11]:
Northwest: H W Gregory
Northeast: C R Marshall
Western: A H Watson
Eastern: W M Maynard

About 1940, Mr Gregory died and the two northern areas were merged under Mr Marshall.

At nationalisation there were 19 districts in the Northmet sub-Area: Royston, Stevenage, Bishops Stortford, Hertford, St Albans, Barnet, Southgate, Enfield, Chingford, Edmonton, Tottenham, Wood Green, Hendon, Harrow, Wembley and the formerly independent Finchley, Hornsey, Welwyn Garden City and Letchworth.

Prior to the Second World War, staff were recruited at junior level and, if they were able, worked their way up through the ranks. Bill Killick was typical, joining the Company at Hertford in September 1928 as a Wireman's Boy at 10/-

---
[10] Report by HM Electrical Inspector of Factories, Fred Clarke, 5/5/1950
[11] PC Mr W J Killick

a week. There were no apprenticeships or day release for studies but he was assured that he would be given the opportunity for training in all aspects of the work in the District. The District Engineer (Mr C R Marshall) arranged for him to attend evening classes at Ware. The classes were not to any recognised certificate but included 'Electricity and Magnetism' taught by a Northmet assistant engineer and mathematics by a master from the local grammar school.

These evening classes went on for two years before Mr Killick started travelling up to Northampton College, London, three evenings a week where he gained Ordinary and Higher National Certificates in Electrical Engineering. Several other youths who rose to become senior engineers also started in Hertford District including Ray Worboys (who became District Engineer at Bedford), Arthur Roat (who retired as District Manager, Norwich), Bill Halls (who became District Commercial Engineer at St Albans) and Dick Gaylard who eventually became Chief Electrical Engineer for the Canadian Navy[12]. However, there was nothing special about Hertford, there are similar accounts of 'boys' being similarly trained in the other districts and reaching senior engineering positions.

The St Albans office was at Ivy House St. Peters Street, a very old building with a staircase by Wrenn. The front of the building became the showrooms, the mains office being in the bedrooms. Offices were built on the side and back with a workshop and garage and stores in the basement. A 120kW AC heating system provided hot water for the radiators. Paintwork was brown and cream. Offices ware for mains, clerical, sales and typists. The only women employed were the showroom assistants in pale green overalls, demonstrators in white overalls and the typists.

When the St Albans and Harpenden undertakings were merged to become the St Albans District, the District Superintendent became the District Manager. Under him there were the District Engineer, District Commercial Engineer, Mains Engineers, Assistant Engineers, Engineering Assistants and Mains Clerks. Assistant Commercial Engineer, Commercial Assistants and Clerks. Chief Clerk, Senior Clerical assistant, clerks, clerical assistants, cashiers, showroom Supervisor, showroom assistants, demonstrators, assistant storeman, stores boys, typists and caretaker. This was typical of a district in the final years of Northmet.

---

[12] PC W Killick

Application and installation cards were received in the general office and processed by each clerk in turn, each one doing a particular job. An account number was issued, the tariff selected and coded. Consumers were advised of the supply AC or DC and the voltage. Details were passed to the mains office to issue a meter works order which was sent to the works. On completion it was returned to the mains office for the meters to be entered on the service card checking the service number and keeping the record of the numbers of each type of consumer. The general office then made out the meter cards and put a card in the file with consumer's correct name and address. Checking back made it possible to put the correct postal address on the service card instead of '4th new house LH side'.

In time the meter book would be issued to a meter reader to read the meters. The meter readings from Harpenden would be returned to the St Albans office in boxes carried on a No 321 bus which was met by the office boy[13]. On return each book was checked and posted to Northmet House in a brown box by parcel post for the account to be prepared and the book returned to the district. The No 84 bus was also used to send packages to Northmet House. Time sheets were made out from Wednesday to Tuesday and the money paid out on Fridays so that wages were always in arrears. The rugby playing-members of the clerical staff walked to the bank to collect the money. Pay envelopes were made out and taken to to all employees on site to sign the pay slip.

Commercial staff sent out quotations for work which were accepted or not. Once a week a return was made of the value of the work received by each assistant. Staff were paid monthly in their bank accounts at the Westminster Bank. Deductions were made for the pension fund.

Many forms were in use, some loose to be typed with copies as required, some made up into pads of different colours to be used with carbon paper, most numbered. Requisitions in triplicate had to be numbered by hand with a special stamp. The titles were gradually changed from the full name to the short name Northmet. Many were retained and changed again to Eastern Electricity Board Northmet Sub Area. Consumers apparatus was returned to the makers for repair, with the appropriate form. Small orders were for stock or directly for consumers, large orders the same. Consumers Orders were for apparatus which went directly, when received, to the consumer.

---

[13] PC A M Gordon

Goods received, goods entered into stock, wiring and lamps had 'T' numbers on white requisitions, showroom stock had 'S' numbers on green requisitions both in debit and credit. Staff used dictating machines fitted with a wax cylinder, The typists objected to engineers' letters which were usually written in pencil. Pen, ink and green blotting paper were available.

Meter cards were in ink, the meter readings in pencil. Consumers would either pay accounts by post or to the cashier who had duplicate copies to know that the correct amount had been paid. Every receipt carried a 2d stamp. For non payment of an electricity account it was usual to fix a slot meter which was calibrated to collect the arrears. There was a different procedure if it was not an electricity account. Deposits could be asked for against future accounts.

Various methods were tried by dishonest customers to stop meters registering by interfering with the wiring or drilling a hole in the meter case to stop the disc with a needle. If nothing at all was registered it was assumed that the meter had stopped and was replaced. Idle services or ones that had been disconnected were checked to see that electricity had not been used illegally. The ultimate step was if a termination could be used without being entered in the meter records. One jointer with a normal service in his house jointed a second service cable under the floor. It was found after he had moved away, leaving the cable in position.

Accounts were kept of units supplied to the City and Rural undertakings, units used on works and offices, accounts for street lighting, traffic and unmetered supplies as well as units lost on the system. Instructions were issued to jointers about recording changes to substations and cables. Councils were notified of excavations in public highways and reinstatement required. Petrol had to be ordered and, during rationing, petrol coupons issued.

The lawn and greenhouse at St Albans were later removed to make a car park and a hut erected behind the showrooms. A new building in St Peters Street became the showrooms so that the old rooms and kitchen became further offices. The show window was covered with a wooden screen, to be offices. Eventually the old mains office was the conference room and the hut was used for serving tea and coffee and to allow staff to eat their own lunches. The main building was divided with fire doors so that anyone trapped could ascend to either of the top floors, open the key cabinet and taking ALL the keys open the door to the roof, walk across to the other top floor unlock the door and descend the other staircase.

The private automatic telephone system now covered most districts and Northmet House. A private cable was laid to the new showrooms. The substation telephones remained on the magneto system. A new office block was then built next to the works which by now had nothing in the engine room which was divided horizontally to form more offices. This move removed all staff, except the Showroom Staff, from any contact with the consumers. Today, even the Showrooms are closed.

Many of the employees in Northmet's districts were craftsmen and labourers carrying out the essential work of installation of mains or customers' wiring. The operatives employed on electrical installations in houses, shops, &c were mostly graded as 'contract wiremen' whose conditions of employment were similar to those of other trades in the construction and building industry. Although they were casual workers who could, in theory, be laid off at an hour's notice, this seldom happened and, as a result, their jobs were reasonably secure[14]. Possibly because of this, Northmet electricians tended to be a very proud group of workers who knew that their workmanship was much better than other electricians. Their 5½ day working week was 47½ hours, pay in the 1930s being around 1/4½p an hour.

There were also, in each district a few 'supply side' electricians who were permanent employees and were paid a slightly higher hourly rate. They fixed meters, inspected installations and connected them. They also carried out some electrical installation work in factories. In later years installation inspectors and meter fixers became separate jobs.

The company employed its own cable jointers for most work, some of the 'mates' graduating to become jointers. The jointers were trained in-house at a jointing school at Hertford. This was a training much prized by engineering apprentices in EEB days, where they learnt the skills of a plumber. Some districts employed their own labourers but these were often hired in, perhaps from a local builder. There was also one, or more, substation fitter and his mate.

Northmet had, apparently, been a leader in the formation of the Electrical Development Association so it is hardly surprising that when the EDA organised a national public speaking competition in 1932, junior staff were encouraged to enter. Northmet had its own competitions to select two men and two women to

---

[14] PC W Killick

go forward to the regional competitions[15]. These competitions continued well into the post-nationalisation period.

As Northmet grew and matured a number of staff welfare and amenity schemes were introduced. Not all these were the result of the Company's altruism, some were the result of Government legislation. For example the 1925 Finance Act prompted Northmet to initiate a group life assurance scheme, up to £100 per man, for the waged staff[16]. At the Chief Engineer's suggestion, it was agreed to provide preferential treatment for older members of staff with long service, the scale of additional compensation being at the discretion of the management.

There were also sick clubs for various grades of staff[17].

Christmas 'boxes' were distributed to those staff not benefiting under the Wages Staff Endowment Scheme[18].

Awards were made to staff who had achieved long periods of service[19].

There were also a series of annual dinners. Some were held locally, others for all salaried staff and one just for Resident Engineers.

Northmet supported the local sports and social clubs by providing the ground and/or the equipment although they were supposed to be self-supporting as far as day to day running costs were concerned[20]. Initially it was considered that, owing to the scattered nature of the company's undertakings, it would be necessary to have two sports grounds, one for the western area and one for the central and eastern area. It was not thought possible to provide for the northern area as regards the general use of a ground[21]. Nevertheless, by nationalisation, most of the districts had some sort of facility for sports, the main Northmet House ground being at Woodcroft in Winchmore Hill. Dinners were held for presentation of the cricket and football trophies, cups and medals being provided

---

[15] PCs W Killick, Marguerite Patten and Gillian Barnett
[16] Northmet Management meeting Item 141 26/6/1925
[17] Northmet Management meeting item 572 25/2/1927
[18] Northmet Management meeting item 236 26/11/1925
[19] Northmet Management meetings item 659 1/7/1927 and item 742 3/11/1927
[20] Northmet Management meetings item 589 18/3/1927, item 657 1/7/1927, item 699 38/8/1927
[21] Resident Engineers' Meetings min 459 13/9/1926

by the Directors of the Company[22]. While part of the Underground Group of companies, Northmet also entered the TOT (tramways, omnibuses and trains) Cup competitions[23] for football, cricket, tennis and swimming. Grants were made by the company for the first year's expenses of the Northmet Sports association which was formed in 1930[24].

33: **Bishops Stortford staff dinner, 1947** [*W Killick collection*]

[22] Resident Engineers' Meeting Minute 547 7/5/1928
[23] Resident Engineers' Meeting Minute 564 2/10/1928
[24] Resident Engineers' Meeting Minute 601 24/6/1930

CHAPTER 11
THE POWER SYSTEM AND ITS OPERATION

The Northmet companies soon established a reputation for being in the forefront of modern developments although they were also renowned for being careful with money. Inevitably there were a few instances where innovation did not pay off. An early example of this was the unsatisfactory performance of 33kV cables which had to be down-rated to 11kV.

Except for the early local installations at Hertford, St Albans and Enfield, Northmet was essentially an AC organisation, relying on the large power stations at either end of its territory. This inevitably led to the use of high voltage to supply local transforming substations.

At various times Northmet had systems which operated at 3kV, 11kV, 22kV and 33kV as well as at normal 'mains' voltages of 240/415V. The original 3kV system, as applied to the rural areas, was interesting in that it had no permanent connection with earth. This allowed an earth fault to persist on the system without loss of supply to consumers.

The 3kV system had three overcurrent coils in the circuit breakers and dust fuses in the indoor substations and 3kV feeder pillars. These fuses were later replaced by more modern high rupturing capacity (HRC) fuses. The 3kV system was provided with three earth voltmeters to show the presence of a fault but nothing happened unless a second earth fault occurred which would then trip on overcurrent.

There was some doubt if the unearthed 3kV system really complied with the electricity supply legislation and it was eventually phased out after nationalisation.

Another system tried in the rural parts of Hertford District involved earthing through Arc Suppression Coils. These devices also allowed faults on the rural system to persist but, as applied to the 11kV system, resulted in overstressing the electrical insulation.

Transformers on overhead lines had wire fuses operated by a pole which was also used to remove and replace the fuses one at a time. Powerful torches were provided for use at night.

In October 1922 it was decided that in each substation there should be a diagram displayed showing the distribution system in the immediate vicinity. It was some years before this decision was finally implemented[1].

In 1926, there were a number of new High Voltage feeders on Northmet's programme of works. These included Chingford-Waltham Abbey, Brimsdown-Barnet (both of which were practically completed) and Brimsdown-Hertford via Cuffley with a view to providing an extension to Royston which would also feed the BC&H Company. There were also to be new overhead lines Potters Bar-Welwyn, Elstree-Shenley-Napsbury-St Albans, Stevenage to Hitchin and Potters Bar-Cuffley[2].

11kV switchgear was delivered with overcurrent relays or Solkor protection which was tested by the Protection Department. 11kV ring main units had glass wire fuses or wire fuses in oil-filled TAP units. HRC fuses were tried under oil but the oil leaked in, partly because they were fitted with trip pins. Later developments produced a unit with the HRC fuses, with trip pins, in a dry compartment. Some faults were not detected by the overcurrent system and were cleared by back-up earth leakage so the middle overcurrent element was altered to earth leakage, producing a combined 3 and 4 wire system. New equipment arrived with a low set earth leakage element and two normal overcurrents.

For transformer circuit breakers, relays were used if there was a trip battery on site. Otherwise AC trip coils were used, again three overcurrents with three fuses in parallel. These were altered in the same way to give earth leakage protection. Trip coils were 5 amp with 5 amp lead wire fuses in parallel but it was possible for the fuse to operate and for the coil impedance then to drop the current enough for the coil not to operate.

All new circuit breakers were then fitted with two 2 amp overcurrent coils with 5 amp fuses in parallel to guarantee tripping. The 2 amp earth leakage coil did not have a fuse and tripped instantly.

---

[1] Resident Engineers' Meeting min 395 5/10/1925
[2] Resident Engineers' Meeting min 447 12/4/1926

Various types of pilot protection were used on the 22 and 33kV systems including split pilot, Solkor and Translay. Overcurrent and earth leakage was also used as well as main transformer protection. 22kV ring main units had transformers protected by glass wire fuses in 'Trip All Phases' (TAP) units, oil fitted. Earthing was by liquid neutral resistances except for the 11kV supply to Stevenage which had a Peterson arc suppression coil and two electric clocks one reading the time a fault started and the second the duration of the fault.

By 1926 it was felt that feeder protective gear was becoming too much to be dealt with by the Districts and it was decided that the oversight of this equipment should be vested in a Relay Engineer. Mr J Piquet was appointed to this role in the Chief Engineer's Office. He looked after the setting and functioning of the relays and all auxiliary gear[3].

After the second world war, there was a lot of new work in hand. The Protection Department required assistance so transformer circuit testing was hived off to the Districts. Suitable Engineers went to Horsley Towers on the Protection Course and then did all the testing in the District, including the trip circuits for consumers' 11kV metered supplies, neutral resistances and occasionally Solkor tests.

Continuing in the spirit of innovation, Mr Smith at Wherstead and Mr Bowerman, one of the District Engineers, devised the 11kV Negative Phase Sequence Protection system. This allowed all transformers to be jointed solid to the substation busbars within the protection area.

Hatfield Grid 33kV circuits were connected in pairs on one circuit breaker each with its own line isolator. Protection and intertripping was by live pilot wires and dead-beat armature relays, type DBA. In later years this was altered to dead pilots.

At St Albans the Gas Board fitted a generator to run in parallel with their 11kV system so the Protection Department tested the reverse power relays, intertripping and interlock circuits. Various types of auto reclose protection were tried on 11kV overhead line circuits.

---

[3] Resident Engineers' Meeting min 466 13/9/1926

Several incidents were investigated and it was found that battery trip supplies were at fault. On Grid circuits a trip circuit healthy lamp was always lit. To prove the 11kV trip circuits an instruction was issued for each circuit breaker operation, to rack in and close, trip on relay, reset and reclose. New relays did not have an external trip button so the cover had to be removed and the disc rotated by hand.

Transformers had been fitted with wire LV fuses but it was decided that these were not necessary and were changed to solid links. Feeders were protected by wire fuses which were changed to HRC. LV protection was provided by continuous bonding to an earth terminal at each termination.

Earth leakage circuit breakers were tried, also a combined neutral/earth system. In Welwyn Garden City, earths had been provided by the water mains but these corroded and bonded service cables had to be provided.

Before the Second World War the Construction Department Test Van and an engineer were available for locating high voltage faults and low voltage when required. This still applied after the war but some instruments were made available locally. The first was a battery operated bridge set which was much better and used a high voltage rotary transformer. Various faults were found, usually 5th core where it was possible to remove all the service fuses. An ex War Department mine detector was provided, altered to listen to the position of live cables. The 'Bimec' test set was next, it passed a heavy current through core to core faults. The detector was carried along the cable to listen to the signal from the lay of the cores.

The Bimec signal was 1000 cycles. This would not be allowed now because of interference with GPO telephones. The detector coil showed a maximum signal over the cable. A flat coil was made for listening to live cables which gave a maximum directly over the cable. Various methods of detection were tried including VHF radio but no results. The Bimec was useful as a source of AC to measure the ratio of capacitance from each end of an open circuit fault. The next procedure was to reverse the Bimec with a large transmitter coil carried along the cable, and the detector connected to the cable panel. The problem was to send the signal back from the detector to the operator with the coil. It could be done now with a radio.

34: **3kV pillar at junction of Hatfield Road and Camp Road, St Albans, 1916** [*M Ferrara*]

The 'Hornsey' test set was devised. This could be plugged into a 15 amp socket and produced an interrupted signal picked up by a detector over the feeder cable. The detector could also be used on its own to locate a live cable. The test set also had a low voltage circuit to be connected to a dead cable to locate its position. Another use not intended was to connect this circuit to a water pipe via the stop taps in the road and in the house and so melt the ice inside the pipe.

Early distribution systems in the 19th Century were provided with service cable fuses in boxes in the footpath but after several explosions these were forbidden and services were jointed direct to the distributor, one result was that the service cable was inadequately protected against faults and could burn out. This was particularly so on DC which did not interrupt the arc inherently. Sometimes the arc stopped at the joint box, sometimes it did not and burnt out the feeder back to the power station with some 10,000 amps.

Callender's cables were used for the distribution system. The feeders were triple concentric and the distributors three–core insulated with vulcanised bitumen and armoured. They were laid in wood troughs, which were filled with bitumen[4].

DC supply in St Albans was provided by 6 core cables, paper insulated, lead covered and steel tape armoured with joint boxes. For example the cores were two 0.5" outers, ½-size mid wire and. 3 voltage pilots. These feeders went to feeder pillars by BI Cables, dark green with the St Albans shield cast into the doors, sometimes coloured. Distributors were 3 core usually 0.05" outers and ½-size mid wire. Distribution pillars by BI were small and later were 4 way path boxes, also by BI. When changes to AC were made DC and AC could exist in the same box and remained so for 20 years. Service cables were over the years of various sizes from 7/.029 to 7/.052 . With the arrival of the Northmet AC system transformers were allocated type numbers as follows, for 33kV type 5, 22kV type 4, 11kV type 3, 3kV 2750 type 2 and LV type 1.

22kV switchgear was BT-H in stone cells with steel doors, cable isolators were at waist height and jam jars were put over the earth contacts while opening the isolators with an insulator on a wooden pole. Voltage transformer isolators were above head-height. The doors opened downwards and then, laying on the floor, the isolators were opened downwards. Circuit breakers were closed by 240 volt DC. 3kV circuit breakers were BT-H. LV feeder panels were BI. The first transformers were type 4/2 in fact 22kV/2850volts reduced to 2750 via a separate ratio regulator with a handle for manual tap changing. Newer transformers had either remote or automatic voltage control and could cover the range to 2750. LV transformers were indoor type 2/1 with radial stampings to reduce noise.

When 33kV arrived at St Albans from Brimsdown it was connected to the Reyrolle form N3T switchgear and then to two 5/4 transformers with one liquid neutral resistance. Transformer neutral isolators were operated with a long wooden pole earthed with a long chain. Five interconnectors at 22kV fed the existing 22kV gear. They were filled with water and glycerin. Closing was by 240 volt DC or an explosive cartridge. When removed, one set of equipment was taken to the Science Museum. With the removal of the generators St. Albans Power Station became St. Albans Main.

---

[4] PC Bourne R after ref: *Electrical Review* vol 53 11/1903

By 1934 the CEB took over the running and programming of the generators at Brimsdown and Willesden, purchasing all the electricity at one price and selling it back to the company at a different price as and when required.

Mr Melling and his staff at Luton were faced with the new Farley Hill housing estate and how to design the electricity supply system. They produced *The Third Report on Post War Housing Estates Electrical Layouts* which introduced a set of formulae, first to find the optimum number of substations and the total cost, including cables, somewhere between one substation for the whole estate and one transformer for each house. Having used this formula, actual substation sites could be found and further calculations made for the low voltage system. A value of 1kW after diversity maximum demand (ADMD) was assumed and used for the transformer sizes (which could be changed later). Cable sizes were based on a figure of 3kW ADMD and 6% voltage drop.

A special slide rule was supplied which worked much better with the slide reversed to bring the variables together. Contrary to expectation, a tapered layout cost more and was not as satisfactory as a uniform cable size which also allowed for three 30% interconnections to adjacent substations. A further consideration was flicker voltage caused by cooker hotplate simmerstat controls. Larger fuses could be used on a uniform cable so that faults would burn clear assisted by a 25MVA fault level.

For houses built with off peak heating the actual load was used. without any diversity. Other research showed that the minimum size of 11kV cable to survive faults was 0.1". All these calculations produced a satisfactory supply, and Mr Melling issued the Report from Wherstead for use in all Districts. Years later the CEGB System Operation Engineer received a student's paper submitted to the IEE for assessment which showed a computer programme solution to the Third Report.

In pre-war days the only guidance had been that large factories provided a substation site with agreement that supply was also given to the adjacent streets. Otherwise, circle diagrams of 1/2500 scale were issued with a 1000 yard radius circle drawn for each substation so that the circles met or showed where gaps occurred. ADMD was ½kW, the Third Report would have produced circles of 250 yard radius had they been drawn.

Communications and Control

35: **Northmet House control room** [*D Willis*]

Northmet Control was established in the top floor of Northmet House and controlled the 33kV, 22kV and 11kV systems. Advice was also given for the 3kV system. Instructions were given verbally, nothing was in writing and permits were not issued. Safety locks were not fitted to switchgear.

It is not known exactly when operational safety was improved but by the early years of nationalisation, the Safety Rules were in place. These took full cognisance of the requirements of the Electricity (Factories Act) Regulations 1908 & 1944 as well as the various Electricity Supply legislation. Although notionally Eastern Electricity rules, they were, in fact, agreed nationally and with minor modifications lasted well over 30 years.

[5]Northmet ran an interconnected HV network from early times, which depended on the use of unit (pilot-wire) protection, and many pilot wire systems were developed by BT-H but the major work was done by Reyrolle; Solkor and Split Pilot were very stable against through faults and induced voltages on the pilot cores. At Reyrolle, E W N Scott, who later joined Northmet just before the war, was the brains behind this work. Accordingly all HV cable systems were laid with pilot and telephone cables, and overhead 33kV lines were provided with underslung pilots.

The cables sizes were typically 3core 7/.029 pilot cores, 2 pairs 150lb conductor (heavy) telephone pairs, and 4pairs 1/19swg. What a mixture of units of measurement! The size of wire expressed in lbs/mile of the conductor was following standard practice in railway telegraph convention, where they wanted the circuit to be good for up to 100miles long. Lighter telephone pairs used standard sizing (1/19 swg). Power engineers were used to dealing with sizes by stranded conductor, each strand being given in swg or diameter.

In addition to being used for pilots between substation, the telephone cores were jointed into each substation and interconnected suitably to provide the telephone routes. Parts of the private telephone system were shared with the Metropolitan Electric Tramways.

There were several permanently manned substations where the telephone circuits were connected to an early type of manual switchboard, and where the attendant had GPO phones to receive calls of no supply from customers. They could also interconnect lines to allow staff in substations to talk to each other, or to Northmet Control.

Because the capacity of each telephone cable was typically 6 pairs, the number of individual lines was severely restricted, and so typically 50 or even more substation telephones had to be connected in parallel onto one "party" line. The phones were "local battery" which meant every one had to have very large dry-cells, and "turn the handle" magneto for ringing out. (Note some Post Office telephones in rural areas had the same. Much Hadham was an example, and they still used wet Leclanche cells!)

---

[5] Much of the following information regarding telephones and remote control was contributed by the late Don Taylor who became Assistant Chief Engineer of Eastern Electricity

In an attempt to improve the loudness of speech, each substation phone was fitted with a cut-out switch which people often forgot to operate when leaving the site unattended. Growing complaints of "can't hear" were tackled by sending telephone electricians out in shared vans to find low insulation on cables or too many switches "left on".

The last attended substations at Hertford and Hatfield were demanned in the mid 1950's, and so all routes had to be diverted into the one remaining manned point at "Wood Green", which was situated in the London Transport trolleybus depot, dating from the common ownership by Metropolitan Electric Tramways and Northmet.

In addition each District office had two lines back to Wood Green, one for the District Manager, and one for the District Engineer. There had been a demand for a small automatic exchange within each District to allow the staff to talk to each other, but the first with a direct dial-out feature was put in virtually at the time of nationalisation. The suppliers, used to Post Office technology, had never done such a thing before, and would not take any responsibility. Northmet House had the largest exchange, some 100 lines at this time, and they could dial out to Wood Green and ask for connection to other offices or substations. These exchanges worked well, and so with confidence the lines from Friern Barnet Office were made to direct dial into Northmet House.

Then Northmet had to vacate Wood Green, centralise the manual "trunk" exchange into Northmet House, and centralise all after hours consumer service. What should the new exchange be called, so as not to confuse it with Northmet PAX?

This important decision could not be determined by engineers, and so was made personally by C C Hill, the Sub-Area Manager, who named it "Walker, after the famous family who had owned Northmet House".

Telephone traffic was growing fast by the 1960's, and the main task was to increase the number of tie-lines between the growing number of PAXs. General managers had this as a problem to be solved, but the 100 or so substations on each shared telephone line was not discussed with much enthusiasm!

The breakthrough was to discover that Army battlefield circuits had the problems of providing more than one circuit over each pair of wires that had been strung across fields under battle conditions. The technique was to use a "carrier" system in which another circuit is provided by sending a radio wave down the cable, without interfering with the original speech circuit. Carrier technology was considered by the Post Office in a very academic way, and was seen to need very special cables to work over. These were laid up as "Quads", ie 2 pairs, and great care was taken in the matching of inter-core capacitance. The Post Office had many thousands of miles of carrier quad, nothing else would do!

The Army showed that an extra channel could be superimposed and did work. Northmet bought a set of ex-army "junk", and showed that it would work from Welwyn Garden City to Northmet House. The Army also developed a system which would superimpose 4 circuits onto a pair, and more "ex-army junk" worked between Stevenage and Welwyn, after suitable modification.

The telephone manufacturers still said no, but at this stage London Underground were short of telephones into Earls Court from Piccadilly, and an entrepreneur from Australia who had dealt with rural telephone small capacity problems, sold equipment to LPTB and Northmet to provide 6 circuits on a telephone paired cable. Northmet's worked perfectly from Welwyn to Northmet, but the LPTB units were unreliable. It transpired that the LPTB equipment had been damaged by "industrial action" during a strike in the Australian factory, and the manufacturer closed down.

All this had been done with electronic valves but by this time early transistor equipment was being developed, making signal processing easier. Ericsson were willing to go ahead and break new ground, and sold 12-channel kit to Northmet. This was developed with suitable isolation equipment to guard against surges, and to cope with less than perfect balance on ordinary telephone pairs. So, other than the cost of buying equipment, the way was clear to extending the size of the PAX network by an order of magnitude.

Substation telephone problems were now solved by fitting a specially developed form of PAX into each grid point, so that there was typically no more than 10 telephones connected to each line. A special feature allowed substations to initiate a ring-back on their own number if the person they wanted was on a shared number, and to arrange a conference of people on different numbers. Magneto phones were now obsolete!

The Eastern Electricity Magazine was able to report: "In all the thousand major substations there is automatic telephone equipment which may be used by staff who visit the substations to telephone System Control; it connects the substations in Northmet with Control and is based on a five-numeral system which can be dialled individually or obtained by pushing two buttons, the first of which gives the initial three numerals and the second the last two.

"Engineers working in a substation may communicate with each other or with Control by telephone but Control can cut into any conversation if any urgent matter arises. It is also possible for a discussion to take place between more than two callers on the system; Control could talk to engineers in four substations simultaneously and the conversation could be five-way."

This development of the use of Carrier Equipment, and of special operational telephone exchanges was the first in the Industry, and people from many other Boards learned from Northmet.

During the War, as more staff were called up for military service, and there were fewer engineers, and others, to deal with supply breakdowns so remote fault alarms from 33kV substations were installed.

The old traditional approach was to wait until a local engineer, or someone else, reported a surge, which might, or might not, have caused a supply failure. Due to the interconnected system, a single fault may have tripped a feeder, but as it was on a ring, no supplies were lost. Engineers had to be sent round all networks, day or night, to see if all circuit breakers were closed. This often involved visiting all 11kv substations fed from the primary substation.

This could not continue, so surges were ignored until routine substation inspection was done, typically weekly, or until a second fault on the same ring caused supply failures triggered calls from consumers.

Extremely costly and elaborate equipment designed by local telephone company, Standard Telephones and Cables, and some by Reyrolle, could provide alarm and remote control of substations. Manchester Corporation had, by the outbreak of war, the start of an STC system but it soon became too costly to extend and became obsolescent,

E W M Scott, working with Stan Dawson, developed very simple equipment which went into all primary substations. In the early form it was a transformer with primary and secondary windings which were connected so that the primary was in the DC trip supply to the common wiring for tripping all circuit breakers. If a breaker was electrically opened, a transient voltage was fed to a telephone pair going to the nearest attended substation. There, a latching relay was released. The attendant reset it and then could report the trip. Mark II was developed by putting another winding on the current transformer in the neutral earthing lead, so that the dropping of the flag indicator might mean that a circuit breaker had tripped, or that there had been a pulse of earth current. Because these systems used a drop relay, they could be triggered by a pulse transferred from another totally independent telephone pair so the attendant had to try to identify the correct alarms from spurious ones.

Mark III accepted the concept that the "safeguarded" trip battery could be used (at some risk to the integrity of the trip supply) to energise a pilot to signal a fault. No supply transmitted signalled no alarm, and then one polarity or the other would transmit separate alarms. These were typically switch trip, or transient earth fault. These signals could be combined, to give separate exclusive identification of fire alarm. To reduce costs, the receive devices were an electromagnet, with a magnetised hack-saw blade hung in front to show polarity!

These alarms had proved acceptable during the war, but by 1950 fault alarms were produced using telephone relay technology. These sent 50V AC to the pilot to monitor the pilot but to show no alarm. Three identifiable signals of DC+, DC-, and no voltage were decoded to light separate lamps for each signal.

During this early stage, the alarms had to be displayed in the control room, as other attended sites had been closed.

It was seen that there would be great advantage if each alarm relay at a substation could be displayed individually, to save the problem of an alarm, one of three, which may have been generated by parallelled alarm contacts, instead of having to inspect the monitor alarm lamps in the substation.

Computers were now being introduced into industry, and a scheme was hatched with Elliott Brothers to produce a transistorised signalling system with telemetry and alarm information to the control room from all Primary and Grid substations. There would be facilities to add remote control at a later date. The politics of introducing each of the three features was tendentious. Unfortunately, the planning engineers, who commented on all capital expenditure, were against spending money on 'non power carrying" equipment'. They were very strongly opposed to remote control facilities, largely argued on the extra cost of fitting power closing mechanisms onto existing and future circuit breakers. Fortunately, the Northmet Group Engineer was not opposed, and the Board's Chief Engineer, who was by that time C C Hill. and later G H Tilbrook, supported the ideas.

In the control room, there was very restricted space for the display of information, certainly not adequate for mosaic panels as used by the CEGB and, indeed, the STC system at Manchester. Accordingly a novel approach was developed, using a printer to display information, and a "punched card" (actually a rigid card with coded teeth along one edge) for input to issue commands, such as to display telemetry reading, or for an instruction to apply control commands to do "voltage reduction" load shedding. This system was christened CATE (Control, Alarm and Telemetry Equipment). The signalling was very slow by modern standards (it could take several seconds for a message to appear) but it gave great resilience against pilot interference.

The Eastern Electricity staff magazine reported on the new system:
"Communications are as important to the engineers of Eastern Electricity as they are to generals during a battle. On the speed with which information about the load on a particular substation or of any fault is sent to the central control will depend the supply of electricity to industry and the homes in the area; the faster information is fed back to engineers, the less likelihood there is of a prolonged or serious breakdown.

"For many years, Eastern Electricity has been striving towards a completely automatic system of communications and in the Northmet Sub-Area, which embraces Barnet, Edmonton, Enfield, Hendon, Hertford, Hornsey, St Albans, Stevenage, Wembley and Wood Green and a great part of the contiguous area, the engineers are on the threshold of securing just that.

"Eastern Electricity obtains its electricity from the Generating Board at grid pick-up points or sub-stations of which there are thirteen in the Northmet Sub-Area, and in seven of which a new electronic device, affectionately named CATE ("Control, Alarm and Telemetry Equipment") has already been installed. Within the next twelve months CATE will be installed in the six remaining grid substations and this will mean that the central Control will have an automatic indication system covering practically all of the several thousand of sub-stations from which consumers take supply.

"CATE, as it appears in the Northmet Control, is a small box with some push button switches and a slot into which plastic "cards" with teeth can be inserted. The electronic "works" are hidden in the basement. The box is the sending device by which the Control Engineer puts questions to CATE; the replies come by an electric typewriter in black type. If CATE communicates with System Control of her own volition, then the electric typewriter operates in red type.

"Mr D J Taylor, one of the Northmet engineers, explained the kind of questions and instructions which Control could put to CATE: "We might want to know the load on the Hatfield sub-station" he said, "and the 'card' for that information would be inserted into the slot. Within seconds CATE would give the answer".

"Mr Taylor carried out the operation and CATE printed the reply of "40 Megawatts", also logging the time, all within three seconds.

""We might want to open a particular circuit breaker at the Harrow substation" went on Mr Taylor, "or we might want to alter the tappings on a transformer, ascertain the oil pressure, or get a reading from the ammeters. We could get all that information quickly; in fact we can obtain any information we want by appropriate adjustments to CATE".

"CATE has been manufactured by the British firm of Elliott Bros. (Boreham Wood) and the Northmet installation, the first of is kind in the country, was modified at the request of Eastern Electricity's engineers by the incorporation of the toothed-card technique. Mr Taylor explained that by having one card for each specific operation the risk of mistakes was reduced to a minimum.

"CATE already has some extraneous duties. At the Harrow grid substation a very wide variety of measurements are taken. For example, the direction of the wind, the light intensity, temperatures, humidity and electrical quantities are all regularly recorded on teleprinter tape for the benefit of Eastern Electricity's research engineer, Mr R S Peacock. "A north wind or a dull day can make a difference to the demand for electricity", said Mr Taylor.

"The resulting paper tape is then analysed by a computer to aid the design of future electricity supply networks."

The report did not, of course, mention the trials and tribulations of being the first in the field. There were no manuals and, although the concepts were straight forward, there had been no in-house experience with this type of transistorised equipment. Two junior power engineers were trained to look after the system but much reliance was placed on the support provided by Elliott Bros. The logic was based on small encapsulated blocks which Elliott called 'Minilog's. The system was programmed by large matrices of plug-in diodes which had a tendency to work loose and lose contact. This was a particular problem in the early days of use as changes were frequently being made during testing and commissioning. Later on it was practicable to solder the diodes in place.

37: **Final version of the Northmet House control room** [*D Willis*]

Not all the problems were electronic. Northmet's telephone pilot system was fairly reliable but there were some cases of problems which the Elliott system was not robust enough to deal with. There were instances where spurious alarms drove the control engineers to such distraction that the equipment was switched off until the cause could be found.

The first applications were for indication of switchgear position and receipt of alarms. There was no check built into these signals, so occasionally spurious alarms were received and an Engineer had to be sent to check. As a control system the system was above reproach. The checks and procedures built into the system meant that it was necessary to send a 'prime' instruction before the final 'operate' instruction could be transmitted.

The advantage of getting rapid alarms of major system abnormalities, hence reducing the duration of many interruptions, and greater knowledge of system loads was appreciated, as were the benefits of being able to implement voltage reductions quickly. (This may have caused the CEGB to ring Northmet to apply emergency voltage reduction, because they had large parts of their area where a member of staff would have to visit the substation to do a manual control.) If the reduction was forecast, those with no remote control had to go from the office to each primary substation to reduce voltage, often getting back just in time to be told to go out again to restore to normal. In the heavy winter of 1961 engineers in areas where remote switching had not been installed Engineers and other 'operational' staff spent many long hours in substations waiting for a message to load shed, sometimes having to switch off supplies to their own homes.

The CATE equipment was demonstrated to the Board at one of their meetings at Northmet House. G H Tilbrook set up a Working Party to recommend the future policy for such equipment throughout Eastern Electricity. Eventually the Board agreed to proposals, and awarded the contract to Ferranti, for "EAC" equipment. There was still little support from engineers in the planning function in support of the concepts, both at Headquarters but also at the other Groups. At this time C C Hill, who was Deputy Chairman, also supported the proposals. Although the Ferranti computers were more highly developed, memory capacity was expensive, and the design said that 64kbit was needed to run an EAC installation, but a small increase was necessary. Much was copied from CATE, including printer displays, with punched card/paper tape for input. However there were small geographic diagrams with one lamp per substation to show any substations with an outstanding alarm. The history of Northmet remote alarms finished when the system was supplanted by a Board-wide system of a standard design, which commenced installation in late 1969.

The decision to vacate Northmet House was complicated by the need to maintain adequate system control. It took a year to transfer the control room functions to the Millfield (Brentwood) offices and during this time EEB had to keep in occupation of the top floor wing of Northmet House. A new communications hub was built over the substation at Tapster Street, Barnet, and microwave links put in. Eventually control passed to Millfield and, effectively, this marked the end of Northmet.

CHAPTER 12: PUBLIC LIGHTING

Public (street) lighting was the original load envisaged by most electricity undertakers and, although Northmet had been founded by a tramway company, it took its lighting load seriously, convincing the local authorities of the benefits of electricity for lighting.

Northmet contracted with the local authorities to supply electricity for the street lighting and, in many cases, also undertook the maintenance of the lights. In the rural areas, this often meant dealing with the individual parishes who were the lighting authorities.

It was reported[1] at the end of 1925 that the number of public lamps in operation were: St Albans 1, Barnet 166, Chingford 7, East Barnet 46, Edgware 108, Edmonton 6, Harrow Weald 36, Hertford 14, Hoddesdon 26, Kingsbury 81, Southgate 130, Tottenham 329, Ware 29, Wealdstone 58 and Wembley 480. New orders for public lighting were reported back to all Resident Engineers, showing how important this work was considered even though the numbers, and the load, seem to be small by modern standards.

Most Northmet undertakings had public lighting sections which, until well after nationalisation, were regarded as an engineering function with a public lighting foreman or chargehand, several public lighting attendants and one or more public lighting electricians. The public lighting attendants saw to the cleaning and functioning of the street lights, the individual contracts with the local authorities specifying how often they should be checked. Although not qualified electricians, the PLAs would change lamps as necessary, leaving any electrical wiring or fault-finding to the electrician.

In 1933, the conditions of work of public lighting attendants were standardised and, in some cases, improved[2]. The 6-day week was adopted, long spread-over of working hours was avoided and mackintoshes were provided at half cost, this giving "the workman a personal interest in the garment".

---

[1] Northmet Monthly Bulletin No 1 Item 1 2/12/1925
[2] Resident Engineers' Meeting 14/2/1933 Item 660

Often, as a public lighting contractor, Northmet chose or recommended the fittings which should be used. In 1910 at Kingsbury there were reflector fittings with no globes, that is the lamps were exposed to the air. This was a novel arrangement at the time although adopted widely subsequently. It saved the expense of the globes which could be cumbersome, expensive to keep clean and a source of light diminution[3].

In 1932 the company introduced the GEC 'Osira' luminaire which was used extensively for main road installations.

Similar contracts were applied to illuminated road signs and, in a few cases, to traffic signals. When the M1 motorway was first opened the PLAs found themselves exposed to new hazards from high speed traffic and it was necessary to devise, with the police, new methods of operation for safety's sake.

Connection of street lights to the low voltage distribution cables left one problem, however. How were the lights to be switched on and off? This could either be done manually or by some automatic device. Early timeswitches were not wholly reliable, leaving some lights unlit or, worse from the company's point of view, lit during the day.

The solution generally adopted by Northmet was the installation in urban areas of underground cables with a 5th core, to which the street lights were connected. The first was laid in Edgware in 1911[4] and the system was standardised by Northmet for its urban areas. The 5th core could then be controlled manually by the power station attendant or by a single timeswitch. A similar system was used in some villages where the overhead lines carried the extra conductor for the street lighting.

As the power system developed the system became a little more complicated but the basic idea was continued with.

Where there were established 4-core underground cable distribution systems it was not economic to install 5-core cables so either the lights had to be

---
[3] *Technical Developments Introduced by the Northmet* Ref JMD/MAY unpublished 2/11/1933
[4] *Technical Developments Introduced by Northmet* Ref JMD/MAY unpublished 2/11/1933

individually switched using timeswitches or, later, photoelectric devices, or some other method of control had to be found.

Pre-war, Hornsey Corporation, a relatively small municipal undertaking not part of Northmet, had installed simple remote signalling system for equipment supplied by LV substations. The signalling technique was developed by Standard Telephones & Cables in the Remote Control dept at New Southgate, apparently in conjunction with the Air Ministry[5]. The system, called DC Bias, imposed a DC voltage onto the LV mains between the transformer neutral and the neutral of the distributors by having a very low resistor in the connection, normally shorted out by a contactor. Six volts DC was injected by opening the contactor, and switching a battery across the resistor. Using either polarity and long or short pulses a small number of codes was possible.

Individual codes were detected by a "personalised" portable receiver unit given to all key personnel so that, provided it was plugged into to "Hornsey" supply, they had an alarm, which notified them to ring the Hornsey duty desk. The obsolescent equipment was not extended after nationalisation, but great effort was made by local staff to keep the equipment workable![6]

The same system was used during the Second World War as a means of calling members of the emergency services. The plug-in portable receiver units were adjustable for 1, 2 or 3 second delay so that Auxiliary Fire Services could have one signal, ARP Wardens another, and so on[7].

The receiving unit incorporated a choke in series with a magnetic relay with two coils and a rocking armature which was side-stable, ie it moved to one position or the other and stayed put. It could, therefore, be controlled by DC pulses of one polarity or the other[8]. The addition of bimetallic strips to delay the movement of the armature allowed the use of time delay codes.

Northmet and other electricity undertakers used DC Bias to control street lighting in those areas where an additional 5th core had not been provided in the underground LV distributor cable for street lighting supply. The same system

---

[5] STC Handbook 524 (courtesy of Nortel Networks historical archive) refers to control from the 'Guard House' and to Air Ministry maintenance procedures.
[6] PC D J Taylor, former Northmet employee
[7] PC A G Walton, former STC employee.
[8] PC L J Day, former STC employee

was also used during the Second World War for remote operation of air raid warning sirens[9].

The changeover contactor was put in the LV neutral-earth connection at the local substation allowing a 6-volt battery to be inserted to raise the whole potential of the local system by this bias voltage, positive for switching the street lights on and negative to switch them off[10]. In use there were either short (less than about 3 seconds) or long (over 3 seconds) pulses. In neither case was the DC bias imposed on the system for long periods. Although these contactors could be controlled remotely, in most Northmet applications they were operated by a timeswitch mounted in a box on the external wall of the substation where they could be adjusted by a public lighting attendant. If the contactors inside the substation needed attention it was a task for the mains department.

By using receiver units with the polarised relays fitted with bimetallic thermal time delays, long or short pulses of each polarity could be detected and used for switching the lighting. It was, therefore, possible to have all-night as well as half-night (ie until around midnight) lighting controlled from one substation. The physical size of the chokes and relays meant that they were rather larger than a timeswitch and were impossible to fit in some lamp columns, particularly gas conversions. The relays were, however relatively cheap, enabling large numbers of street lamps to the switched at the same time.

Initially the systems worked satisfactorily. Batteries needed maintaining but, as there was maintenance regime for substation tripping batteries, this was not much of a problem. However, as things developed, two problems arose. The neutral contactors were rated at 150A, less than the phase current in some installations. The contactors started burning out, and it was found that neutral currents were an increasing nuisance. Harmonics were extremely high, particularly where the load was primarily fluorescent and gas discharge lighting. The ballast units and the non-linearity of gas discharge tubes were extremely high. DC in the neutral was also being imposed by domestic television sets as the power units used half-wave rectification direct of the 240v supply. This spurious DC could cause the receiver units to switch the street lamps on or off[11].

---

[9] PC H R Olphert, former STC employee.
[10] STC Handbook No 524.
[11] PC L J Day, former STC employee.

A surprise was the number of complaints from users of IBM computers which took supply through 115/240V transformers. These large transformers, ran at high core flux densities, and any DC arising from the switching of a DC Bias street lighting command, could cause the transformer to saturate, and play havoc with the computer. Court action for damages by a large consumer determined that the technique was not allowable, so it was back to individual tine-switches. In any case the introduction of Consac and similar combined neutral-earth (CNE) cable types forced a widespread change to time switch or photoelectric control for street lighting. Fortunately, photoelectric units were becoming cheaper and more reliable.

It is believed that production of DC bias units finished in November 1961[12]

Other techniques for remote control of street lights (and other loads) were tried out by other undertakings but, as far as is known were not used by Northmet prior to Nationalisation. After that time, however, Letchworth, which was another small undertaking, merged into the Northmet sub-area of Eastern Electricity. They used "Ripple Control" to inject audio frequency tones onto the supply network, avoiding frequencies which were close to system harmonic frequencies. Tuned relays set to detect the frequency, and the speed of repetition of the pulses, were used to control the street lighting. This system, although in fair use in other parts of the country, including Norwich, was never used by Northmet. The injection points were at the 11kV (primary substation) source so, as the network expanded, more injection points were required, one for each new Primary Substation. Trials of injecting at Grid points and hoping that signal would be coupled through the 33kV/11kV transformers were unreliable. The system was abandoned in Letchworth in the 1950s.

---

[12] PC L J Goddard, former STC employee.

CHAPTER 13: TRACTION SUPPLIES[1]

When the Middlesex light railways were planned it was intended to have a local electricity generating station for each group of routes. However, this was a time of rapid strides in electrical technology and British Electric Traction saw the advantages in serving the whole area from a central power station and distributing by AC to local converting substations. This was the origins of the first North Metropolitan Electric Power Supply Company, registered on 19th January 1899. Metropolitan Electric Tramways (MET) was formed on 12th October 1901[2]. MET, itself a BET company, had an agreement, dated 16th November 1900, with MCC to provide power for the light railways. So Met acquired the supply company from BET.

At the MET Board meeting on 30th January 1901[3], it was reported that relations between MET and both Northmet companies (the Distribution company and the Supply company) were 'discussed at length' but not recorded. A meeting was arranged with MCC regarding land for a generating station.

By the Board meeting on 30th October 1903[4] it was said that "the Power Supply Co is already supplying us with all the power required for our tramways and light railways....".

An agreement between the MCC, MET and Northmet was signed on 13 October 1903[5] and authorised the MET to buy all its power from the Northmet at a rate of 1.4d per unit for the first five million units per half-year, reducing by 0.04d per unit for each additional million units with a minimum price of 1d per unit for the total current used. A similar agreement was signed with Hertfordshire on 6 November 1903, but in their case the starting price was 1.5d per unit. In October 1904 the MCC had asked that power used on the Middlesex Light Railways be metered separately from that used on the MET tramways, but were told that this was impracticable and that power costs would be apportioned between MCC, MET and Hertfordshire on the basis of car miles worked.

---

[1] The two main sources for this chapter are Smeeton CS, *Metropolitan Electric Tramways*, LRTL & TLRS (ISBNs 0900433949 and 094810600X) and Croome D and Jackson A, *Rails through the Clay*, Capital Transport Publishing (ISBN 1854141511)
[2] London Metropolitan Archive Acc/1297/MELT1/8
[3] London Metropolitan Archive Acc/1297/MELT1/1
[4] London Metropolitan Archive Acc/1297/MELT1/8
[5] Northmet Board minute 23 27/7/1903

Electricity was distributed from Brimsdown to traction substations at Edmonton, Finchley, Hendon and Wood Green depots by high voltage cables supplied by British Insulated & Helsby Cable Co Ltd. Each substation was equipped with BT-H rotary convertors. There were three 250kW and one 500kW at Wood Green, two 250kW and one 500kW at Finchley, two 250kW at Hendon, three 250kW at Edmonton and two 300kW at Barnet (which also supplied local DC load) after the power station closed[6]. BT-H negative boosters were provided for the remote sections. BT-H was, at that time, associated with the BET group of companies. Finchley and Wood Green also had an 800Ah battery each.

Because of Finchley Council's opposition to Northmet as a rival electricity supplier, there was some delay in laying the cables to Finchley depot. This was not completed until after Northmet obtained an authorising Act of Parliament in 1905. In the meantime, to supply the tramway from Highgate to Whetstone, temporary electricity supply for about three years was taken from Finchley Corporation's Squires Lane power station.

MET's western lines were supplied from Taylors Lane power station at Willesden, to a traction substation at Hendon and direct to nearby tram lines on the Harrow Road.

The Traction substations were owned by Northmet but the DC mains were MET property. The original feeder cables sufficed until about 1911 when additional cables were authorised to deal with increased loads. Another traction supply (with one 300kW and two 100kW convertors) came from Enfield (Ladysmith Road) in 1914[7].

Although some western routes of the MET were outside Northmet territory and supply was taken from the Metropolitan Electric Supply Co (METESCO), it was done through an agreement whereby Northmet bought the power from METESCO and resold it to MET. This was probably for accounting convenience.

There was apparently some bargaining on power costs, for in 1911 the MET offered to reduce the unit charge to 0.8 pence if Middlesex would extend the company's lease from 1930 to 1946. However, no agreement resulted.

---

[6] Garcke's Manuals 1907 and 1908
[7] Garcke's Manual 1914-15

By 1915 things had changed and on 30 December 1915 the Northmet wrote to the MET asking for a revision of the power tariff because of increased coal prices, but no change was made at that time. By July 1919 wages had doubled since 1914 and coal had increased by 70% since 1915, and Northmet proposed a new tariff with a fixed charge per quarter subject to a wage clause linked to the pay of substation attendants, and a price of 0.7 pence per unit subject to a coal clause with a mid-point of 30/- per ton. The MCC committee sought an independent opinion from J H Rider of Preece, Cardew, Snell and Rider, who found the company's request justified, and a new agreement including coal and wages clauses and a maximum demand charge came into force in July 1921.

The introduction of a maximum demand clause in the tariff made it desirable to check power consumption on the cars, and eight Arthur power recorders were bought for £59 in 1921, to indicate to motormen the power consumed by the car. Following trials the entire MET passenger fleet was equipped, costing £1,885, but their use was discontinued in 1925 because armature and magnetic brake defects had increased as a result of motormen's attempts to reduce current consumption. When the recorders were removed, armature and brake defects reverted to their 1921 level.

So long as the MET owned the power company, profits from high power charges came back to the MET in the form of dividend. The MET held 40,000 of the 40,002 Northmet shares, and this investment of £400,020 had yielded £281,750 in dividends between 1910 and 1917, the dividend for 1917 being 6%. No dividend was paid in 1918, possibly because of new plant being charged to revenue, but the position soon recovered, to 4½% in 1919, 7½t's in 1920 and 10% in 1921-4. The Northmet dividend was of vital importance to the MET, since the financial position of the tramways was steadily deteriorating. Some shares were sold to London & Suburban Traction in 1926, but the MET's holding was still £387,707.

Up to the year 1914 the units sold to the Tramway Company represented more than 50% of the total output of the Company but then the consumption by the Tramways and, after conversion, by the Trolleybuses, gradually became of comparatively less importance.

In 1920, in preparation for through running with London County Council trams, a new traction substation was built at West Green Lane (South Grove) in

Tottenham. Northmet owned the substation which was equipped with two 500kW rotary converters which may have come from Wood Green, which was re-equipped with 1000kW machines about that time. Wood Green was also the home for another convertor acquired second-hand from the 'never-stop' railway at the 1924-5 Wembley British Empire Exhibition.

To meet the demand from higher-powered trams an additional substation was commissioned at Llanvanor Road, Cricklewood on 7th March 1927. This was described as 'semi-automatic', consisting of a 300lW Hewittic mercury arc rectifier supplied by a 11kV 0.05 sq in feeder switched from Childs Hill substation. On the DC side there was an Igranic auto-reclose circuit breaker which automatically disconnected the supply from the track in the event of excessive load and reconnected it as soon as conditions returned to normal. To enable tramway staff to switch the substation in and out of commission, a push-button was fitted to one of the tramway section pillars to control the auto-reclose circuit breaker[8].

There were a number of failures in traction supply in 1929[9] leading to correspondence between Northmet and Frank Pick of MET. The majority of these were said to be due to causes over which Northmet had no control but Captain Donaldson had an uneasy feeling that one or two of them might be put in the category of 'avoidable failures' where substation attendants had not noticed that circuit breakers had come out. In another case the alarm bells did not work properly.

The Chief Engineer "wished Resident Engineers tactfully to indicate to substation attendants their responsibility in these matters".

Tramway load continued to increase[10]. Subsequent reinforcement took the form of mercury arc rectifiers installed in Northmet substations at Kensal Rise and Elmhurst Road, Enfield Wash in 1930.

MET power costs in 1926 averaged 1.46 pence per unit, the tramway load (23¼ million units in 1925) being about one-fifth of Northmet's total output, though originally the proportion had been much higher. The MCC noticed, however, that power costs on the MET in 1925 were 2.659 pence per car mile, against 1.579

---
[8] Northmet Monthly Bulletin 3/27 item 123 March 1927
[9] Resident Engineers' Meeting 30/9/1929 Min 587
[10] Northmet Management meeting item 15 11/1/1929

pence on the LCC and only 1.401 pence in Glasgow. Of the ten largest tramways, only Liverpool at 2.761 pence paid more than the MET for its power, and this was eventually reduced. Challenged by Middlesex, Emile Garcke said that no two power companies were alike and the comparison was therefore unreasonable.

In 1927 the MET was in arrears with its rent to the county, and the MCC asked that the shares in the power company should be lodged with the county council as security for the rent due. Emile Garcke explained that since the MET itself had no physical assets, its holding in the power company was almost all pledged as security for the debenture holders. The issue became embroiled in negotiations for a new lease, but a result was that the average price per unit, already reduced to 1.20 pence per unit in 1927, was further reduced to 0.8197 pence per unit from 1 January 1928, facilitated by the commissioning of more efficient generating plant. The new tariff was known as the Donaldson/Mason tariff[11], presumably as they were the men who had thrashed it out.

The size of the 1927-28 tariff reductions shows that there was some truth in the county council's view of the power charges, and their committee chairman said in 1926 that it now appeared to him that building up the profitable power company based on the monopoly concession granted by the county council may have been the real objective of the BET group when the Middlesex lease was obtained. Two years later, the BET sold its interest in the MET and in London and Suburban Traction to the Underground group, and on 6 November 1930 the MET board voted to sell all its remaining shares in the power company (then valued at £351,820) to the UERL, who were planning to use Brimsdown power for the tube railway extension to Cockfosters. Part of the proceeds were invested in government securities on behalf of the debenture holders, and the rest was used to help buy modern tramcars.

In 1933 it was decided to put the traction substations under unified control[12]. Mr E A Elliott of Wood Green was designated Traction Substation Engineer, reporting to the Chief Engineer (with copies to the Resident Engineers). Experience gained in one substation would be pooled for use in all other substations on the system. Emergency repairs would still be done locally but there should be no difficulty working in this way. It was recognised that

---

[11] Northmet Management meeting item 915 9/6/1928
[12] Resident Engineers' Meeting 14/2/1933 item 657

Assistant Engineers would have to visit the traction substations in order to be familiar with the equipment. For 'pay and discipline', staff at traction substations would still be under the control of the Resident Engineers.

One 'perk' lost by certain members of Northmet staff were the passes which were issued for use on the MET system. These were withdrawn at the end of 1933 and was thought by management to be of little consequence except, perhaps, for Juniors using their passes to attend evening classes and for the workers at Brimsdown power station[13].

The Northwood Electric Light & Power Co had had an agreement for the supply of electricity with the District Railway. When that expired, Northmet took it over (in September 1921) by means of a 10kV feeder run from Pinner Substation.

When London Transport took over the MET tramways in 1933 it embarked on a programme of conversion to trolleybuses. The tramway traction substations were retained, some, like Wood Green, with their old rotary convertors. Others were fitted with mercury arc rectifiers and additional substations were similarly equipped (eg at Barrowell Green).

In 1945 the units supplied for the operation of the Trolleybuses amounted to 36 millions which represented 3.2% of the total output. DC metering for supplies to the trolleybuses had to be checked and tested on site periodically. This was a two-man job for safety reasons. The method of testing was to install a temporary meter and allow it to run for a week against the two meters on site. The most difficult part was installing heavy copper the 4000 amp shunt in the substation live busbars and then opening the links while service continued. The supply was 650V DC arranged with earth at the mid-point so touching the earthed framework at the same time as fitting the shunt would result in being thrown off and could lead to muscle stiffness[14]. Such work was always dirty because of the dust which was drawn into the substation by the cooling fans of the mercury arc rectifiers.

All trolleybuses were withdrawn from the Northmet supply area by January 1962 but, by then, Eastern Electricity had long lost interest in this traction load.

---

[13] Resident Engineers' Meeting 20/11/1933 item 673
[14] PC F Greenwood

London Transport took over from the Underground Group in 1933 and continued with the completion the extension of the Piccadilly tube line to Cockfosters. Supply was taken from Northmet's Watsons Road substation (behind the tram depot) for the Piccadilly at Wood Green. The installation included some unusual 11kV BT-H minimum oil switchgear controlling the three six-phase traction transformers and their steel tank rectifiers as well as supplies to other substations along the line.

As part of a government-sponsored initiative to provide employment, London Transport launched its 'New Works' programme which included taking over and electrifying some of the LNER suburban lines. As a result, Northmet also supplied the Barnet branch of the Northern Line at East Finchley from Watsons Road (Wood Green) via 11kV cables laid through Alexandra Park and alongside the railway branch line. East Finchley, like Wood Green, had three steel-tank mercury arc rectifiers and supply feeders to other lineside substations. One of these was newly constructed at Cranley Gardens but was never used for traction purposes as the electrification of the Alexandra Palace branch was abandoned after the war.

The Railway supplies steadily increased from 22 million units in 1933 to 71 millions in 1945[15].

Eventually London Transport decided that after converting its power stations to 50Hz working, it wanted all its traction supplies to be taken from them. The Northmet traction supplies then finished.

In April 1958, British Railways electrified the line to Enfield Town and in 1960 to Hertford East and Bishops Stortford. Supply to the railways' 25kV overhead line system was obtained from the CEGB at Silver Street and Rye House with a supply for emergencies only at Bishops Stortford. All British Railways traction supplies, regardless of the actual system connection were the subject of a special agreement between the railway and CEGB. Eastern Electricity only had an indirect interest in these supplies until the 132kV system passed to them after the demise of the Northmet Sub-Area.

---

[15] Outline History of the Northmet Power Co Kingsbury & Boyes, 1947

CHAPTER 14: BIOGRAPHICAL NOTES

Many of the most important and best remembered employees of Northmet are mentioned elsewhere in this history. However, the following biographical notes will help to bring some of these characters to life.

LORD ASHFIELD

Albert Henry Stanley was born in the Rosehill district of Derby, England, on 8th August[1] or 8th November[2] 1874 as Albert Knattriess. His father, Henry, worked as a coach painter. The family emigrated to the USA when Albert was 11 and he was educated in Detroit, Michigan. After a few years the family name was changed to Stanley because it sounded more English. At the age of 14 he got a job working in the stables of the Detroit Citizens' Street Railway Company, one of Detroit's seven tramway undertakings. He spent a year working as a messenger and was then promoted to a clerical post in the schedules department. The tramways were being converted from horse to electric traction. In January 1900, the Citizens' Street Railway formed a new holding company to acquire the other undertakings. Stanley was appointed superintendent with responsibility for the whole of Detroit's tramways. Four years of steady progression found him in the post of general manager of the Public Service Corporation of New Jersey in 1904. The same year he married Grace Lowrey Woodruff by whom he had two daughters.

In 1907 the American shareholders in the UERL persuaded him to return to Britain as UERL general manager (a director from 1908, managing director from 1910). With Sir Edgar Speyer he brought about the mergers of 1911-1913 between UERL, LGOC, MET, LUT and SMET, becoming Managing Director of the Underground Group of companies in 1912. He was knighted in 1914. He was Conservative MP for Ashton-under-Lyne from 1916 to 1920. In 1916 he became director-general of mechanical transport at the Ministry of Munitions, and was chosen as President of the Board of Trade later that year. On returning to the UERL in 1919 as chairman and managing director, he was elevated to the peerage, becoming Lord Ashfield of Southwell.

---

[1] *Metropolitan Electric Tramways* by C S Smeeton, LRTL and *The Man Whole Built London Transport* by Christian Barman (David & Charles) ISBN 0-7153-7753-1
[2] *WHO WAS WHO* 1941-1950 vol IV

He was chairman and managing director of the London & Suburban Traction Co (owners of the MET) for most of its life and of Northmet[3], and managing director of the MET from November 1919, though his many other commitments meant that James Devonshire usually acted on his behalf. As Lord Ashfield he became chairman of the LPTB on its formation in 1933 and continued in this post until 1947. He became a Member of the British Transport Commission in 1947. During the War, he was Hon Col 84th (LT) AA Regt, RA, and he was Colonel Engineer of the Railway Staff Corps. He was also a director of Midland Bank Ltd and Imperial Chemical Industries Ltd. He was a member of a Royal Commission on Railways and Transportation In Canada, 1931. He was a member of the Carlton and Royal automobile clubs. He died on 4th November 1948.

He lived at The Crossway, Sunningdale and his recreation was golf. On one occasion Ashfield saw Marshall, the Northern Superintendent, playing golf on a working day and afterwards remarked on this. Marshall apologised and said it would not happen again. Ashfield's reply was that he accepted the apology for Marshall's look of guilt but if Marshall thought it beneficial to the Company's interests that he should play golf on a working day with an important consumer, there was certainly no cause for shame[4].

EVELYN BOYS

Evelyn Boys was one of the longest serving members of the Northmet officers. He joined the MET as assistant to James Devonshire and was present at the sixth General Meeting of the Supply company[5]. He became secretary to Northmet in 1908. He saw active service in the First World War, gaining an MC. After the war he rejoined MET becoming assistant secretary in 1919 and company secretary in 1921. From that date he was also secretary of London & Suburban Traction.[6] Little is known of his personal details. When L&ST was wound up and The Underground Group became part of London Transport he remained with Northmet, being company secretary until shortly before nationalisation when he was replaced by J E Blair. With E T Kingsbury he wrote an outline history of the company but this was not published.

---

[3] London Metropolitan Archive Acc/1297/UER1/6
[4] PC the late C T Melling
[5] Minutes of Northmet Supply Co General Meetings 30/12/1903
[6] Metropolitan Electric Tramways by C S Smeeton LRTA, p220

SIR JAMES DEVONSHIRE

James Lyne Devonshire began his career in 1888 with the Laing, Wharton & Down Construction Syndicate, predecessor of the British Thomson-Houston Co Ltd, of which he became manager and secretary in 1891. He was manager and secretary of the BET group from 1896 to 1900, and was one of the original directors [presumably the director nominated by BT-H under the terms of the 1898 agreement] of the MET, becoming managing director in July 1902. He became managing director of the Northmet power company in 1905, chairman of the SMET in 1906, managing director of the Tramways (MET) Omnibus Co Ltd in 1912 and of the LUT and SMET from 1913. During the war he served on the Board of Trade Committee on Tramways, for which he received a knighthood. In 1919, following the integration of the MET into the Underground group, Sir Albert Stanley (Lord Ashfield) became managing director of the three 'combine' tramway companies, but in practice the duties of that office were still carried out by James Devonshire. He remained a director of the MET until 1933. As chairman and managing director of the Northmet power company he was a leading figure in the electrical industry[7]. Like Evelyn Boys (qv) he was involved with Northmet for all of its independent life. He shared with Lord Ashfield the distinction of having a 'fireless' steam locomotive at Brimsdown named after him.

CAPTAIN DONALDSON

John Muir Donaldson was born on 21st October 1877 at Kenley, three miles south of Croydon, the son of Alexander Donaldson, merchant, and Mary Isabella, nee Muir. He had the benefit of a good education. Following school at Whitgift, Croydon, he gained his technical education from 1894 at Finsbury Technical College, spending two years in the physics department and securing the Huxley scholarship (tenable for three years at the Central Technical College) awarded by the Fishmongers Company. After two years at the latter institution he obtained the college diploma, ACGI and the Siemens Memorial Medal. Later he gained the Students Premium of the Institution of Electrical Engineers.

---

[7] Metropolitan Electric Tramways by C S Smeeton, LRTA p221

38: Captail Donaldson at Criccieth, 1933 [*D B Welbourne*]

On leaving Finsbury in 1898 he joined the British Thomson-Houston Co Ltd, where he remained for three years in the engineering department at Cannon Street under Mr Eustace Thomas and, later, under Mr Frank Wallis. and then at the City and Guilds College, South Kensington. This was followed by a spell of work in Schenectady, USA, where he gained experience in the testing and foreign departments of the General Electric Company, and in Canada with the Montreal Light Heat and Power Co. In 1904, Capt Donaldson returned to England, rejoining BT-H to handle switchgear on the commercial side of its traction and lighting departments at Rugby.

In 1906 Donaldson was appointed technical assistant to E T Ruthven-Murray, who was engineer-in-chief of the Northmet Company which had major generating stations at Brimsdown and Willesden (Taylors Lane). Off duty he was an officer in the Church Lads Brigade. During the first world war Donaldson served in the King's Royal Rifle Corps (16th Battalion) from 1914 to 1918. He rose to the rank of captain, was wounded in the battle of the Somme, and was awarded the Military Cross. It is said that he was hard of hearing, probably as a result of exposure to gunfire. After a sojourn in hospital he was still able to perform useful military service as instructor to the 1st Cadet Battalion of the RFC (afterwards the RAF). In November of 1918 he resumed his civil duties with Northmet.

In 1920 he succeeded Ruthven-Murray as chief engineer. The office may have carried the same title over the years but it is quite evident from the following comparative data that the scope very greatly increased.

He was chief engineer of the Bedfordshire, Cambridgeshire and Huntingdonshire Electricity Co from its inception in 1925 to its disposal to Edmundsons.

In 1926 a new power station was designed under Donaldson's direction. Brimsdown B was alongside the existing station which became Brimsdown A and 33 kV outdoor switchgear was installed to handle the increased output. Captain Donaldson was an engineer who believed very strongly that the Company should be at the forefront of available technology and under his direction the Company was one of the first users of 33 kV switchgear and cables. Some of these items especially cables were a little before their time and frequent failures resulted in some of them being downgraded. A new type of 33 kV metalclad outdoor switchgear was installed before the power station extension was commissioned in 1932. Shortly afterwards Donaldson decided to rebuild Brimsdown A with new generating plant and two forced-circulation boilers in a new boiler house. The Loeffler boilers of all-welded construction were the first of this type to be installed in the country and were designed to operate at 2,000 psi and 9400F.

Meanwhile Donaldson increased the generating plant at Willesden and introduced pulverised fuel firing in 1926. To make best use of the existing space, compact Brush Ljungstrom generating sets were installed, the last in 1932.

In 1931, Donaldson became President of the IEE and in celebration of this and of ten years as Northmet's Chief Engineer, his senior staff presented him with an engraved silver salver. After his death on 14th January 1963, it was donated to St Albans City Council and is now part of the City plate.

Donaldson became General Manager of Northmet in 1936. He would go to 55 Broadway for regular meetings with Lord Ashfield. Donaldson would be dressed in a country tweed suit in contrast to the conventional black or grey suits worn by LT Officers and staff. When Donaldson was asked how things were going with Northmet, he used to reply "Plenty of load". His cheerfulness was a welcome change from the usual mood at 55 Broadway, where the finances of the LPTB were not satisfactory (and the finances of the United Railways of Havana , of which Lord Ashfield was also the Chairman, were much worse than those of the LPTB). Supplying electricity during the continuous housing and industrial development of the north London suburbs was a rewarding business.

Lord Ashfield, having seen the press report of a power failure caused by a mistaken operation, asked Captain Donaldson the name of the engineer responsible. Captain Donaldson's immediate reply was "Donaldson, Sir." Ashfield, suspecting that Donaldson was disguising something, asked him again. Donaldson's reply was "Donaldson, Sir: I am responsible for all the accidents of my engineers".

Before his retirement in 1942 Donaldson had planned Northmet's last generating station at Rye House which was completed by the British Electricity Authority.

Apart from his technical duties, Capt Donaldson played an active part in the promotion of the interests both of his professional and of the electrical industry generally. He was Chairman of the Council of the Electrical Development Association in 1929/30 at the time when the late Dr S Z de Ferranti was President, and during his term of office a committee was set up to report on the possibility of securing the general adoption of a two-part tariff with a uniform low secondary charge. Mr E Auckland at St Albans helped with calculations for the new two-part tariff based on the floor area of the house. At nationalisation this became a standard charge.

The application of the Whitley Council principle to the electricity supply section of the industry proved an outstanding success. For some five years Capt Donaldson was one of the representatives of the Power Companies Association on both the National Joint Board and the National Joint Industrial Council. He was also for nearly 10 years a representative on the No.10 JIC (ie, the London district) for the Provincial Electric Supply Corporation. He also represented the power companies on the London and Home Counties Joint Electricity Authority.

Donaldson was brought out of retirement at Nationalisation and appointed to the Board of Eastern Electricity, where his membership helped to reassure his former staff that their traditions and interests would be protected. His final retirement from the Board came at the end of 1954.

Captain Donaldson was a bachelor, but had about a dozen godchildren who, when young, called him Don John. Each Christmas he would give a party for Godchildren Unlimited, which consisted of a theatre matinee followed by tea at his club, the Junior Army and Navy.

One of his Godchildren writes of vivid memories of staying with him in St Albans in Jan 1929 for the AGM of 'Godchildren Unlimited', when there was an enormous snow storm. He decided that he had better inspect the damage to overhead lines for himself, and give direct support to his staff. "We were driven in his enormous aluminium-bodied Lanchester by his devoted chauffeur, Reed, who had, I think, been his batman during the war, right up to St.Neots, stopping frequently to talk with staff, and then across to Rugby, where he put me on the train for Liverpool".

"Skipper" (as many people called him) Donaldson had a 28ft gaff rigged river cruiser yacht *Kenmure* on the Broads, in which he had substituted batteries in place of the ballast, and had an electric motor driving a propeller, which caused the boat to glide along quietly with no signs of what was propelling it[8]. Each winter the batteries were stored in Northmet's St Albans Works. The first thing to do each season was to lift the batteries into the car and then put them in the yacht, returning them at the end of the year. In 1953 when Mr Donaldson sold the yacht he was in his 75th year. He had made 77 cruises in her totalling 5,137 miles. The boat is still in existence. He also had a smaller yacht, *Morning Calm* from 1939 but, as it was wartime, it got little use and he sold it after the war.

The District Manager persuaded the St Albans Sports Club to alter the rules to allow for four outside members to be picked by the Manager. The result was that for several years St Albans won the tennis tournament. Captain Donaldson was asked if he would look in his attic for a suitable trophy. He produced a metal model of a Spanish galleon, sails set, complete with a candle holder and candle labelled "In case of cuts". This then appeared in a glass fronted case as the trophy.

Donaldson had a grass tennis court at his St Albans home but he did not play tennis very well.

Donaldson was a liveryman of the Fishmongers Company and a governor of Christs Hospital. He liked pretty girls around him but never, as far as is known, made advances to any of them. He later admitted that when in his late teens he thought that women were anatomically different with feet more like duck's flippers on the end of legs about a foot long (in the days when women wore skirts to the ground).

Donaldson was an active member of Toc H, a diligent prison visitor and worked with the Prisoners' Aid Society to rehabilitate ex-offenders. In the depths of the Depression it was said in Northmet that it was easier to get a job if you had been in prison than if you had had a blameless career.

After his retirement, he interested himself in local politics and, bringing his business experience to bear, radically reorganised the running of municipal

---

[8] This may not have been Donaldson's first electric boat. On 28th September 1927 he reported to the Northmet Management Meeting (ref min 704) that he had purchased two of the electric launches from the BEE at Wembley, including fresh batteries at a cost of about £250. On 24th November it was recorded that one of these had been handed over to the Lee Conservancy (ref Min 754) but no mention is made of what happened to the other.

affairs in St Albans. He was elected Mayor after only a very short period on the town council. He was also heavily involved with St Albans Abbey for many years. His last years were sad, since he developed Alzheimer's disease. When he died, he was cremated and his ashes buried in the north churchyard of St Albans Abbey. Two fine electric chandeliers were made in his memory and hung for many years above the shrine of St Alban.

This account has been prepared from information supplied by Messrs A Bull, P C Bourne, B Eady, N Newbold, D B Welbourne, E Wright, Miss M Thody, the late C T Melling and The Electrical Review *5th June 1931.*

EMILE GARCKE

Emile Garcke was born in Saxony in 1856 and became a naturalised British subject in 1880. He joined the Anglo-American Brush Electric Light Corporation Ltd as secretary in 1883, becoming manager in 1887 and managing director of its successor company, The Brush Electrical Engineering Co Ltd, in 1891. He was a firm believer in the possibilities of electric traction and, with his financial friends, including other Brush directors, set up the British Electric Traction Co Ltd in 1896, becoming its managing director. By 1904 the BET group consisted of 66 companies, mostly concerned with tramways and electric power, with Emile Garcke as the moving spirit of the whole vast enterprise, which in 1906 operated 15% of all British tramways and carried 11% of passengers. He was chairman of the MET from its formation to 1929 and then deputy chairman until his death on 14 November 1930[9].

He was a Member of the Institution of Electrical Engineers; Member of the Institute of Transport; Member of the executive committee of the Federation of British Industries; President of the British Electrical and Allied Industries Research Association; Chairman of the Electrical Section of the London Chamber of Commerce; Vice President of the Tramways and Light Railways Association; Chairman Brush Electrical Engineering Co; Director of Electrical and General investment Co; Past President of British Electrical Federation; Deputy Chairman of British Electric traction Co; Deputy Chairman of the British institute of Philosophical Studies; Chairman of executive of Industrial co-partnership Association.

---

[9] Metropolitan Electric Tramways by C S Smeeton, LRTL p221

His publications included: 'Factory Accounts, Their Principles and Practice'; article on Commercial Aspects of Electricity in 'Encyclopaedia Britannica'; 'Individual Understanding: A layman's Approach to Practical Philosophy'. Probably his best known publication was his 'Manual of Electrical Undertakings' published annually from 1896. Publication continued after his death until electricity nationalisation.

He lived at Ditton Meads, near Maidenhead and was a member of the Garrick, Authors' Club and the RAC

WILLIAM MADGEN

William Leonard Madgen was born in 1862 and became a pupil at the School of Electrical Engineering in London. In 1882 he became a district manager with the National Telephone Company, and in 1892 founded the journal *Lighting*, later the *Electrical Times*. From 1893 he was engaged in developing the Ferranti meter business, and in 1896 helped to found the Municipal Electrical Association. He helped to set up the original BET-owned North Metropolitan Electrical Power Distribution Co Ltd, becoming a BET director in 1899. After the Brush Electrical Engineering Co Ltd joined the BET group he became a director of Brush in 1902, managing director from 1903 to 1908, then vice-Chairman until 1924. He was one of the original directors of the MET, continuing in office until 22 June 1923. He died in January 1925[10].

JOE SALTER

A man of diverse interests, Mr Salter's linguistic inclinations may have stemmed from his descent from a distinguished Armenian family. Born in Guernsey and educated at Exeter, he followed family wishes to become an officer in the Regular Army, but in 1920 he resigned his commission to take a four-year course at Faraday House where his application to his studies gained him both gold and silver medals. Not content with this he took an external BSc while involved for a short time with private industry, eventually taking an appointment as a junior engineer at Enfield, later becoming relay engineer at Northmet House.

---

[10] Metropolitan Electric Tramways by C S Smeeton, LRTL p221

Recalled as a Reservist in 1939, Captain Salter worked in the London area on electrical and mechanical installations, "building them up as the Germans knocked them down". Meanwhile, he took the Foreign Office course in Russian, passing the Royal Society of Arts advanced examination so that when the war ended he was in demand as an interpreter on vessels engaged on the repatriation of Russians taken prisoner in various parts of Europe by the Nazis.

Back at Northmet House, Joe Salter assumed his job as third assistant engineer (relays) but his Russian came into use for the visit, with a party of engineers, of Mr Malenkov. "I think we were the only people who were able to give them descriptive material in their own language" he said. "Much of my work on languages has had to be shelved but I am looking forward to going ahead with it all in my retirement." He possessed a working knowledge of Esperanto and "dabbled", as he put it, in Chinese. He was known to have left messages written in vertical format Chinese characters on substation door pillars.

Even if he was to weary of roots, conjugations and declensions he had plenty of alternative interests. A large gauge 1 model railway included engines and control gear of his own design and construction. He also had an interest in edible fungi and was well-known for visiting rural substations in the autumn to satisfy his interest. "There are almost unlimited numbers of fungi which are quite pleasant to eat and there is really only one deadly species, Phalloides, of the genus Amaneta."[11]

One day Mr Salter was testing the protection on a 22kV line parallel to the main railway line. The railway track circuits all failed. Next morning he produced a newspaper cutting "Unusual sun spot activity yesterday interfered with communication circuits".

He was renowned for the number of driving accidents he had, He kept a file of all the insurance claims. On one occasion an engineer and a fitter were to go with Mr Salter to a remote substation. The fitter and engineer were in another car, "Don't drive in front of Mr Salter", the fitter said, " he is sure to run into you". They arrived at the substation, the engineer pulling safely in behind Joe's car, whereupon Joe reversed smartly into the engineer's car[12]!

---

[11] From EEB *Magazine*
[12] PC W Killick

He retired to Bury St Edmonds.

CHRISTOPHER SPENCER

Christopher John Spencer was born in 1876, the son of a tramways manager, and in 1889 was apprenticed to the Blackpool Electric Tramway Company. Whilst there he devised the carbon brush for use in traction motors, which had hitherto had brushes of brass, and the directors awarded him a sovereign for this invention. In 1892 he became electrician to the South Staffordshire Tramways, where his father was resident engineer, and in 1898, at the early age of 22, he became general manager of Bradford Corporation Tramways. During his 20 years at Bradford he designed, with the help of his father, the Spencer Slipper Brake for use on steep gradients, and the variable-gauge equipment which enabled cars to work from the 4 ft. Bradford system onto the standard gauge Leeds tramways. He was President of the Municipal Tramways Association in 1910.

During the 1914-18 war Spencer was seconded to the Admiralty as an assistant director of its labour division. Whilst there, he doubtless met Sir Albert Stanley (later Lord Ashfield), chairman of the Underground group of companies, who was then President of the Board of Trade. During 1918 Bradford Corporation pressed for Spencer's release from the Admiralty but it seems probable that Spencer was approached by Sir Albert Stanley and invited to accept the post of tramways manager to the London & Suburban Traction group.

Spencer's appointment took effect from 1 November 1918, at a salary of £1,500, as manager of the MET and LUT; on 24 January 1919 he was also appointed manager of the SMET. His name thereafter appeared on the cars, and his title was changed to General Manager from 28 January 1921. The many developments on the MET during his managership are evidence of his progressive outlook and his 1926 paper on tramcar design foreshadowed the research programme which culminated in the Feltham cars. On the formation of the LPTB in 1933 he was designated Tramways Manager (Northern and Western Areas) but resigned later that year, becoming a Resident Director at Northmet's Brimsdown power station. Before taking up his duties with Northmet, he went on a tour of South Africa. He retired from Northmet in January 1941 and moved to Swansea. He died in 1950.[13]

---

[13] G E Badderley *The Tramways of Croydon* LRTA 1973 ISBN 0900433 906

CHAPTER 15: NORTHMET AT WAR

Records of the effect of the Second World War on Northmet are sparse. It is possible that some reports and records would have been regarded as sensitive but it is much more likely that records were disposed of and that little was published.

An Ordinary General Meeting of the Northmet Power Company was held on 12th March 1940 and gives an idea of the impact of the early stages of the Second World War. Lord Ashfield had influenza so his speech was read to the meeting by Sir James Devonshire, the Deputy Chairman.

"I think that at the commencement of my remarks to you this morning I should refer to the fact that this is the first Annual General Meeting of the Company under its new name, The Northmet Power Company. The Company's Bill of last Session received Royal Assent on 25th May and our new title became law. We are happy that the cumbrous designation with which we have lived for so many years is now a thing of the past. We are happy, too, that the change has been so widely welcomed.

"When last we met I do not suppose that any of us thought that war would, in fact, come before our next Annual Meeting. The threat of war had been for months hanging over our heads, but there was a feeling that a way out would be found and that a rational solution of the international difficulties which had arisen would be forthcoming and the tragedy of war averted. Our hopes were not, however, realised and we are here to-day in circumstances very different from those which we then contemplated. The clouds of war have once more descended upon our activities and last September we of the Northmet were conscious of having reached the end of an epoch in our history and of entering upon a period the outcome of which could not clearly be seen.

"Before I review the financial results which are now before you, it will I know be your wish that I should deal briefly with the steps which have been taken to meet the conditions which inevitably arise from war and to refer to the effect of those conditions upon the Company's position in so far as it can be ascertained at this point in time.

"The outbreak of war divided the year 1939 into two distinct and sharply contrasted parts. During the first eight months of the year our business continued to develop in accordance with the trends which had prevailed for many years. The rate of growth in the revenue was comparable with previous experience. The number of units of electricity sold to consumers either directly or indirectly showed an increase of about 18 per cent over the number sold in the corresponding period of the previous year. The number of new consumers connected by the Company was 12,349. Development continued and our distribution system was expanding at the rate to which we have become accustomed in recent years. The general operating conditions were typical of previous years. The prospects seemed favourable and had normal conditions been experienced throughout the year there is little doubt that the gross revenue for 1939 would have shown an increase in keeping with previous years.

"Whilst the rate of expansion in consumption was satisfactorily maintained in the first eight months of the year, there was one disturbing factor in our experience and that was the continuous rise in the price of coal. The price of coal has been rising progressively during the last three years. You will remember that I drew attention to this factor in my speech to you in 1938 and that Sir James Devonshire also referred to it in the course of his remarks at the last Annual Meeting. By August last the average price of coal purchased by the Company had increased since 1936 by no less than 44 per cent. Apart from wages, coal constitutes the largest single element in the Company's working expenses; the high level to which the price had risen was causing your Directors concern and it may have been, even if normal conditions had continued, that some upward adjustment in charges would have been necessary to ensure that a part of the burden which the increase imposed upon the Company was shared with the consumers. Nevertheless, the results up to the end of August were to be regarded as generally satisfactory, and as we look back we see how fortunate we were to have raised when we did the additional capital monies required by your subsidiary, the North Metropolitan Power Station Company, Limited, to finance the extension of Brimsdown "B" Generating Station and the reconstruction of the Willesden Generating Station.

"Whilst the coming of the war meant the frustration of our hopes, we were ready to place the undertaking upon a war footing at a moment's notice. Preparations had been made for the establishment of a war organization. The Company's obligations under the Civil Defence Act, 1939, had been discharged. Air raid precautionary measures had been undertaken for the protection of the staff at the generating stations and sub-stations and at the Head Office, branch offices, showrooms and repair depots, and steps had been taken to ensure the maintenance of supplies under all conditions. Emergency stocks of coal, cable and other essential requirements had been assembled. Schemes for the training of the staff in first aid, fire fighting and in gas protection had already been introduced. In fact, all measures had been taken to enable the undertaking to withstand the strain which war conditions would impose and to be in a position to carry on its essential public service. The organization which has been set up has, fortunately, not yet been tested. but if the time should come when our area is subject to enemy attack from the air I am sure that this organization will prove its worth. These precautionary measures have involved the Company in considerable expenditure, but some part of this expenditure may be recouped by grants from the Government under the Civil Defence Act.

"London, in common with all the great cities of the country, was bound to feel the impact of modern war to a greater extent than other areas. Your Company is fortunate in possessing an area which, while mostly within the Metropolitan zone, consists mainly of suburban and rural districts on the outskirts of the more densely populated sections which comprise central London. Nevertheless, a not inconsiderable portion of the Company's area is classified under the Government's scheme as an evacuation area, and the coming of war saw the evacuation or "scattering" as Mr A P Herbert would have us say, of a large number of the consumers in the nearer London districts from which we derive the greater part of our revenue from domestic supplies. This loss was to some extent offset by an influx of population into the more northerly reception areas, but the consequential additional consumption of electricity in those areas was small in proportion to the reduction sustained in the areas nearer the centre.

"With the war there also came the blackout which in turn led to a considerable reduction in the consumption of electricity. Street lighting was cut off; shop windows could not be illuminated. The general restriction of lighting tended, in any event at the outset, to impose a limitation in the use of electricity in the home. The fall in consumption in the first months of the war due to the blackout was of serious dimensions and it was greatly intensified by the provision contained in the original Fuel and Lighting Order that consumption should be reduced by 25 per cent. This Order was subsequently modified, but during the time it was in force the effect was harmful from the revenue point of view, for the greatest economy in the use of electricity became the rule in practically every home. I would not go so far as to say that there is no case for economy in the use of electricity in time of war, for care in the use of fuel may be necessary in the National interest. All I am doing here is to point out the consequences of restriction so far as your Company is concerned.

"It is noteworthy, however, that as lives and habits were adjusted to wartime conditions there was a revival in the demand for electricity. Methods of blacking out windows in houses improved. A determination to defeat the blackout seemed to take possession of most people and a well lighted home came to be recognised as a sure antidote to the depressing effect of the absence of lighting in the streets. Then recently shop window lighting has been restored in modified form and now experiments in the illumination of the streets under blackout conditions are being made. The war has also stimulated in certain directions the consumption of electricity for industrial purposes.

"The fall in the total demand during the opening months of the war was in the neighbourhood of 20 to 25 per cent. As I have already said the output to the end of August was approximately 18 per cent, higher than in the previous year. In normal circumstances the increase during the whole of the year would not have been less than this, whereas in point of fact the actual increase over the year was less than 10 per cent. The financial results for the last four months of the year therefore stand in sharp contrast to those for the first eight months. Consumption declined; the number of new consumers was, of course, reduced to relatively small proportions; revenue lacked buoyancy; working expenses increased; the rise in the price of coal continued and the prices of other materials also rose; wage increases took place, and payments began under the Company's scheme for allowances to members of the permanent staff serving with the fighting services. In consequence of these conflicting movements the margin between revenue and expenditure diminished."

The report then went on to record the absorption of the Hendon Electric Supply Company (as from 30th September 1939). The accounts were examined in some detail before concluding:

"Now in looking at the results for 1939 it must be remembered that the year essentially falls into two parts and that the outbreak of war altered, to some extent at least, the course of our affairs. The wartime reduction in consumption and also the increase in working expenses, which goes back to before the war, have had a disturbing effect upon our economy. It is impossible to forecast the trend of events in the future for there are many factors whose influence might be felt and many contingencies for which provision should be made. It is to be anticipated, however, that during the current year the consumption of electricity will be less than for 1939, and it must be assumed that the present enhanced level of prices for coal and other materials will be maintained if, indeed, the level does not rise still further; rates of pay may also be subject to further advance and the total amount of the allowances to members of the staff serving with the Forces will increase, for not only will such allowances be operative throughout the year but additional staff will be called up for military service.

"In these circumstances, it was obvious to your Directors that unless steps were taken to improve the revenue the Company's financial position would be seriously prejudiced. It has therefore been decided that the rates of charge to all consumers who are not supplied under agreements which contain a coal clause shall be increased by 12.5 per cent in respect of electricity consumed as from the meter readings taken on or after 1st March 1940. The increase will not be fully applicable to the year and, owing to the Company's system of continuous meter reading, will only apply on the average to consumption after mid-April. All consumers who are supplied under agreements containing a coal clause are, of course, already paying increased charges for their electricity.

"In view of the Company's previous record of progressive reductions in charges, I need hardly tell you that this decision was reached only after a careful review had been made of the Company's position and after every alternative and its consequences had been exhaustively considered. The decision was taken with regret, for it involved the reversal of a policy which had been followed for many years and which had produced such a marked expansion of our business. We left the decision as long as we could, but in the end there was no escape from the fact that the cost of producing the commodity sold had increased beyond what the Company could in fairness be called upon to bear, and it was clear that if we were to maintain a secure financial basis for the conduct of the business the consumers must take up some part of the burden which had been placed on the Company. The Company can justly claim that it has always dealt fairly with its consumers; their interests have at all times been of first importance in the fashioning of our policy and the direction of our undertaking. Whenever it was possible, charges have been lowered. The average revenue per unit from those supplies which will now be subject to the 12.5 per cent increase was reduced as a direct result of the policy of lowering rates from 3.03d in 1929 to 1.35d in 1939, or by 55 per cent. And here I may perhaps remind you that the maintenance of sound financial position for your Company is as much in the interest of the consumers as of the stockholders, for upon it depends not only the credit of the Company and its ability to raise fresh capital for extensions at a low rate of interest but also the efficient maintenance and operation of the undertaking. There can be no expansion without capital and the demand for additional facilities which will undoubtedly follow upon the conclusion of the war can only be met on a basis satisfactory to the consumer if the Company's credit in the money market stands high and its general financial position is strong.

"During the war we shall seek to provide the same standard of service to our consumers as we did before the war. There will be no relaxation on our part and the high reputation which the Company has had for so many years will be jealously guarded. It must of course be recognised that restrictions may be imposed upon us and that capital expenditure will be reduced to a minimum in the National interest. But I would earnestly assure all concerned that we seek no advantage from the present emergency. The aim of the Company is and will be the same as it has always been in the past, namely, to supply electricity at the lowest possible prices consistent with the proper and efficient maintenance of their undertaking.

"It is not possible for me this morning to say very much about the future. For each and every one of us it contains an element of uncertainty in greater or less degree and so it is with your Company. The war will inevitably produce problems of great complexity, but we shall face them resolutely and however great the difficulty endeavour to find a satisfactory solution, so that when peace is restored the Company will be in a position to take its part in the work of National reconstruction and the progress in our affairs which the war would appear to have interrupted may be resumed. We are fortunate in many ways; in the situation of our area, in the diversified character of the demand made upon us, in the strength and resiliency of our finances and in the resource and ability of the officers and staff who serve us. For my own part I view the future with hope and with confidence.

"I think you will wish to know that at the present time over 500 members of the Company's staff are serving with HM Forces. Early in the war we decided that those members of our permanent staff who were serving with the fighting services should receive from the Company an allowance equivalent to one-half of their normal standard rate of pay. Such a scheme was in operation during last war and my colleagues and I are certain that you will approve our decision to revive the scheme during the present war.

"If I may take up a few more minutes of your time there are one or two other matters that I should mention to you. In the first place, I would refer to the subsidiary companies. The capital expenditure of the North Metropolitan Power Station Company during the year; mainly in connection with the extension of the Brimsdown B Station and the purchase of the Willesden Station, amounted to £481,94&. After deducting cost of plant written off, the total capital expenditure of the Station Company at 31st December last was £2,955,189. To provide for the cost of acquisition and reconstruction of the Willesden Station and to complete additional works at the Brimsdown Stations, a £1,700,000 issue of 3.5 per cent Second Mortgage Debenture Stock 1965 was made in June 1939, at a price of 89 per cent. For convenience, this issue and the previous issue of £1,000,000 have been consolidated and amalgamated into one issue called 3.5 per cent Second Mortgage Debenture Stock, Series "B" 1965. The reconstructed Brimsdown "A" Station has been on commercial load throughout the year, and much of the building work in connection with the extension of the Brimsdown "B" Station has been completed.

"The results of the Bishop's Stortford, Epping & District Gas Company for the past year have been satisfactory. The number of consumers increased by 2.7 per cent, and the number of therms of gas sold showed an increase of 3.8 per cent. compared with 1938. The balance from operating is £3,646 more than in 1938 and the Company has been able to maintain the same dividends as in the previous year and to carry forward a slightly increased amount. Improvements have been carried out at the gasworks at Bishop's Stortford and Epping and to provide an increased effective capacity the gasholder at Harlow has been reconstructed.

"Before I conclude I should like to pay tribute to the work of our officers and staff during the past year. Preparation for war in the first eight months and the particularly trying conditions since the war began have imposed no small strain. In one way or another, practically the whole of the staff have had additional work and responsibility placed upon them and from the highest to the lowest they have carried out these extra duties with cheerfulness and industry. I have no hesitation, therefore, in asking you to join with my colleagues and myself in placing on record our sincerest thanks and our appreciation of their splendid services."

This was the 'phoney war' period before there had been many air raids. A few months later, things would be very different. Because of Government restrictions on the issuing of accounts and annual reports there is no corresponding report for the subsequent war years. However, later in 1940, Captain Donaldson wrote a departmental letter to his staff:

"As I look through the War Damage reports every day and go round the District, I cannot help feeling that I should like to express individually to that devoted body of men whom I refer to above as 'Duty Engineers' the appreciation and gratitude of the Management for the really arduous work which is being put in day by day, or perhaps I should rather say "night by night". There seems some prospect of a lull in enemy action although, of course, one cannot bank on this, but it may afford some measure of relief from the strain which must be particularly felt in some of the nearer London undertakings, which have suffered more heavily than other Districts

"The duties of these men call them out at very uncomfortable times in the black-out in order to make sure that there is no danger from electricity to the unfortunate people whose houses have been shattered or demolished and not infrequently also to restore interrupted supply. The former duty often involves witnessing what must be extremely harrowing scenes, while the other involves a very thorough knowledge of the Supply System and a considerable degree of judgement.

"On more than one occasion, outsiders have expressed their surprise at the manner in which supply was got on again during the dark hours, when work in a substation must be exceedingly difficult, and such implied congratulations are undoubtedly well deserved.

"I have been particularly struck with the handling of very difficult situations by the control staff at Northmet House who, I think, are heartily to be congratulated on the efficiency with which they rapidly size up and deal with them, and I think that the cooperation between them and the Outside Staff is extraordinarily good.

"In referring particularly to the Duty Engineers, I do not wish, in any way to deprecate the work of what I might call the Shift Engineers at the Power Stations and so forth, who continue to work round the clock in what are very noisy and disturbing conditions, nor of the Superintendents, who have a greater burden of responsibility than their Juniors.

"The work of the repair gangs has been speedy and invaluable and they certainly have had their hands full, both with overhead lines and cables.

"I cannot, from the nature of things, speak to everybody personally, but I shall be glad if you will make the contents of this letter known to those who are concerned, at the same time expressing the hope of all of us that conditions may become easier as time goes on."

The Company was justly proud of the part the staff played in the war. Out of a pre-war male staff of 4020, 1566 or 39%, had by June 1944 joined the Forces or taken on some full-time Civil Defence or war work[1].

Northmet was unable to provide the same standard of service to its consumers as it did before the war because, in common with every other undertaker, the Company's activities were regulated or restricted by a large number of emergency measures introduced by the Government. The staff was considerably curtailed by the calls of the Forces and the Civil Defence Services.

New or additional supplies of electricity could only be afforded in cases where they were clearly shown to be required for or in connection with the war effort or for domestic or other purposes where serious or exceptional hardship would result if the supply was not provided. This considerably interfered with the Company's development policy and practically stopped the sale of electrical apparatus and appliances.

The clerical staff was most seriously affected by the calls of the Forces. No less than 83%, of the Company's male permanent clerical staff were serving with the Forces in June 1944. The vacancies thus caused were temporarily filled mainly by women and there were then 734 women on the staff compared with 280 pre-war. In addition to undertaking clerical duties the women worked in the

---

[1] Kingsbury & Boys *Outline History of Northmet*

showrooms, the power stations, in the meter repair department and as meter readers.

The meter test station also became involved in some semi-official work in conjuction with ERA on the detection of flaws in the plywood used for making Mosquito aircraft and in testing devices to record the accuracy of gun turret control in tanks[2].

Several members of the staff serving with the Forces earned distinctions; two were awarded the DFC, one of whom had previously been awarded the DFM and Bar; three earned the MBE; two the DSM and one the MM and a number attained senior rank in the Services. Regrettably by August 1943, 33 members of the staff had lost their lives whilst serving their country and 51 had been reported missing or were prisoners of war.

The problems affecting the Electricity Supply Industry during the war years are described fully by Dr Leslie Hannah[3] and Northmet were as much affected as any other undertaking.

At the beginning of the war the workshop at St Albans was converted to an air raid shelter, the windows blocked and sandbagged. The caretaker made tea only, twice a day, and had a large tray for about 60 cups which he filled and then carried the tray down the stairs and to all the offices. With the war more and more women staff were employed and, wanting something better, brought their own kettles to make tea and coffee. This resulted in blown fuses and a ban from time to time. In a change of policy the women stayed on after the war as more and more staff were required.

Four engineers were available during the war for office work and stand-by duties. The charge engineer and his assistant were available to take telephone calls, there was one lorry driver and two jointers. Office staff were on duty at night, sleeping in the offices. Cables for air raid warning bells were laid over the roofs of the buildings in the city centre. The Commercial engineer and his family were killed by a bomb. Cars were provided with identification plates REPAIR PARTY ELECTRICITY.

---

[2] F Boysen.
[3] Hannah L *Electricity Before Nationalisation*, Macmillan, 1979 ISBN 0333 220862

The neon signs at the showrooms were removed and the show window was used for display but without any lighting.

After the war, St Albans offices were, by now, not large enough so a third floor was added at the back of the building. Space in the office was very limited so some plan chests were removed and the 1/500 plans were hung in a long cupboard. Shelves carried a set of electricity standards in green files and all the wayleave agreements. Critical Path Analysis was introduced as a new technique but did not help with the type of work carried out.

During and after the war, everything was in short supply. Certificates were required for the use of iron and steel so existing houses could not be fitted with new wiring. A few cables were laid for pre war housing developments and for essential supplies. The direct labour gangs had long gone so a gang was formed from Italian prisoners of war, laying unarmoured cables covered with clay tiles.

Prefabricated houses were designed and erected on new estates with 3kV kiosk substations connected to the existing system. The new estate at Welwyn Garden City was outside the old boundary and was therefore supplied from the adjacent Northmet 3kV system. This meant that the consumers had to travel to Hatfield to pay their accounts so a mobile showroom was provided. When the boundary was altered supply changed to the new Welwyn 11kV system and the phase colours were changed, it also became the only estate in Welwyn Garden City with 5 core cables.

The 'prefabs' had an electric cooker and a dual element immersion heater to provide a large or small amount of hot water. The house was so compact that it was possible to stand in the bath and cook your breakfast. 'EDA' consumer units were fitted with the new 30 amp ring main and 13 amp plugs and sockets. These were of two types the Dorman Smith round pin with the fuse in the pin and the MK rectangular pin with the fuse inside the plug. The round pin version gradually disappeared and was replaced by the MK in brown and white, sockets with and without switches and plugs with and without switches. The slot for inspection of the earth wire connection was still provided. A contractor wiring a bungalow said that he would provide a ring main all round the roof space and drop spurs to each socket outlet, but no, this was not in accordance with the regulations which said that half the sockets had to be directly on the ring.

Another query was about the practice of taking the cooker wiring in a house up to the roof, across the loft and all the way down to the cooker.

Mr Grierson at Northmet House designed the Northmet immersion heater which was fitted from inside the tank via an 8" hand hole. The hole for the heater was plain so that the heater element could be turned to the correct position relative to the water, the thread was outside as was the nut so that the thread did not corrode, It is not known if this design was used in quantity. In 1947 everything went wrong. There was very severe weather, A shortage of coal which arrived in the railway wagons frozen solid and a shortage of generating plant at the same time as everyone wanted more electricity. Drastic measures were taken usually by shedding domestic consumers every evening and running at 48 cycles during the day then attempting to catch up at night. Both of these methods upset the Southern Railway whose track circuits were tuned to 50 cycles. The catching up was abandoned and the system ran at 48 cycles for several weeks resulting in a loss of 5½ hours which was never recovered and was finally 'written off'.

Consumers did not know, as their supply was on and off several times. This slow running was found years later to have permanently damaged the generators. As well as these problems everybody had their turn at strikes, some very extended, and in total occupied about 10 years. One strike at Brimsdown was covered by engineers from the districts volunteering, and Royal Navy stokers (not volunteers) to run the generators for one week but it was never done again. The Conspiracy and Protection of Property Act was repealed so engineers could now have their turn at a strike, for one day, and finally received a 25% pay rise.

CHAPTER 16: NATIONALISATION

Legally the two Northmet companies ceased to exist on 1st April 1948, the Power company passing to the Eastern Electricity Board and the Power Station company to the British Electricity Authority, later CEGB. However the legacy of Northmet lived on as EEB's Northmet Sub Area.

A Local Advisory Committee was formed and the Suggestion Scheme introduced. Some engineers were authorised to use their private cars receiving an allowance and Mr Dunkerley at Northmet House accepted insurance as an agent for the White Cross Insurance Company. In turn he paid back half of his commission. It was said that he used to insure the company vehicles.

The new management decided that, rather than throw the whole enterprise into turmoil, they would build on what they had inherited. Cecil Melling, the first EEB Chairman, wrote[1] that the Board acknowledged the good work performed by the employees of the 38 undertakings, and their approach to impending nationalisation was a recognition of the importance of the human aspects of electricity supply in effecting smooth transition to the new regime. Most of the Board's employees had been engaged in the work of the former undertakings, each with its own historical development, traditions and loyalties; undertakings which, in most cases, had expanded rapidly in the previous decades to the general satisfaction of consumers, employees and owners.

Among employees, there was pride, though generally unspoken, in the work of their undertakings and, on the whole, satisfaction in their own work. This resulted from feelings of mutual dependence among employees working in the smaller undertakings and in the relatively small operating units of the large ones as well as on good relations between management and employees. Of course, in the pre-vesting undertakings, as in all organisations, there were times of frustration and grumbling, but, in general, there was satisfaction and good feeling and, with good feeling, good work.

Pride was felt particularly by senior and middle management in the larger undertakings, such as Northmet Power Company. Senior employees were justifiably proud of their company, which was widely regarded as one of the best

---
[1] Melling CT: *Light in the East* Eastern Electricity 1987 ISBN 0904 064 14X

undertakings in the industry, and the staff were conscious of that distinction. They had little or no wish to be nationalised and there was sorrow and some resentment at the prospect of being absorbed into a new Board, which, it was feared, might have little sympathy with Northmet traditions.

The Board felt that it would have been an act of folly to attempt to extinguish or diminish these traditions and that it was important to safeguard and build on the loyalties and goodwill of the company's employees. Fortunately, J M Donaldson, general manager for many years until his retirement in 1942, had generously agreed to a personal appeal to accept nomination to the Board, where his membership helped to reassure his former staff that their traditions and interests would be protected[2].

Apart from Captain Donaldson, the other last Directors of the Northmet Company (Sir Reginald Blair, Mr G W Spencer Hawes, Mr K A Scott Moncrieff and the Rt Hon William Morrison) seem to have had nothing further to do with EEB. However, the Chief Commercial Officer was Mr G E Barrett, formerly commercial manager, Northmet Power Co. Mr Barrett died 8 July 1948 and was succeeded by a Mr E A Fowler who was not a Northmet man. The Board's Chief Accountant was J E Blair, formerly Northmet Secretary and Accountant.

Northmet's last General Manager was Mr W N C Clinch who did not join EEB but became Eastern Divisional Controller, British Electricity Authority.

At the lower levels of the hierarchy, most of the local Resident Engineers became District Managers or District Engineers in the new organisation. From then on, engineers seem to have been gradually squeezed out of management roles in the organisation.

The final list of Resident Engineers and Engineers in Charge before nationalisation was:

Barnet H P Guy	Friern Barnet W McL Philip
B Stortford W H Hatton Ward	Harrow N Axford
Chingford F G Bromley	Hendon G C Chamberlain
Edmonton G F Halton	Hertford R F Winder
Enfield F H Long	Royston F J Drake
	St Albans R A Voit

---
[2] Melling CT *Light in the East* EEB, 1987 ISBN 0904064 14X

Southgate W R B Wood
Stevenage J C Horell
Tottenham C A Baker

Wembley T Hollis
Wood Green C E Hollingsworth

The new districts were Finchley (C Bradley), Hornsey (C March), Letchworth (H C Sumner) and Welwyn Garden City (P T Bullen). Northmet had 19 out of the new Board's 43 districts[3].

Not everyone came quietly into the EEB fold. It was said that some of the non-Northmet undertakings were resentful of losing their independence and useful records were maliciously destroyed. This is said to have happened at Welwyn Garden City and Hornsey which, together with Letchworth, Hitchin and Finchley became part of the new sub-area.

The Board's new area was essentially rural, in contrast to the southern part of Northmet. EEB initially kept to small, manageable districts. It was decided that no work should be centralised unless it was clear that centralisation would result in a very real improvement in operational efficiency. The sub-area was under the control of a sub-area manager, Mr C C Hill, who had been Northmet's assistant general manager. He was directly responsible to the Board's Chairman and Deputy Chairman. He was assisted by the sub-area Engineer, the sub-area Commercial Officer, the sub-area Accountant and the sub-area Secretarial Officer, each receiving technical instructions from, and reporting to, the corresponding Chief Officer at Headquarters.

EEB's Districts had a District manager, A District Engineer, a District Commercial officer and a District Clerk. Some of the Districts had branches or outstations depending on local needs. The whole arrangement was dynamic in that it changed over the following years.

Although, in the original arrangement, a few small undertaking areas had been amalgamated with larger ones, it became clear, when cost data became available, that many of the Board's original districts were too small for economic operation. Analysis of districts' costs showed that taking all factors into account, a district of 20,000 consumers had materially higher costs per consumer than one of 30,000, which in turn, was somewhat more costly than a 50,000 consumer district. Beyond that size, there seemed to be a further, though smaller economy

---

[3] EEB *First Report and Accounts, 1948–49*

but the data then available on costs and service were insufficient to justify conclusions on the optimum sizes of urban and rural districts.

In amalgamating small districts with one another or with larger neighbouring districts, the Board had regard to their original intention, namely "securing Districts small enough to make it possible for the District Manager and his senior officers to maintain close contact with all consumers and with all employees in the District, thus avoiding any loss of that personal touch in consumer service, which was one of the most valuable achievements of the former undertakings." As far as could be judged, contacts with consumers and employees were satisfactory in medium and larger districts and there seemed to be no reason why, under good management, such conditions should not be achieved in districts which were to be merged, although, inevitably, there would be a period of some disturbance before amalgamations could be successful.

Although there was a clear case for the merging of small districts, caution was necessary. At the least, a merger would cause inconvenience to staff and, in the majority of cases, concern about a possible change in their work. More serious would be worry about the possible need to move home or change occupation. The trade unions, employees and joint committees involved in forthcoming mergers were therefore consulted on the processes of implementation, and care was taken to minimise inconvenience and disappointment to staff whose place of work would be changed. Some, having reached retiring age, left the Board. Others, the majority, elected to take up work in the new location, but some, wishing to avoid removal or longer travel, transferred to work elsewhere. Care was taken to avoid feelings, by staff in a small district, of having been absorbed, or, on the other hand, feelings in the larger districts of having absorbed the smaller one; such feelings were minimised by rearrangement of accommodation in the offices of larger districts in which the new districts would be stationed, so that all staff shared a sense of innovation. Merger operations were well handled by the sub-area managers and others concerned and, in achieving economies, they had careful regard to welfare of staff.

It did not always work. For many years the staff of the former Southgate district were resentful towards their Wood Green colleagues following a merger and there was still a tendency for outside staff to continue to work in their old area.

The Board had inherited an industry that was still feeling the effects of the war and post-war economies. Everywhere, including the ex-Northmet districts, there were reports of overloading and the need for reinforcement of the distribution system. Thus the first few years of nationalisation in the Northmet sub-area were a time of expansion and development. New mains were laid, new substations were installed. A more scientific way of designing low voltage distribution systems was developed for Farley Hill, Luton, and adopted by the rest of the Board, including Northmet.

There was an additional challenge in the designation of six new towns in the Board's area and four of these (Harlow, Hatfield, Stevenage and Welwyn) were in the Northmet Sub-Area.

The connection of New Towns and new housing estates was capital expensive and the Board saw little prospect of a profit, or even of breaking even, unless many consumers used electric cookers water-heaters and other appliances. Where, as in some cases, the wiring installation was inadequate for the use of electrical appliances, or the housing authority discouraged such use, or provided free gas cookers or gas water-heaters, there was no prospect of covering the Board's costs by the sale of electricity on normal tariffs, and such a housing estate would require a continuing subsidy from the general body of consumers. Consequently, in 1950, the Board decided that the provision of supplies to new housing estates could not be given without a capital contribution, "unless it seemed reasonably probable that as soon as the present need for stringent economy had passed, the occupiers of the new houses would make adequate use of the supply afforded to them". The Board were prepared to assume that if the new houses were suitably wired so as to give tenants a free choice in the matter, consumers would choose in the long run to take full advantage of the supply of electricity made available to them. A "Freedom of Choice" formula was therefore agreed with officers of the New Town Corporations in the Eastern area. In other words, if their tenants were free to choose electricity for cooking and if wiring installations were suitable, with a minimum of one socket-outlet per room, then, except in exceptional circumstances, the Board would waive their right to require a capital contribution towards the cost of connecting supply.

Electricity undertakings were required by law to provide a supply of electricity on the request of any owner or occupier of premises within 50 yards of any distribution main, and in doing so, to provide without charge an electric line for connection up to a length of 60 feet not on property owned by or in possession of the occupant. The Board decided, however, to offer terms which were more generous than the legal requirement. For the connection of a new consumer by underground cable, the Board provided, without charge, the necessary service cable up to 60 feet in length on property owned or occupied by the consumer plus up to 60 feet not on the consumer property. For a connection by overhead line, the length of service line provided without charge on the consumer's property was 90 feet. At the request of a consumer, payment for excess lengths of cable or overhead line could be spread over five years.

For connection of supplies in rural areas, the Board offered generous terms which required a subsidy for some years from the general body of consumers. Villages and hamlets of six or more premises were connected without a charge towards the cost of mains extension, other than a charge for excess lengths of service line.

For some years prior to Vesting, undertakers had been prevented by Government policy from raising prices charged for electricity. At the same time. wages were increasing. The Eastern Board therefore decided to increase their tariffs. Estimates of the anticipated financial result for the year commencing 1st April 1948 were prepared for each undertaking, on the assumption that undertakings continued as before; i.e. that there had been no nationalisation. These estimates (prepared in most cases by the former owners) showed that, allowing for the effect of a wage increase agreed a month before nationalisation, 21 undertakings expected to make losses and that, including the profit estimated to be made by the other 17 undertakings, the total net loss was expected to be £1,610,000 ie approx. 10% of the revenue expected from the sale of electricity in the year.

First-aid measures were necessary and the Board decided that those tariffs which were unduly low should be increased, instead of making an increase in all tariffs. Allowing for the time to make the detailed examination and estimates, to report to the Board and advertise the proposed increases in the local press, with reasonable notice to consumers, the earliest practicable date of increase was 1 July 1948, but, as meters were read on a continuous rota, it was expressed as an increase in charge for electricity consumed by domestic and commercial consumers in the localities concerned following the first normal meter reading after 30 June 1948. Only about 70–75% of a full year's extra revenue, if operated for a full year, would accrue to the Board in the year ending 31 March 1949 and, in order to moderate the effect of increases on consumers, it was decided not to attempt to correct the whole of the deficiency in the first year. The full effect of tariff increases was not seen until 31st March 1950. This was followed by a gradual alignment of tariffs to bring in a degree of uniformity and standardisation.

Examination showed a variety of accounting practices and procedures. In a few undertakings, accounting machines were used, in others, accounting was done entirely by hand. Even in the Northmet Company, consumers' bills were handwritten, the calculations being on what was described as a "peg-board", a method which, after personal examination of billing practice in the USA by the company's chief accountant (later chief accountant of the Board), was claimed to be as economical as the mechanised billing methods then available, taking all factors into consideration. There was variety, too, in the cost-accounting practices and stores procedures and, of course, in the size of accounting departments, ranging from the large, well-organised department of the Northmet Company to the single bookkeeper, with assistant, in the smallest undertakings[4].

Northmet had taken care to keep the local press on their side and this was continued under the new regime. It was pointed out to District Managers that: "Readers of Newspapers are also consumers of electricity and they should be kept properly informed...". Because of the parlous state of the system, newspaper advertisements were initially concerned with exhorting consumers to use less electricity during peak hours but gradually this changed to advertisements encouraging further development of the Board's business.

Northmet had built up a healthy business carrying out contracting work and hiring out apparatus to consumers. This continued after nationalisation although there continued to be unfounded allegations from other contractors that the Board had some sort of unfair advantage.

An important means of communication with employees was through the Board magazine, containing social and sporting news, personal news of employees and other items contributed by correspondents in each district and sub-area, together with a small ingredient of Board news on developments. Before nationalisation, a magazine had been published on behalf of employees in Northmet and was jealously guarded by contributors and editor. The magazine was welcomed and read by those whom it served. It would have been divisive to have two

---

[4] C T Melling *Light in the East*

competing magazines in a sub-area, the former one and the new Board magazine, so it was agreed, after negotiating with the editors and their colleagues in each of the former magazines, that the Board magazine would be in two parts, namely, a section common to all sub-areas, and a section for each particular sub-area, this special sub-area section being contributed, in the case of Northmet , by those responsible for the former magazine.

The area-wide section of the magazine was occasionally enlivened by articles of a general nature, including contributions by employees who were well known in the sporting world. If the magazine had been given free to employees it was inevitable that a few copies would have been thrown away and left on the ground, so instead a nominal charge of 3d was made. About 9,000 copies of each issue were bought; ie by about 70% of employees, but, when a worrying situation arose, such as the forthcoming merger of two small districts, there was a reduction in sales of about 10% for the next few months in the places concerned, although sales soon came back to about their previous numbers. This was an interesting indication of temporary loss of morale. A further means of communication with employees was the popular edition of the Annual Report. This was short and addressed to employees, presenting information on progress, so that its importance could be appreciated almost at a glance.

By statute, the Industry had to have joint consultation with the trade unions as representatives of the workers. These included local Works Committees under the National Joint Industrial Council for manual staff, Joint staff committees for NJC (administrative) staff and a District Joint Board for technical staff. There were also joint advisory committees which covered health, safety, welfare, education and training. Pay was determined on national scales, some of which depended on units sold, making the Northmet sub-area very attractive for some technical staff.

District or office mergers were clearly a matter for joint consultation, but in what form should a merger be raised in consultation with employees and the joint bodies on which they were represented by their unions? If a statement, supported by relevant data, were put to unions as merely a possibility of merger, it would most likely be judged on the subjective grounds of the feelings of the employees concerned, and the view expressed to the Board would be against merger. The joint consultative bodies were advisory only and unions and employees would most likely feel and maybe say that it was for the Board to make economies and the unions' duty to protect employees.

This method of consultation was in line with a statement made to trade unions on behalf of the Board, defining the scope of joint consultation to be anything to do with the Board's work, except:
(a) Matters of national security, on which the Board had to maintain confidentiality.
(b) Matters which were the province of the negotiating bodies.
(c) Matters which were the province of the Eastern Electricity Consultative Council.
(d) Matters on which premature disclosure would be likely to cause undue concern and alarm to employees.

These formal structures were supplemented by a suggestions scheme, various sports and social clubs and an ambulance branch of first aiders. Some of these facilities had been initiated by the pre-nationalisation Northmet.

Electricity and gas were produced from coal, oil came from the British owned oilfields and refineries so that tankers carried petrol, heating oil, diesel and lubricating oils. Several countries took over the refineries so new ones were built in this country and crude oil was carried in the tankers. The Gas Board started using oil to convert to gas and the CEGB asked the oil companies what they could offer. After passing through the refineries residual oil was left over and was put back in the tankers, taken away, and pumped down the dead oil wells. They were amazed to hear that the CEGB would buy this residual. Several new 2000 kVA coal fired power stations had been built and so the same design was used for oil fired stations with oil tanks which required trace heating to keep the oil warm. The first tanker arrived and so did the inland revenue demanding the oil tax. "Tax? But the Gas Board don't pay any tax for their oil."
"No, they don't burn the oil so they don't pay the tax."
The Government then stepped in and said that more oil tanks should be built, filled with oil, and tax paid.

All this oil was very useful when the coal mines had their strikes. Even so, various types of load shedding was required, mostly based on stages switched by District staff or other arrangements like the 3 day week. The last long strike was met by burning fuels as available so that, if it had come to the bitter end all the power stations would have run out of fuel at the same moment. Attempts were made, by the strikers,to stop chemicals getting to the nuclear stations. The CEGB had their own schedules issued to their substation operators based on two stages of voltage reduction, two stages of automatic disconnection by low frequency and further stages as required by reducing the frequency. Railway supplies were always kept on as long as possible. Stages were restored on the rise of frequency. Further schedules allowed for black starts without any external supply, Some power stations had their own gas turbines which were adapted for this purpose.

Conditions became better, and two gangs of Irish labourers were contracted to lay cables and then to build outdoor substation foundations. Houses without electricity in St Albans City were wired all ready for connection but there were so many that a waiting list about a year long was started for "gas conversions". Complaints that consumers were taken out of turn were sometimes true. If a move was made from an electric house the question was 'do you have an electric cooker?' which received priority. So, having provided supply, the next question was 'but where is your electric cooker?'. Answer: Its a new one still in the showrooms.

The part time fireman who wanted to get up in the middle of the night was told that he could have two lights, one in the bedroom and one in the hall. Years later came the request to connect the rest of the wiring.

To reduce winter demand a new tariff was devised, increasing the price of electricity in the winter and reducing it in the summer. However, this did not go down well with consumers who had new electric cookers and water heaters but often had no electricity. It was left to the cashiers to try and explain that the total was the same and it only lasted one year.

Budget allocations were made for new developments, housing business, factories and reinforcement. The company forms were still used, white 'GM' forms signed by the Sub Area Manager up to £1000, and pink 'BD' up to £3000, signed by the Board. St Albans serial numbers were A, Welwyn was N. A schedule was provided with the cost of all the items and a complete development was assembled on paper. Decisions had been made previously as to the type and equipment of each substation. The District Commercial Engineer produced a revenue estimate, 20% for housing, 33% for factories against the capital cost. Anything over was allocated to reinforcement or else deferred where possible. Years after the work was finished the accountants would close the job and compare the results;

Budgets were prepared for other work, mainly repairs. The accountants did not seem to worry about the amounts entered. Stock lists were examined and reductions made in quantities so that work carried out once a year was regarded as using slow moving stock and the items returned to Central Stores. The solution was to order the items and hold them in the engine room, together with equipment for new substations.

New equipment had to be ordered 2 years ahead of requirements so arrangements were made to produce all the parts which were then assembled to the exact requirements for the job. Therefore all different makes and types were used. Switchgear for 11kV was standard but for the same design to be used at 3kV was a special order and more expensive. To use this gear later at 11kV was again a special requirement and, again, cost money.

The same applied to cable which was drawn as required and was often delivered on the back of an 8 wheel lorry to the office address. The driver was then shown the site and the drum was lowered down skids with the aid of a rope. A tip (10 shillings) was given and claimed from petty cash.

The two year wait also applied to cable for commercial jobs. The commercial assistants were not engineers so that, when the Deep Well Boring Company wanted to test their water pumps, they bought second-hand 11kV switchgear, a transformer, liquid starter and 400 HP motor. A mains Engineer had the job of assembling and testing (including calibrating the starter) and then starting the motor[5].

A new wind generator was designed by De Havilland with the turbine vertical and air drawn up the tower by the hollow propeller blades. Lord Verulam of Gorhambury Estate was a director of Enfield Cables and the generator was erected on his estate for testing, complete with two sets of metering. It was later taken to the Hebrides.

The Rural Electrification Budget was relaxed and more staff were taken on. At the same time the New Towns were proceeding and a monthly return was made of equipment required and substations commissioned. The District Engineer

---

[5] PC E Wright

offered a barrel of beer for completing 20 substations in a month but the highest figure was 18. New forms were used for substation apparatus details which were then entered on the new Kardex system. Defects were discovered, sometimes during maintenance, and reported to Sub Area and to Wherstead. In turn the makers produced new parts which had to be fitted and, again, reported on completion. The office was, in effect, divided between construction and maintenance with fault repairs. Contractors were taken on for high voltage jointing, not always as successful as the Board's own staff.

After nationalisation there was an initial catching up to be done following the lean post-war years. Gradually development slowed down until almost everyone in the Northmet sub-area had an electricity supply. At nationalisation, Northmet had nearly half a million consumers. By 1973 that had reached 625,000 but hardly increased at all thereafter. The number of district offices was reduced by mergers to four (Barnet, Enfield, Hertford and St Albans before Northmet was itself carved up to merge with the three other groups of districts in Eastern Electricity. When this happened there were still 32 showrooms in the former Northmet area, emphasising the value that was still put on sales and service to the consumer.

This, essentially, marked the end of Northmet as an entity. The Sports Association held a 'Farewell Northmet' party on 4th October 1974, there having already been a farewell party at Woodcroft, the Northmet sports ground on 20th September. Although the administration moved out of Northmet House, the Northmet control remained there. Even after the purchase by the Legal & General Assurance Society Ltd in 1975, Eastern Electricity's new control room at Millfield, near Brentwood, was not ready so Northmet Control remained as lodgers until 4th September 1978.

That really was the end.

39: Frank Erridge closes the doors of Northmet House for the last time [*Eastern Electricity*]

INDEX

Acme Electric Company 95
Acton Lane 43, 51, 60
AEC 32
Agricultural shows, local 171
Air raid precautionary measures 241
Alarms 207
Alarms, fault 206
Alarms, spurious 213
Alderman's Hill 82-3
Alexandra Palace 30, 171
Alexandra Park 10, 226
Alperton 114-15
Apparatus Repair Department (ARD) 160, 181, 187
Appliances 3
Arc lamps 79, 99
Arc Suppression Coils 195-7
Area Superintendents 188
Arkley 180
Arnold's 145
Arnos Grove 147
Arnos Grove Estate 145
Ashfield, Lord 32-3, 53, 180, 227, 232, 240

Badge, corporate 175
Baldock 32
Barnet 9, 11, 24, 29, 31, 36, 79, 163-4, 172, 177-8, 180, 188, 221, 263
Barninghams 103
Barring gear 58
Barrowell Green 83, 225
Battery trip supplies 198
BC&H Company 141, 196
Bedfordshire, Cambridgeshire & Huntingdonshire Electricity Company 25, 139, 231
Bentley Priory 105
BET 30-32, 224, 229, 236
Billing 258

Biographical Notes 227
Bishop's Stortford, Epping & District Gas Co. 25, 129, 246
Bishops Stortford 129-30, 134-5, 137-8, 162, 172, 175, 180, 188, 226, 246
Blackbird Substation 104
Blackout 242
Bomber Command 105
Booklets 178
Borehamwood 105, 172
Bourne Hill 83
Boys, Evelyn 150, 228
Brent Street 107
Brimsdown 1-2, 11-12, 23, 26, 34, 43, 46, 51, 80, 121, 128, 134, 175, 181, 200-201, 221, 224-5, 229, 231, 238, 241, 246, 251
Brimsdown Factory 66-7
Brimsdown North 132/33kV Grid Substation 65, 67
Brimsdown South 66-7
British Electric Traction Co (BET) 7, 29, 37, 119, 144, 220, 235
British Electrical Federation 144
British Electricity Authority 253
British Empire Exhibition 1, 104, 111, 114, 116, 152, 223
British Oxygen 71-2, 111, 114
British Railways 226
Broadway, 55 144, 232
Broxbourne 180
Buntingford 172
Bush Hill Park 88-90
Byculllah 89

Cable jointers 192
Cables, 33kV 195
Cables, 5 core 216, 250
Calender 178
Cambridgeshire 139
Camp Field 120

Campfield Press 42
Campfield Road, St Albans 161
Captain Donaldson 33, 58, 180, 223, 229, 253
Carrier technology 205
Carterhatch Lane 93, 100, 102
Cashiers office 157
CATE (Control, Alarm and Telemetry Equipment) 208, 211
CEGB 226, 252
Central Electricity Board (CEB) 33-4, 46, 54, 70-2
Central Stores 181, 187
Cheshunt 11, 13, 16-17, 24, 29-30, 180
Childs Hill 107, 223
Chingford 172, 180-81, 188
Christmas party 152
Church Lane, Tottenham 94-5
Churches 177
Cinemas 84, 99
Civil Defence Act, 1939 241
Clinch, W N C 253
Coal handling 52
Coal, price of 241
Cockfosters 226
Colebrooke, James 147
Colin Deep 103, 107
Colne Valley 25
Colne Valley Electric Supply Co Ltd 32, 108
Commercial 176
Communications and Control 202
Conditions of employment 192
Conspiracy and Protection of Property Act 251
Construction Department 181-2, 198
Consultation, joint 259
Consumer service, after hours 204
Contracting 3, 176
Control, Northmet 202
Control Room 4, 152, 208, 214
Council housing 100, 176
County of London Electric Supply Co Ltd 25

Cranley Gardens 226
Crompton & Co Ltd 107
Cuffley 41, 128
Current limiters 176

DC Bias 217, 219
Delta Enfield 66-7
Demonstration kitchen 157
Demonstrator 164-5
Devonshire, Sir James 53, 229, 240-41
Digswell 181
District offices 188
District Railway 109, 225
Donaldson, Captain 33, 58, 69-70, 72, 180, 223, 229, 253
Donington House 144
Drake, S T 125

East Barnet 13, 17, 19, 30, 172, 178
East Barnet Valley 9, 80, 180
East Finchley 226
Eastcote 109
Eastern Electricity Board 35
Edgware 104, 106, 172, 180-81
Edison Swan Electric Company 12, 90
Edmonton 10-15, 20, 24, 29, 52, 86, 93, 157, 172, 176, 178, 180, 188, 221
Edmonton Cooperative Society 83
Edmonton Green 94
Edmundson's 118, 142
Electric Lighting Act of 1882 5
Electric Lighting (Clauses) Act, 1889 the 8
Electric Lighting Manufacturers' Association 176
Electric lighting orders 6
Electric Power Distribution Co 128
Electric Railway House 31, 144
Electric Supply Corporation 107
Electrical Apparatus Co 121, 123
Electrical Association for Women 164
Electrical Development Association 177, 192, 233

INDEX

Electricity Act, 1882 3
Electricity Commissioners 34-5, 47, 73
Electricity House 165
Electricity (Supply) Act 33
Electricity Supply Co (of Scotland) 24
Elliott Bros 208, 211
Elmhurst Road 88, 223
Elstree 105, 181
Enfield 9-14, 29, 31, 81, 86, 163, 165, 172, 178-80, 188, 195, 221, 263
Enfield Cable Works 91
Enfield Highway 88
Enfield, London Borough of 147
Enfield Rolling Mills 66, 91
Enfield Town 226
Enfield Wash 88
Epping 129-30, 137, 246
Ericsson 205
Evacuation 242
Evelyn House 144
Evening classes 189
Excavators, electrically powered 41

Farewell Northmet' party 263
Farms 177
Feeders, High Voltage 196
Finchley 10-12, 15, 29-30, 32-3, 188, 221
Fireless steam locomotive 53, 229
Firewatch duties 152
First aid 260
First Garden City Ltd 32
Fore Street 95
Fox Lane 82
Freemasons' School 100
Friern Barnet 8, 10, 172, 180

Garcke, Emile 8, 32, 235
Gas Supplier 129
Gas turbines 68, 76
General Electric Co 111
Generating stations 10
Generator, double current 44-5
Gilbert Scott, Sir Giles 35, 73

Golders Green 104
Grange Park 82
Great Northern Railway 41
Green Lanes 82, 84
Green Street 88

Hadley Wood 177
Hammond, Mr B 93
Hammond, Robert 119
Harlow 137, 256
Harlow New Town 138
Harpenden 172, 180, 189
Harringay 172
Harrow 10-11, 25, 29, 108, 116, 172, 188
Harrow Electric Light & Power Co 110, 116
Harrow Road and Paddington Tramways Co 23
Harrow Weald 105, 172, 180-81
Hatfield 24, 121, 162, 172, 178, 180, 204, 250, 256
Hawtayne, W C C 92-3
Head Offices 144 st seq
Heaters, thermal storage 3
Heating, Electric 177
Heating, off peak 201
Hedge Lane 82
Hemstonery 108
Hendon 10-12, 24-5, 29, 32, 103-4, 107, 172, 188, 221
Hendon Electric Supply Company, absorption of the 243
Hendon Rural 30, 181
Hertford 1, 9, 11, 13, 24, 29, 31, 36, 41, 121, 126, 128, 134, 136, 138, 169, 172, 176, 178-81, 188, 195, 204, 263
Hertford East 226
Hertfordshire County Council 31, 35, 73, 118
High Barnet 17, 80
High-pressure 54, 58, 64
High voltage test van 182
Hill End 121
Hitchin 17, 24-5, 32-3

HM Forces, staff serving with 245
Hoddesdon 11, 29, 34, 72, 129, 167, 172, 180
Holden, Charles 145
Hoppers Road 82
Hornsey 9, 11, 14, 20, 29-30, 32-3, 93, 188
Hornsey' test set 199
House of Commons, Select Committee of the 30
Huntingdonshire 139

Industrial metering 186
Inverforth, Lord 145, 149
Ivy House 124

James Bruton & Sons 82
Joint Electricity Authorities 33, 86
Jointers 192
Julius Caesar, Triumph and Apotheosis of 154

Kensal Rise 223
Kenton 115, 172
King George Reservoir 61
Kingsbury 24, 30, 103, 172, 180, 216
Kingsway, London WC 144

Ladysmith Road 87
Lanscroon, Gerrard 147
Lanscroon murals; A Description 154
Laundries 178
Lea Valley 34, 73, 152
Legal & General Assurance Society Ltd 153
Legislation, early 5
Letchworth 32, 188
Light railway orders 10
Lighting, Public (street) 215
Lincoln Road 90
Little Barford 139
Ljungstrom 1-2, 41, 45, 50, 52
Llanvanor Road, Cricklewood 223
LNER 226

Load shedding 260
Local Advisory Committee 252
Local Government Board 6
Locomotive, fireless shunting 51
Loeffler 2, 55-6, 58-9, 62-4
Logo 175
London & Home Counties Enfield District Council minute 1843 (vol 68), 19/1/1931.Joint Electricity Authority 92
London & Home Counties Joint Electricity Authority 33
London & Home Counties Joint Electricity District 86
London & Suburban Traction Co Ltd (L&STCo) 30, 32, 222, 224, 228
London Hosiery Factory 84
London Passenger Transport Act, 1933 33
London Transport 32, 59, 69, 225-6, 228
London Underground 205
Long service awards 161
Lonsdale Drive 67
LPTB 228, 238
L&STCo 31
Luton 1, 43, 121

Madgen, William Leonard 236
Magazine 258
Manns' Road 105
Manor House 144, 149, 180
Marion 82
Marion & Co 82
Marshalswick 122
Melling, Cecil 252
Mercury arc rectifier 223, 225-6
Mercury arc rectifiers 223
MET 30, 224-5, 228-9, 235-6, 238
Meter Testing Laboratories 181, 183
Meter Testing Station 181
Metering 186
Metropolitan Electric Supply Co (METESCO) 43, 221

INDEX

269

Metropolitan Electric Tramways 7, 11, 23, 51, 87, 203-4
Metropolitan Electric Tramways Co (MET) 29, 144
Metropolitan Electric Tramways (MET) 220
Metropolitan Railway 69-70
Metropolitan Water Board 61
Middlesex County Council 8, 10, 15
Middlesex light railways 220
Mill Hill 172
Ministry of Supply 138
Mobile showroom 169
Motor Repair Section 181
Motors, electric 6
Much Hadham 134, 137
Municipal Electric Supply Co 126
Muswell Hill 172

National Electric Construction Co 108
National Joint Industrial Council 259
NATIONALISATION 252
Neasden 69
Negative Phase Sequence Protection, 11kV 197
Neverstop Railway 152
New Barnes Mill 120, 123
New Barnet 17
New Southgate 1, 80, 145
New Towns 256, 262
Newmarket 139
North Enfield 67
North London exhibition 171
North Metropolitan Electrical Power Distribution Garcke's Manual 1902-3 gives the date as 12th AprilCompany, Limited 7
North Metropolitan Power Station Co Ltd 26
North Metropolitan Tramways 180
Northern Line 226
Northmet House 145, 214, 247, 251, 263
Northwick 115

Northwood Electric Light and Power Co Ltd 32, 225
Northwood Hospital 109

Oil fired stations 59, 260
Old Welwyn 173
Organisation 180
Outside Department 1, 181
Overhead Line Department 181
Overhead Line Engineer 182
Overhead Line section 183

Palmers Green 82, 163, 173
Palmers Green Grid 67
Patten, Marguerite 164
Pension 165
Permits 202
Piano factories 98
Piccadilly Line station, Wood Green 101
Piccadilly tube line 226
Pick, Frank 69-70
Pilot and telephone cables 203
Pilot protection 197
Pinner 32, 108, 225
Ponders End 12, 88
Potters Bar 81, 163, 167, 172, 176, 180
Potters Bar 177
Power Station Company 34
Power system 195
Prefabricated houses 250
Private automatic telephone 192
Protection, unit (pilot-wire) 203
Provisional Order 5
Public Lighting 84, 98, 215
Public speaking 192
Pulverised coal firing 60
Purchase rights 34, 91

Queen's Avenue (Winchmore Hill) 81

Railway Supply 75
Refuse destructor 41-3
Resident Engineers 180, 188, 253
Ridgeway 89

Ringslade Road, Wood Green 187
River Lea 29, 52
Roundel 175
Royal National Orthopaedic Hospital 105
Royston 128, 172, 188
Ruislip 109
Ruthven-Murray, Ethelbert 44-5, 180, 231
Rye House 3, 27, 34-5, 72, 226, 232

Safety locks 202
Safety Rules 202
Sales 3, 176
Salter, Joe 236
Salvation Army 42, 120, 123
Sandridge 121
Sangamo Weston 184, 186
Saracen's Head Yard 122
Sawbridgeworth 137
Second World War 3, 152, 188, 197, 240
Sewage works 178
Sheepcote 110
Shop lighting 176
Shotter, Mr G F 184
Show house 167
Show houses 165
Showhouse 89
Showroom 82-3, 86, 90, 94, 101, 106, 116, 121, 124, 128, 130-31, 135, 157, 162, 172, 188, 263
Showrooms 3, 93, 172
Signalling system, remote 217
Signalling system, transistorised 208
Silver Street 226
Solkor protection 196
Southgate 12, 14, 16, 24, 30, 81, 173, 179-80, 188, 255
Southgate Council 145
Spencer, Christopher John 238
Sports and social clubs 193, 260
St Albans 1, 11, 17, 20, 24, 29, 31, 42, 68, 118-21, 123, 157, 167, 172, 179-80, 188-9, 195, 200, 249-50, 261, 263

St Neots 140
Standard Telephones & Cables Ltd 80, 217
Stanley, Albert Henry 227
Stanmore 105, 180-81
Stanstead 138
Station Road, Wood Green 101
Stevenage 1, 17, 24-5, 32, 41, 43, 173, 180, 188, 256
Stevenage Electric Light & Power Co Ltd 68, 125
Still & Sons Ltd, W M 83
Stoke Newington 25, 30, 32-3
Street lighting 137, 242
Strikes 260
Sudbury 114
Suggestion Scheme 252
Superannuation 165
Supply, DC 200
Switchgear, 11kV 196
Switchgear, 22kV 200
System, 3kV 195
Systems, battle of the 6

Talbot, Frederick G 184
Tapster Street 79, 81, 214
Tariff increases 258
Taylor, Sir Robert 147
Taylors Lane 34, 43, 54, 58, 60, 115, 121, 221, 231
Telephone, Substation 205
Telephone system, private 203
Test station 188
Test Van 198
Thermal efficiency, highest in 47
Thorley Junction 134
Tottenham 11-16, 24, 29, 86, 95, 173, 179-80, 188, 223
Tottenham & District Gas Co 20, 25, 32, 100, 163
Tottenham District Light Heat and Power Co 100
Totteridge 80, 180
Traction Substation Engineer 224

INDEX

Traction supplies 220
Trade Facilities Acts, 1921-26 26, 34
Trades unions 259
Training 189
Tramway Avenue, Edmonton 80
Tramways 6
Trinity College, Cambridge 51
Trolleybuses 81, 87, 222, 225

Underground Electric Railways Company of London Ltd (UERL) 31-2, 69, 144-5, 157, 175, 224, 226-9

Vehicles, electric 83
Voltage reductions 213

Walker 204
Walker, Isaac 148
Waltham Abbey 180
Waltham Cross 11, 29, 88, 172
Walthamstow 11, 29-30, 32-3
War Damage 247
War, Second World 240
Ware 11, 17, 24, 29-30, 129, 137, 173, 178, 180

Watsons Road 226
Wealdstone 30, 108-9, 115-16, 180
Welwyn 24, 256
Welwyn Garden City 25, 32, 188, 205, 250
Welwyn Rural 181
Wembley 30, 104, 108-9, 111, 115-16, 167, 173, 179-81, 188
Wembley, North 111
Wembley Stadium 112
West Green Lane (South Grove) 222
Western Area 108
Whetstone 173, 221
White Horse Inn 131
Willesden 1-2, 12, 15, 21, 23, 34, 43, 104, 108, 201, 241, 246
Willesden (Taylors Lane) see Taylors Lane
Willesden UDC 107
Winchmore Hill 10, 173
Wind generator 262
Wood Green 10, 12-15, 20, 25, 30, 32, 81, 93, 100, 152, 163, 173, 188, 204, 221, 223, 225-6, 255
Woodall House 100
Works Committees 259

ACKNOWLEDGEMENTS

After the initial disappointment of finding that neither Eastern Electricity nor The Electricity Association had kept any historical records, I was pleased with the extensive help which I received from other sources. The London Transport Museum and the London Transport archive were both helpful as were the record offices at the House of Lords, London Metropolitan Archive and the London Boroughs of Enfield and Haringey. One unexpected find was the Company's minute books in the Hertfordshire record office.

There were also records in the Manchester Museum of Science and Technology and at the Tramway Museum at Crich. At both places the staff were very helpful. Volunteers at the museums at Bishops Stortford and Hertford helped fill in a few gaps and, although a minor part of the story, I was very impressed with the response from Northern Telecomm, successors to Standard Telephones and Cables. Clearly not all modern companies consign their past to the waste bin.

This history would not have been possible without the help of many individuals, mostly former employees of Northmet and Eastern Electricity. Many of their contributions are signalled in the footnotes. I am very grateful to Alick and Gillian Barnett, D Battlebury, Roy Boune, K Bolton, Chris Buck, Anthony Bull, J M Burgess, D Burnett, Mrs R Catlin, Ken Chandler, Brig J Clinch, F Crawley, Fred Cutts, Eric Davies, Chris Dawes, Brian Dillingham, B Eady, Owen Elias, F Erridge, Dr K B Everard, Eric Fase, Ted Garnham, Gareth Key, Geoffrey Gillam, Alan Gordon, Frederick Greenwood, D F Gunning, W O Haythorne, G F Hill, Peter Howe, Dr Geoff Hughes, Tony Jackson, R W Jenkins, Hugh Jones, Bill Killick, C J Knight, Kenneth and Leonard Lambert, George Lawrence, S J Little, Glen McBirne, Graham McKenzie, Garry Matthews, Alan Newberry, Derek Newbold, Marguerite Patten, Alf Phillips, Stan Pollikett, Alan Ray, Ken Sheale, George Sibley, Cyril Smeeton, Fred Smith, Norman Smith, Ian Souter, Chris Taylor, C J Thody, Marion Thody, Ron Thomas, R G Whillock, John Whittington and Alex Winyard. Particular thanks go to those individuals and organisations who allowed me to use their illustrations.

Regrettably C T Melling and Don Taylor both died during the preparation of this book and are a sad reminder of how time is running out for recording great industrial enterprises such as Northmet.

Particular thanks goes to Eric Wright who supplied much material and practical support in the production of this book.

I have tried very hard to check the facts contained in this book, however it is possible that errors have crept in. I take full responsibility for the final text.